주한미군지위협정(SOFA)

서명 및 발효 17

주한미군지위협정(SOFA)

서명 및 발효 17

머리말

미국은 오래전부터 우리나라 외교에 있어서 가장 긴밀하고 실질적인 우호 · 협력관계를 맺어 온 나라다. 6 · 25전쟁 정전 협정이 체결된 후 북한의 재침을 막기 위한 대책으로서 1953년 11월 한미 상호방위조약이 체결되었다. 이는 미군이 한국에 주둔하는 법적 근거였고, 그렇게 주둔하게 된 미군의 시설, 구역, 사업, 용역, 출입국, 통관과 관세, 재판권 등 포괄적인 법적 지위를 규정하는 것이 바로 주한미군지위협정(SOFA)이다. 그러나 이와 관련한 협상은 계속된 난항을 겪으며 한미 상호방위조약이 체결로부터 10년이 훌쩍 넘은 1967년이 돼서야 정식 발효에 이를 수 있었다. 그럼에도 당시 미군 범죄에 대한 한국의 재판권은 심한 제약을 받았으며, 1980년대 후반 민주화 운동과 함께 미군 범죄 문제가 사회적 이슈로 떠오르자 협정을 개정해야 한다는 목소리가 커지게 되었다. 이에 1991년 2월 주한미군지위협정 1차 개정이 진행되었고, 이후에도 여러 사건이 발생하며 2001년 4월 2차 개정이 진행되어 현재에 이르고 있다.

본 총서는 외교부에서 작성하여 최근 공개한 주한미군지위협정(SOFA) 관련 자료를 담고 있다. 1953년 한미 상호방위조약 체결 이후부터 1967년 발효가 이뤄지기까지의 자료와 더불어, 이후 한미 합동위원회를 비롯해 민 · 형사재판권, 시설, 노무, 교통 등 각 분과위원회의 회의록과 운영 자료, 한국인 고용인 문제와 관련한 자료, 기타 관련 분쟁 자료 등을 포함해 총 42권으로 구성되었다. 전체 분량은 약 2만 2천여 쪽에 이른다.

2024년 3월

한국학술정보(주)

| 일러두기

· 본 총서에 실린 자료는 2022년 4월과 2023년 4월에 각각 공개한 외교문서 4,827권, 76만 여 쪽 가운데 일부를 발췌한 것이다.

· 각 권의 제목과 순서는 공개된 원본을 최대한 반영하였으나, 주제에 따라 일부는 적절히 변경하였다.

· 원본 자료는 A4 판형에 맞게 축소하거나 원본 비율을 유지한 채 A4 페이지 안에 삽입하였다. 또한 현재 시점에선 공개되지 않아 '공란'이란 표기만 있는 페이지 역시 그대로 실었다.

· 외교부가 공개한 문서 각 권의 첫 페이지에는 '정리 보존 문서 목록'이란 이름으로 기록물 종류, 일자, 명칭, 간단한 내용 등의 정보가 수록되어 있으며, 이를 기준으로 0001번부터 번호가 매겨져 있다. 이는 삭제하지 않고 총서에 그대로 수록하였다.

· 보고서 내용에 관한 더 자세한 정보가 필요하다면, 외교부가 온라인상에 제공하는 『대한민국 외교사료요약집』 1991년과 1992년 자료를 참조할 수 있다.

| 차례

정/리/보/존/문/서/목/록					
기록물종류	문서-일반공문서철	등록번호	943 9616	등록일자	2006-07-27
분류번호	741.12	국가코드	US	주제	
문서철명	한.미국 간의 상호방위조약 제4조에 의한 시설과 구역 및 한국에서의 미국군대의 지위에 관한 협정 (SOFA) 전59권. 1966.7.9 서울에서 서명 : 1967.2.9 발효 (조약 232호) *원본				
생산과	미주과/조약과	생산년도	1952 - 1967	보존기간	영구
담당과(그룹)	조약	조약	서가번호	--	
참조분류					
권차명	V.45 토의 의제 및 합의사항				
내용목차	* 일지 : 1953.8.7 이승만 대통령-Dulles 미국 국무장관 공동성명 - 상호방위조약 발효 후 군대지위협정 교섭 약속 1954.12.2 정부, 주한 UN군의 관세업무협정 체결 제의 1955.1월, 5월 미국, 제의 거절 1955.4.28 정부, 군대지위협정 제의 (한국측 초안 제시) 1957.9.10 Hurter 미국 국무차관 방한 시 각서 수교 (한국측 제의 수락 요구) 1957.11.13, 26 정부, 개별 협정의 단계적 체결 제의 1958.9.18 Dawling 주한미국대사, 형사재판관할권 협정 제외 조건으로 행정협정 체결 의사 전달 1960.3.10 정부, 토지, 시설협정의 우선적 체결 강력 요구 1961.4.10 장면 국무총리-McConaughy 주한미국대사 공동성명으로 교섭 개시 합의 1961.4.15, 4.25 제1, 2차 한.미국 교섭회의 (서울) 1962.3.12 정부, 교섭 재개 촉구 공한 송부 1962.5.14 Burger 주한미국대사, 최규하 장관 면담 시 형사재판관할권 문제 제기 않는 조건으로 교섭 재개 통고 1962.9.6 한.미국 간 공동성명 발표 (9월 중 교섭 재개 합의) 1962.9.20~ 1965.6.7 제1-81차 실무 교섭회의 (서울) 1966.7.8 제82차 실무 교섭회의 (서울) 1966.7.9 서명 1967.2.9 발효 (조약 232호)					

마/이/크/로/필/름/사/항				
촬영연도	*롤 번호	화일 번호	후레임 번호	보관함 번호
2006-11-24	I-06-0071	05	1-268	

0001

1962. 9. 20. 하오 3시
이전에 발표함을 금함.

1962년 9월 20일 한미간 주둔군지위 협정
교섭 회의개최에 즈음한 외무부장관 식사

버거 대사, 여러내빈 그리고 교섭대표 여러분,

본인은 공동방위를 위하여 대한민국에 주둔하고 있는 미합중국 군대지위에 관한 협정체결 교섭을 재개함에 즈음하여 12 년전 미국을 위시한 자유국가의 연합군이 한국군과 긴밀한 협조하에 공산 침략자와 싸웠다는 사실을 자랑스럽게 상기하고저 하는 바입니다.

본인은 또한 오늘의 이교섭재개가 직접적이고 긴급한 공산 침략의 위협에 직면한 가운데서 자유세계가 보여주는 또하나의 고귀한 협조의 실예임을 기쁨으로 주목코저 하는 바입니다.

특히 이회담은 전통적 한미관계의 오랜특징인 가장 화목한 우의와 협조의 정신 그리고 부동한 상호 신뢰의 웅변적 상징인 것입니다.

본인으로서는 우리양국 국민간에 발생하는 개개사건의 방지나 또는 일국의 타국에대한 주권의 주장이 이번회담에 있어서 본질적문제가 되는것이 아니라고 생각하며 오히려 이번 회의의 참된 의의와 주둔군 지위협정 교섭의 중대한 사명을 다루는 엄숙한 목적은 자유국가간의 관계는 평등과 상호 존중의 명예로운 원칙위에 서야하고 또한 실제로 서있다는 사실, 그리고 그러한 원칙위에 기반을둔 여사한 관계야말로 참으로 위대하며 영구히 평화속에 지속된다는 사실을 만방에 시위하려는 우리의 공동관심에 있는 것입니다.

본인은 오늘의 회담재개가 구체적 행동과 결과로서 한 자유의 선봉국가와 현세기의 가장 위대한 국가간의 관계가 바로 그러하다는 것을 증명하게 될것으로 확신하는 바입니다.

0002

협정체결이 실현되기까지에는 허다한 난관을 극복해야 하며 복잡한 많은문제를 해결해야 할것입니다. 그러나 우리들은 우리들의 목적, 단결과 인내에 있어서 결코 실패하지 않을것입니다.

본인은 이자리에 계신 여러 교섭대표들의 노력이 조속히 협정을 성공적인 체결로 이끌어 한미간의 우호관계의 역사에 또하나의 이정표를 마련할것을 충심으로 원하는 바입니다.

0003

Strictly not to be
released before 3 p.m.
on Sept. 20, 1962

STATEMENT BY FOREIGN MINISTER CHOI DUK SHIN AT THE OPENING OF STATUS OF FORCES NEGOTIATION BETWEEN THE GOVERNMENTS OF THE REPUBLIC OF KOREA AND THE UNITED STATES, SEOUL, KOREA

SEPTEMBER 20, 1962

Mr. Ambassador, guests and negotiators,

On this occasion of the resumption of negotiations for an agreement covering the status of United States Forces that are stationed in the Republic of Korea for the purpose of common defense, I wish to note with pride that it was barely a dozen year ago when the united forces of the United States and other free nations, shoulder to shoulder with their Korean ally, fought back the Communist aggressors. I wish further to note with pleasure that today's resumption of negotiations represents another of many noble examples of Free World cooperation in the face of direct and immediate threat of Communist aggression.

In particular, this gathering eloquently symbolizes the most amicable spirit of friendship and cooperation as well as the unshakable mutual confidence that have long been characteristic of traditional relations between the Republic of Korea and the United States.

It is, to me, not so much the prevention of this or that incident involving nationals of our two countries, nor the assertion of one's sovereignty over that of another that is at stake in this coming negotiations. Rather, the true significance of this occasion and the solemn purpose with which we are to engage in the exacting task of the status of forces negotiations lie

0004

in our joint resolve to demonstrate to the world that the relations of free nations shall be, and in fact are, based on an honorable principle of equality and mutual respect, and that only such relations founded on such principle are truly great and lasting in peace.

I am confident that today's reopening of negotiations will prove, through concrete action and results, that such is the case of relations between a frontier state of freedom and the greatest nation of the century.

Many difficulties will have to be overcome; and many a complex problem must be solved, before an agreement can be effected. But, in our purpose, unity and patience, we cannot fail.

I sincerely hope that the efforts of these negotiators present here will soon lead to the successful conclusion of an agreement, which will lay another milestone in the annals of the friendly relations between the Republic of Korea and the United States.

0005

Strictly not to be
released before 3 p.m.
on Sept. 20, 1962

OPENING SESSION, SOFA NEGOTIATIONS

REMARKS BY AMBASSADOR BERGER

Mr. Minister, Friends and Colleagues -

1. As we begin negotiations today it is important that we have a clear view of our common objective, That objective is to strengthen further the already close ties existing between Korea and the United States. Our joint task is to conclude an agreement which will contribute to this objective in a manner satisfactory to both sides. The United States Government is entering these negotiations with the earnest intent to conclude an agreement which will meet this objective.

2. My country is aware of the great interest of the Korean people in these negotiations. There is the same intense interest, I can assure you, among the people of the United States and my government.

3. A Status of Forces Agreement covers many kinds of activities. It encompasses extensive, complex and varied administrative arrangements. The areas to be discussed include postal facilities, port and airplane facilities, servicing of ships and aircraft, customs regulations, tax regulations, the use of facilities for the defense of Korea, and matters of jurisdiction over personnel. These are intricate and complicated matters. They posed complex problems between the United States and other countries. Complicated problems are a challenge to the skills of the negotiators, but they are not necessarily barriers to agreement. The wide

the same intense interest, I can assure you, among the people of the United States and my government.

3. A Status of Forces Agreement covers many kinds of activities. It encompasses extensive, complex and

range of questions which will arise and will need to be resolved in the course of these negotiations will provide the fabric to fashion a mutually satisfactory agreement.

4. Difficult and complex though the problems may be, we expect to draw up a Status of Forces Agreement which will further those amicable associations between the United States and Korea that have historically provided the power and the will to resist threats to freedom. This task calls for unity of purpose, mutual respect and a real effort to understand each other's problem. On this our common security depends. It is in this spirit and with this purpose, that the United States enters these negotiations for a Status of Forces Agreement with the Republic of Korea.

보도자료 62 — 22 호

9 월 20 일

외 무 부 발 표

한미 주둔군 지위협정 고섭회의

제 1 차 회의 한미 공동 성명

오늘 회의에서 대한민국측을 대표한 외무부 최덕신 장관과 미국측을 대표한 사뮤엘 디 버거대사는 한미간 주둔군 지위협정에관한 고섭 회의의 재개를 환영하였다.

양측의 식사에 이어 외무부장관과 버거대사는 한국측과 미국측의 실무자들을 소개하였다.

최초회의에서는 고섭회의 절차사항과 여러가지 기타 예비적인 행정사항을 도의하였다. 금번 토의에서는 차후 고섭의 신속한진행을 위한 기초를 닦아놓았다.

이번회의에서는 고섭의 진전상황을 일반국민에게 주지시키기 위하여 수시로 공동발표를 하는데 양측의 합의 하였다.

다음 회의는 9월 28일에 개최하기로 합의 하였다.

0008

NEGOTIATION OF STATUS OF FORCES AGREEMENT RESUMED

At today's meeting the Minister of Foreign Affairs, Choi Duk Shin, speaking for the Republic of Korea, and Ambassador Samuel D. Berger, speaking for the United States, welcomed the resumption of negotiations for Korea and the United States of America. Following these openning remarks, the Foreign Minister and Ambassador Berger introduced the members of the Korean and American negotiating teams.

The initial discussions dealt with the procedures to be followed and various other preliminary administrative matters. These discussion laid the groundwork for the expeditious conduct of subsequeut negotiations. It was agreed that joint press statements would be issued from time of time in order to keep the public informed of the progress of negotiations.

By common agreement, the next meeting was shheduled for Sept. 28 .

0003

미 주둔군 지위협정 실무교섭

제 2 차 회의 의제

1962. 9. 10. 오후 2 시

협정의 범위 및 내용 (제목)

1. 전문 및 용어의 정의

가. 목적과 이유

나. 용어의 정의

(ㄱ) 미군대 구성원

(ㄴ) 군속

(ㄷ) 가족

2. 출입국 관리문제

가. 면제

나. 요건

다. 신분의 변경 및 의거

3. 시설 및 토지문제

가. 사용허가

나. 보상 (사용료 혹은 임대료) 문제

다. 유지비 문제

라. 시설 및 토지의 반환문제

마. 임시 사용권

바. 시설, 운영, 안전 및 통제조치 문제

사. 원상회복 및 개선에 관한 문제

4. 선박 항공기의 출입과 교통 통제및 통신체계 문제

가. 선박 항공기의 출입 및 이용료 면제, 출입에관한 통고

나. 통제 및 통신체계에 관한 조정과 협조

0010

다. 기상정보

5. 형사재판 관할권 문제

가. 일반적 관할권의 원칙

나. 전속적 관할권

다. 경합적 관할권

(ㄱ) 미국의 제 1 차 적 관할권

(ㄴ) 한국의 제 1 차 적 관할권

(ㄷ) 공무와 비공무 집행중 여부의 결정

라. 관할권의 포기

마. 체포 수사 증거 수집상의 상호협조

바. 구금

사. 형집행 문제

아. 2중처벌 방지문제

자. 한국법원에 기소된자의 재판상의 권리

차. 헌병의 사용문제

6. 민사재판 및 청구권 문제

가. 한국법원의 민사재판권 및 판결집행의 면제 범위

나. 양국 군용재산 손해에 대한 청구권

다. 양국 비군용재산 손해에 대한 청구권 및 중재인사용 문제

라. 제 3 자에 가한 손해에 대한 청구권

마. 공무집행중 입은 인적손해에 대한 청구권의 포기

바. 미군대 구성원 혹은 고용자의 불법적 작위 혹은 부작위로 인한 손해청구권

사. 차량의 불법사용으로 인한 손해청구권

아. 강제집행을 면한 사유동산의 인도

0011

자. 공무 혹은 비공무집행중 여부의 결정에관한 증거수집에
있어서의 협조

차. 중재인을 통한 분쟁의 중재

카. 계약상의 분쟁 해결문제

7. 관세문제

가. 관세통제의 일반적 원칙

나. 용관세의 면제범위

다. 세관검사의 면제범위

라. 무세통관 물품의 국내에서의 처분문제

마. 특권 남용방지

8. 조세문제

가. 군용재산에 대한 면제

나. 소득에 대한 면제범위

다. 특정 부동산에 대한 면제문제

9. 세출의 자금기관

가. 일반적 허가

나. 면세범위

다. 세출의 자금기관 물자의 처분에대한 제한

라. 수입량에 대한 제한

마. 한국 관헌에대한 정보제공

10. 물자구입, 용역 및 노무 문제

가. 구매업무 등에관한 한국법운의 적용문제

나. 채의무적 조정문제

다. 사적 목적을위한 구매에대한 세금의 분면제

라. 일반적 노무 기준

마. 제 3 국 국민의 고용금지

바. 한국 노무자의 고용 및 해고문제

0012

11. 미군의 계약자 문제

가. 한국법령의 적용에관한 일반적 규정

나. 계약자 지정에대한 제한

다. 특권과 면제 범위

라. 계약자에 대한 형사재판 관할권 문제

12. 외환관리

가. 일반적 원칙

나. 한국내에 있어서 혹은 한국외로의 외환이전에 대한 허가문제

다. 특권남용 방지문제

라. 일정지역내에서의 군표사용 허가문제

마. 비인가자의 군표사용 단속문제

바. 군용은행 시설의 설치

13. 합동위원회

가. 기능

나. 구성

14. 군사우편

가. 군사우편국의 설치 및 업무

나. 특권남용 방지를위한 조치

15. 기타조항

가. 전시특례 조항

(1) 전시에 있어서의 협정적용에 관한 수정을위한 협의

나. 운전면허

다. 무기휴대

라. 예비역 훈련

16. 최종조항

가. 발효 나. 만기

다. 개정 라. 본협정과 양립하지 않는 기존협정의 폐기문제

0013

0014

A COMPARATIVE TABLE OF AGREEMENTS CONCERNING STATUS OF FORCES

ITEM \ AGREEMENT	US-JAPAN 1952	UN-JAPAN 1954	US-JAPAN 1960	NATO 1951	US-ICELAND 1951	US-PHILIP. 1947	US-LYBIA 1954	US-ETHIOPIA 1953	ROK-UN 1955(Draft)	ROK-US 1962(Draft)
1. Definitions	1	1	1	1	1	-	28	24	1	1
2. Facilities and Areas	2,3,4	5	2,3,4	-	-	1,3,17,19,21,22, 25,26, Annex A&B	1,2,4,6, 7,10,11	1,2,3,4, 7,10	3	4,5,6,7, 8,9
3. Access by Vessels and Aircraft	5	4	5	-	-	4	3,8,9	-	-	10
4. Control of Navigations & Meteorological Services	6,8	-	6,8	-	-	-	-	-	-	11
5. Use of Public Utilities and Services	7	6	7	-	-	7	5	6	-	-
6. Entry and Exit	9	3	9	3	-	11	16	14	2	3
7. Driving Permits, Number Plate and Uniforms	10	7	10	4,5	3,4	-	21	15	11,12	22
8. Carrying of Arms	-	-	-	6	5	-	22	21	13	23
9. Customs Duties	11	13	11	11,12,13	8,9	5	25	18	8	14
10. Procurement of Materials, Services and Labour	12	14	12	9	6	-	13,23	16,22,23	6	17
11. Taxation	13	12	13	10	7	12	24	-	7	15
12. US Contractors	14	-	14	-	-	-	-	-	-	18
13. Non-appropriated Fund Organizations	15	9	15	-	-	18	17	13	9	16
14. Respect of Receiving State's Law & Criminal Jurisdiction	16,17	2,16	16,17	2,7	2	13,14,20	20,27	17	4,14	2,12
15. Civil Jurisdiction and Claims	18	18	18	8	12	23	19	19	5	13

16. Foreign Exchange Control	19	10	18	14	10	-	-	-	-	19
17. Currency	20	11	20	-	-	-	26	20	-	20
18. Military Post Office	21	8	21	14	-	16	15	12	10	21
19. Training in Reserve Organization	22	-	22	-	-	28	-	-	-	24
20. Mutual Cooperation	-	-	-	-	-	2	-	-	-	-
21. Security of Forces and Properties	23	17	23	-	-	15	-	-	-	-
22. Maneuvering Areas	-	-	-	-	-	6	-	11	-	-
23. Health and Sanitation	-	-	-	-	-	8	18	5	-	-
24. Aurveys	-	-	-	-	-	9	14	8,9	-	-
25. Cemetries, Historical Sites, and Mineral Resources	-	-	-	-	-	10,24	-	-	-	-
26. Voluntary Enrollment	-	-	-	-	-	27	-	-	-	-
27. Expenditures and Accounting	25	15	24	-	-	-	-	-	-	-
28. Consultation for Joint Defense	24	-	-	-	-	-	-	-	-	-
29. Adjustment in the Event of Hostilities	-	-	-	15	-	-	-	-	15	25
30. Joint Committee and Settlement Disputes	26	20	25	16	-	-	29	-	16	26
31. Privileges for NATO Forces	-	-	-	-	11	-	-	-	-	-
32. Other Obligations	-	-	-	-	-	-	12	-	-	-
33. Final Clauses	27,28,29	19,21,22 23,24,25	26,27,28	17,18, 19,20	-	29	30	25	17,18,19	27,28,29

0015

October 10, 1962

STATUS OF FORCES AGREEMENT - MAJOR TOPICS

1. PREAMBLE
2. DEFINITIONS
3. FACILITIES AND AREAS
4. AIR TRAFFIC CONTROL AND NAVIGATIONAL AIDS
5. JOINT COMMITTEE
6. ENTRY AND EXIT OF PERSONS
7. CUSTOMS AND DUTIES
8. VEHICLE, VESSEL & AIRCRAFT ACCESS TO PORTS AND AIRPORTS, ACCESS OF VEHICLES AND PERSONNEL TO FACILITIES AND AREAS
9. UTILITIES AND SERVICES
10. MILITARY PAYMENT CERTIFICATES
11. APO's AND MAILING
12. ENROLIMENT AND TRAINING OF RESERVISTS
13. MEASURES TO INSURE SAFFETY AND SECURITY OF US ARMED FORCES, ITS MEMBERS, DEPENDENTS, AND PROPERTY
14. METEOROLOGICAL AND RELATED SERVICES
15. VEHICLE AND DRIVER LICENSES; MARKINGS
16. CURRENCY CONTROLS
17. NONAPPROPRIATED FUND ACTIVITIES
18. RESPECT FOR LOCAL LAW
19. CRIMINAL JURISDICTION AND ADMINISTRATION
20. CLAIMS
21. TAXES
22. LOCAL (OFF SHORE) PROCUREMENT OF SUPPLIES, MATERIALS AND CONSTRUCTION
23. CONTRACTUAL DISPUTES
24. ARMED FORCES CONTRACTORS

0016

25. LABOR

26. NATIONAL APPROVAL, EFFECTIVE DATE, AND IMPLEMENTING LEGISLATION TO BRING AGREEMENT INTO FORCE

27. REVISION OR AMENIMENT OF AGREEMENT

28. DURATION AND TERMINATION OF AGREEMENT

(29) Health and Sanitation

0017

ARTICLE ________

3. Upon certification by appropriate United States authorities as to their identity, such persons shall be accorded the following benefits of this Agreement:

(a) Accession and movement, as provided for in Article Vessel, Aircraft & Access, paragraph 2;

(b) Entry into Korea in accordance with the provisions of Article Entry & Exit;

(c) The exemption from customs duties and other such charges provided for in Article Customs; paragraph 3, for members of the United States armed forces, the civilian component, and their dependents;

(d) If authorized by the Government of the United States, the use of the services of the activities provided for in Article PX;

(e) Those provided in Article currency control, paragraph 2, for members of the United States armed forces, the civilian component, and their dependents;

0018

(f) If authorized by the Government of the United States, the use of military payment certificates, as provided in Article MPC; —OK

(g) The use of postal facilities provided for in Article MPO; —OK

(h) The use of utilities and services in accordance with those priorities, conditions, rates, or tariffs accorded the United States armed forces by Article Util. & Services paragraph 3, relating to utilities and services; —OK

(i) Those provided to members of the United States armed forces, the civilian component, and their dependents by Article ____, relating to driving permits and registration of vehicles;

(j) Exemption from the laws and regulations of Korea with respect to terms and conditions of employment, and licensing and registration of businesses and corporations. —OK

Contractors 700
20 — Private vehicle
50%

0019

Preamble

Wherease the United States forces were originally disposed in and about the territory of the Republic of Korea pursuant to the resolutions of the United Nations Security Council of June 25, 1950, June 27, 1950 and July7, 1950 to repel the Communist armed attack;

Wherease, the Article IV of the Mutual Defense Treaty between the Republic of Korea and the United Srates of America signed on October 1, 1953, following the conclusion of the Armistice Agreement on July 27, 1953, states that the Republic of Korea grants, and the United States of America accepts, the right to dispose United States land, air and sea forces in and about the territory of the Republic of Korea as determined by mutual agreement;

Wherease, pursuant to the aforesaid provision of the Mutual Defense Treaty, the United States of America has disposed its armed forces in and about the territory of the Republic of Korea, and;

Wherease the Republic of Korea and the United States of America are desirous of providing for practical administrative arrangements which shall govern the disposition of the United States forces in and about the territory of the Republic of Korea in order to strengthen the close bonds of mutual interests between their two countries;

Therefore, the Governments of the Republic of Korea and of the United States of America have agreed as follows:

0020

序文

合意된것

"Whereas the United States of America has diposed its armed forces in and about the territory of the Republic of Korea pursuant to the resolutions of the United Nations Security Council of June 25, 1950, June 27, 1950, and July 7, 1950, and pursuant to Article IV of the Mutual defense Treaty between the United States of America and the Republic of Korea signed on October 1, 1953.

Therefore, the United States of America and the Republic of Korea, in order to strengthen the close bonds of mutual interest between their two countries, have entered into this Agreement regarding facilities and areas and the status of United States armed forces in the Republic of Korea in terms as set forth below:"

0021

Original

PREAMBLE

The United States of America and the Republic of Korea, pursuant to Article IV of the Mutual Defense Treaty between the United States of America and the Republic of Korea signed at Washington on October 1, 1953, have entered into this Agreement regarding facilities and areas and the status of United States armed forces in the Republic of Korea in terms as set forth below:

0022

P

Revised

"Whereas the United States of America has disposed its armed forces in and about the territory of the Republic of Korea pursuant to the resolutions of the United Nations Security Council of June 25, 1950, June 27, 1950, and July 7, 1950, and pursuant to Article IV of the Mutual defense Treaty between the United States of America and the Republic of Korea signed on October 1, 1953.

Therefore, the United States of America and the Republic of Korea, in order to strengthen the close bonds of mutual interest between their two countries, have entered into this Agreement regarding facilities and areas and the status of United States armed forces in the Republic of Korea in terms as set forth below:"

0023

Definition

In this Agreement the expression--

(a) "members of the United States forces" means the personnel on active duty belonging to the land, sea or air armed services of the United States of America when in the territory of the Republic of Korea.

(b) "civilian component" means the civilian persons of United States nationality who are in the employ of, serving with, or accompanying the United States forces in the Republic of Korea, but excludes persons who are ordinarily resident in the Republic of Korea or who are mentioned in Article XVIII. For the purposes of this agreement only, dual nationals, Korean and United States, who are brought to theRepublic of Korea by the United States shall be considered as United States nationals.

(c) "dependents" means

(i) Spouse, and children under 2I;

(ii) Parents, and children over 2I, if dependent for over half their support upon a member of the United States forces or civilian component.

0024

Agreed Minute to Definition of Terms

Members of the United States armed forces referred to in Paragraph (a) exclude the military attaché to the Embassy of the United States of America and those for whom status has been provided for in the Agreement between the Government of the Republic of Korea and the Government of the United States on January 26, 1950 regarding the establishment of a United States Military Advisory Group to the Republic of Korea, as amended by the exchange of Notes between the Foreign Minister of the Republic of Korea and the Charge D'Affairs of the Embassy of the United States dated October 21, 1960.

0025

Agreed Minute to Article ____ (Definitions)

The expression "except for those for whom status has otherwise been provided" in Paragraph (a) refers only to personnel on active duty belonging to the United States land, sea or air armed services for whom status is provided in the Military Advisory Group Agreement signed on January 26, 1950, and personnel of service attache offices in the Embassy of the United States of America.

0026

Definition

In this Agreement the expression --

(a) "members of the United States forces" means the personnel on active duty belonging to the land, sea or air armed services of the United States of America when in the territory of the Republic of Korea.

(b) "civilian component" means the civilian persons of United States nationality who are in the employ of, serving with, or accompanying the United States forces in the Republic of Korea, but excludes persons who are ordinarily resident in the Republic of Korea or who are mentioned in Article XVIII. For the purposes of this agreement only, dual nationals, Korean and United States, who are brought to the Republic of Korea by the United States shall be considered as United States nationals.

(c) "dependents" means

(i) Spouse, and children under 21;

(ii) Parents, and children over 21, if dependent for over half their support upon a member of the United States forces or civilian component.

skills
3rd states
nationals

NATO

Japan
Joint Committee
administered

0027

Entry and Exit

I. The United States may bring into the Republic of Korea persons who are members of the United States forces, the civilian component, and their dependents, subject to the provisions of this Article.

2. (a) Members of the United States forces shall be exempt from laws and regulations of the Republic of Korea governing the passport and visa. Members of the United States fo ces, the civilian component, and their dependents shall be exempt from laws and regulations of the Republic of Korea governing the registration and control of aliens, but shall not be considered acquiring any right to permanent resid4nce or domicile in the Republic of Korea.

(b) Members of the civilian component, their dependents, and the dependents of the members of the United States forces shall be in possession of passports with their status descrbed therein, upon their entry into or departure from or while in the Republic of Korea.

3. Upon entry into or departure from the Republic of Korea members of the United States forces shall be in possession of the following documents:

(a) personal identity card issued by the authorities of the United States forces showing name, date of birth, rank and number, service, and photograph; and

(b) individual or collective travel order issued by the authorities of the United States forces certifying to the status of the individual or group as a member or members of the United States forces and to the travel ordered.

For the purpose of their identification while in the Republic of Korea, members of the United States forces

0028

shall be in possion of the foregoing personal identity card which must be presented on demand of the appropriate authorities of the Republic of Korea.

4. (a) If any person brought into the Republic of Korea under paragraph I of this Article is, by reason of alteration in his status, no longer entitled to such admission provided for i in the foregoing paragraphs, the United States authorities shall immediately notify the authorities of the Republic of Korea and shall, if such person be required by the authorities of the Republic of Korea to leave the Republic of Korea, be responsible for the transportation from the Republic of Korea of such person within a reasonable time at no cost to the Government of the Republic of Korea.

(b) If the Government of the Republic of Korea has requested the removal from its territory of a member of the United States fo ces or the civilian component or has made an expulsion order against an ex-member of the United States forces or of the civilian component or against a dependent of a member or ex-member, the United States authorities shall be responsible for receiving the person concerned within its own territory of otherwise disposing of him outside the Republic of Korea. This paragraph shall apply only to persns who are not nationals of the Republic of Korea and have entered the Republic of Korea as members of the United States fo ces or the civilian component or for the purpose of becoming such members, and to the dependents of such persons.

0020

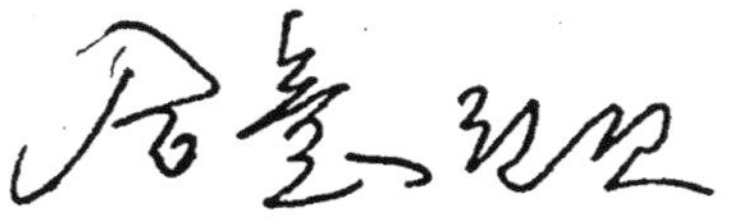

1. The United States may bring into the Republic of Korea persons who are members of the United States armed forces, the civilian component, and their dependents, subject to the provisions of this Article. The Government of the Republic of Korea will be notified at regular intervals, in accordance with procedures to be agreed between the two Governments, of numbers and categories of persons entering and departing.

2. Members of the United States armed forces shall be exempt from Korean passport and visa laws and regulations. Members of the United States armed forces, the civilian component, and their dependents shall be exempt from Korean laws and regulations on the registration and control of aliens, but shall not be considered as acquiring any right to permanent residence or domicile in the territory of the Republic of Korea.

3. Upon entry into or departure from the Republic of Korea members of the United States armed forces shall be in possession of the following documents:

0030

(a) personal identity card showing name, date of birth, rank and service number, service, and photograph; and

(b) individual or collective travel order certifying to the status of the individual or group as a member or members of the United States armed forces and to the travel ordered.

For purposes of their identification while in the Republic of Korea, members of the United States armed forces shall be in possession of the foregoing personal identity card which must be presented on request to the appropriate Korean authorities.

4. Members of the civilian component, their dependents, and the dependents of members of the United States armed forces shall be in possession of appropriate documentation issued by the United States authorities so that their status may be verified by Korean authorities upon their entry into or departure from the Republic of Korea, or while in the Republic of Korea.

5. If the status of any person brought into the Republic of Korea under paragraph 1 of this Article is altered so that he would no longer be entitled to such admission, the United States authorities shall notify the Korean authorities and shall, if such person be

0031

required by the Korean authorities to leave the Republic of Korea, assure that transportation from the Republic of Korea will be provided within a reasonable time at no cost to the Government of the Republic of Korea.

6. If the Government of the Republic of Korea has requested the removal from its Territory of a member of the United States armed forces or civilian component or has made an expulsion order against an ex-member of the United States armed forces or the civilian component or against a dependent of a member or an ex-member, the authorities of the United States shall be responsible for recoiving the person concerned into its own territory or otherwise disposing of him outside the Republic of Korea. This paragraph shall apply only to persons who are not nationals of the Republic of Korea and have entered the Republic of Korea as members of the United States armed forces or civilian component or for the purpose of becoming such members, and to the dependents of such persons.

0032

Agreed Minutes to Article

(Entry and Exit)

1. With regard to Paragraph 3(a), United States Armed Forces law enforcement personnel (such as MP, SP, AP, CID and CIC), who engage in military police activities in the Republic of Korea, will carry a bilingual identity card containing the bearer's name, position, and the fact that he is a member of a law enforcement agency. This card will be shown upon request to persons concerned when the bearer is in the performance of duty.

2. The United States Armed Forces will furnish, upon request, to Korean authorities the form of the identification cards of the members of the United States Armed Forces, the civilian component, and their dependents and descriptions of the various uniforms of the United States Armed Forces in the Republic of Korea.

3. The final sentence of Paragraph 3 means that members of the United States Armed Forces will display their identity cards upon request but will not be required to surrender them to Korean authorities.

4. Following a change of status purusant to Paragraph 5, the responsibilities of the United States

0033

authorities under [redacted] arise only if the expulsion order is issued within a reasonable time after the notice under Paragraph 5 has been communicated to the Korean authorities.

0034

Article____(Enrollment and Training of Reservists)

The United States may enroll and train eligible United States citizens residing in the Republic of Korea in the reserve organizations of the United States armed forces.

A.M.에 Residing 이란 Int'l Law.에 따라 한국의 出入口管理法에
따라서 一般外國人으로 간주한다 는 것을 約束

0035

#1

JOINT COMMITTEE

1. A Joint Committee shall be established as the means for consultation between the two Governments on all matters requiring mutual consultation regarding the interpretation and implementation of this Agreement.

2. The Joint Committee shall be composed of a representative of the Government of the Republic of Korea and a representative of the Government of the United States, each of whom shall have one or more deputies and a staff. The Joint Committee shall determine its own procedures, and arrange for such auxiliary organs and administrative services as may be required.
The Joint Committee shall be so organized that it may meet immediately at any time at the request of the representative of either Government.

3. If the Joint Committee is unable to resolve any matter, it shall refer that matter to the respective Governments for further consideration through diplomatic channels.

0036

A.M.에 다음을 挿入 提議.
"The exception provided for in the first sentence of paragraph 1 is relevant only to paragraph 2, subparagraphs (b) and (c) of Article —."

ARTICLE

F&A (B)
2.(1)b c

1. A Joint Committee shall be established as the means for consultation between the Government of the United States and the Government of the Republic of Korea on all matters requiring mutual consultation regarding the implementation of this Agreement ~~unless~~ except where otherwise provided ~~for~~.* In particular, th Joint Committee shall serve as the means for consultation in determining the facilities and areas in the Republic of Korea which are required for the use of the United States in carrying out the purposes of this Agreement.

2. The Joint Committee shall be composed of a representative of the Government of the United States and a representative of the Government of the Republic of Korea, each of whom shall have one or more deputies and a staff. The Joint Committee shall determine its own procedures, and arrange for such auxiliary organs and administrative services as may be required. The Joint Committee shall be so organized that it may meet immediately at any time at the request of the representative of either the Government of the United States or the Government of the Republic of Korea.

3. If the Joint Committee is unable to resolve any matter, it shall refer that matter to the respective Governments for further consideration through appropriate channels.

* This phrase "unless otherwise provided for" has been substituted with the phrase "except where otherwise provided."

0037

我口側案

Customs Duties

1. Except as provided expressly to the contrary in this Agreement, members of the United States forces, the civilian component, and their dependents shall be subject to the laws and regulations administered by the customs authorities of the Republic of Korea. In particular customs authorities of the Republic of Korea shall have the right, under the general conditions laid down by the laws and regulations of the Republic of Korea, to search members of the United States forces, the civilian component and their dependents and to examine their luggage, and to seize articles pursuant to such laws and regulations.

2. All materials, supplies and equipment imported by the United States forces or by the organizations provided for in Article ______ exclusively for the official use of the United States forces or those organizations or for the use of members of the United States forces, the civilian component and their dependents shall be permitted entry into Korean free from customs duties and other such charges. When such materials, supplies and equipment are imported, a certificate issued by the authorities of the United States forces in the form to be determined by the Joint Committee shall be submitted to the customs authorities of the Republic of Korea.

關稅

3. Property consigned to and for the personal use of members of the United States forces, the civilian component and their dependents, shall be subject to customs duties, except that no such duties or charges shall be paid with respect to:

(a) Furniture, household goods and other personal [illegible] for their private use [illegible]

0038

effects for their private use imported by the members of the United States forces, the civilian component and their dependents at time of their first arrival in Korea.

(b) Reasonable quantities of clothing and household goods which are mailed into the Republic of Korea through the United States military post offices.

4. (c) The exemption granted in paragraphs 2 and 3 shall apply only to cases of importation of goods and shall not be interpreted as refuning customs duties and domestic excises collected by the customs authorities at the time of entry in cases of purchases of goods on which such duties and excises have already been collected.

5. Customs examination shall be exempted only in the following cases:

(a) Units of the United States forces under orders entering or leaving the Republic of Korea;

(b) Official documents under official seal;

(c) Official mail in United States military postal channels;

(d) Military cargo shipped on a United States Government bill of lading.

6. Goods imported free from customs dutues and other such charges pursuant to paragraphs 2 and 3 above:

(a) May be re-exported free from customs duties and other such charges;

(b) shall not be disposed of in the Republic of Korea, by way of either sale or gift, to person not entitled to import such goods free from duty, except as such disposal may be authorized on conditions agreed between the authorities of the Republic of Korea and the United States.

0039

7. (a) The authorities of the United States forces, in corporation with the atuthorities of the Republic of Korea, shall take such steps as are necessary to prevent abuse of the privileges granted to the United States forces, members of such forces, the civilian component, and their dependents in accordance with this Article.

(b) In order to prevent offenses against customs and fiscal laws and regulations, the authorities of the Republic of Korea and of the United States forces shall assist each other in the conduct of inquiries and the collection of evidence.

(c) The authorities of the United States forces shall render all assistance within their power to ensure that articles liable to seizure by, or on behalf of, the customs authorities of the Republic of Korea are hanced to those authorities,

(d) The authorities of the Unted States forces shall render all assistance within their power to ensure the payment of duties, taxes and penalities payable by members of the United States forces or the civilian component, or their dependendents.

(e) The authoritaes of the United States forces shall provide all practicable assistance to the customs officials dispatched to military controlled piers and airports for the purpose of customs inspection,

3. (c) Vehicles and parts imported by members of the U.S. armed forces or civilian component within two months after their first arrival in Korea for the private use of themselves or their dependents.

0040

8. Vehicles and articles belonging to the United States armed forces seized by the customs authorities of the Government of the Republic of Korea in connection with an offense against its customs or fiscal laws or regulations shall be handed over to appropriate authorities of the force concerned.

0041

D

Definition

In this Agreement the expression —

(a) "members of the United States forces" means the personnel on active duty belonging to the land, sea or air armed services of the United States of America when in the territory of the Republic of Korea.

(b) "civilian component" means the civilian persons of United States nationality who are in the employ of, serving with, or accompanying the United States forces in the Republic of Korea, but excludes persons who are ordinarily resident in the Republic of Korea or who are mentioned in Article XVIII. For the purposes of this agreement only, dual nationals, Korean and United States, who are brought to the Republic of Korea by the United States shall be considered as United States nationals.

(c) "dependents" means

(i) Spouse, and children under 21;

(ii) Parents, and children over 21, if dependent for over half their support upon a member of the United States forces or civilian component.

0042

관 세 조 항

1. 관세관계 제법령의 적용

가. 미합중국 군대 구성원,군속 및 그가족은 본 협정에 명백히 반대의 규정이 있는 경우를 제외하고 대한민국 세관당국이 집행하는 법령에 복종하여야한다.

나. 본 협정에서 규정된 관세에관한 면제특전은 군사목적의 수행을 원활히 하는데 있는바 만약 특정군사 시설 및 구역내에서의 대한민국 관세법상의 이유로 관세경찰권을 행사할 사유가 발생할때에는 미합중국 군당국은 협조하여야 한다.

다. 미합중국 군대구성원 군속및 그가족이 대한민국에 또는 대한민국으로부터 입출국할때에 대한민국 세관은 그들의 휴대품을 조사하고 필요할때에는 수색을 함과 동시에 범칙물품을 압수할 권한을 갖는다.

2. 관세면제특전 및 증명

가. 다음의 물품은 관세 및기타 과징금을 면제한다.

(1) 미합중국 군대가 수입하는 공용품

(2) 미합중국 군당국이 허가하고 규제하는 해군판매소, PX, 식당보급소 사교크럽 극장 및 기타의 세출외 자금에 의하여 운영되는 기관이 수입하는자용품.

(3) 미합중국 군대 구성원 군속 및 그가족의 사용을 위하여 또는 그들에게 판매하기 위하여 전기 (2) 항에서 말한 제기관 또는 미합중국 군대가 수입하는 물품.

나. 전항의 물품은 자재공급품 및 비품등으로서 미합중국 군기관이 직접 수입

하는 경우에 면세하는 것이며 이의 수입자는 미합중국 군대 및 미합중국군대의 공인 조달기관 이다.

다. 전항의 사실은 합동위원회에서 결정된 소정 양식에 의하여 미합중국 군당국이 발행하는 증명서를 첨부하여 대한민국 세관에 신고하여야만 한다.

(1) 세관에대한 신고는 미합중국 군기관의 명의와 책임하에 행하여야 한다.

(2) 따라서 수입행위에 대하여 제3자의 개입이나대리는 인정하지않는다.

마. 대한민국 정부가 공인하는 자선단체에 증여하기 위하여 수입하는 자선용 구호물품에 대한 관세및 과징금은 면제 한다.

마. 미합중국 군대의 구성원 및 군속이 사용으로 수입하는 자동차에 대하여 그들이 최초로 한국에 도착할때 반입하는 경우에 한하여 관세및제세를 면제한다. 단 본인이 도착한날로 부터 2개월 내에 한국내에 반입되어야 한다.

3. 재 산 반 입

가. 원칙적으로 미합중국 군대의 구성원군속 및 그가족의 사용재산의 반입에 대하여는 관세를 부과한다. 단 다음 경우에는 관세및 과징금을 면제한다.

(1) 미합중군 군대의 구성원군속 및 그가족이 한국에 최초로 도착할때에 반입하는 그들 개인의 사용에 공하는 가구 가정용품 및 기타 개인용품.

(2) 미합중국 군사우체국을 통하여 한국에 우송되는 합리적인 양의 피복류와 가정용품.

4. 수입물품의 관세참반려

가. 미합중군 군대 또는 미합중국 정부의 세출외자금에 의하여 운영되는

0044

군인용 판매기관 등이 한국내에서 본 협정에 의하여 관세및과징금을 면제받는 것은 당해 물품 수입시에 한한다.

나. 관세및과징금이 이미 납부된 수입물품을 한국내에서 미합중국군 또는 미합중국 정부의 세출외자금에 의하여 운영되는 제기관이 공용으로 구매조달할 경우에도 당해 관세및과징금을 반려하지는 않는다.

~~이는 일반의 국산품 보다 수입품이 유리한 혜택을 받게되는 결과로서 야기되는 일반국내 제조업에 대한 부당한 압박이 되는 까닭이다.~~

다. 미합중국 군대 구성원군속 및 그가족이 사용하고저 하는 물품을 한국내에서 관세및과징금을 이미 납부한 수입품을 구매할 경우에도 전항과 같이 당해 관세및 과징금을 반려하지 않는다.

5. 세관검사의 면제

가. 수출입 물품에 대하여 세관에서 필요로하는 모든 검사는 본 협정에 의하여 다음의 경우에 한하여 면제 한다.

(1) 명령에 의하여대한민국에 출입국하는 미합중국 군대의 부대

(2) 미합중국군대의 공문서로서 공식봉인으로 공용임이 표시된것.

(3) 미합중국 군사우편 선로상에 있는 공용우편물

(4) 미합중국 정부의 선하증권에 의하여 미합중국 군대 앞으로 운송되는 군사화물

그러나 본 협정에서의 세관검사의 면제는 본래의 수출입신고 및 수출입면허 절차 까지를 면제하는것은 아니다.

나. 명령에 의하여 대한민국에 출입국하는 미합중국 군대의 부대및 구성원

0045

의 휴대품에 대하여는 각각 그지위관 및 본인의 구두신고에 의하여 사정을 감안하고 세관검사를 면제하며 공용의 봉인이 있는 공문서에 대하여는 그의 공용의 표시를 확인하고 세관검사를 면제한다.

다. 미합중국 정부의 선하증권에 의하여 미합중국 군대 앞으로 운송되는 군사화물은 합동위원회에서 결정한 소정 양식에 의거 미합중군 군대가 수입 신고를 하고 정부 선하증권 사본 또는 이에 대치할 미합중국 군대수송부의 증명서를 첨부하여 세관검사를 면제한다.

라. "미합중국 정부의선하증권" 이라 함은 미합중국 정부가 발행하는 것을 말하며 선박회사가 미합중군 정부를 위하여 발행하는것은 포함하지않는다.

마. 본 협정에서 "군사화물" 이라 함은 무기및비품에 한정하는 것이 아니고 합중국정부의 선하증권에 의하여 미합중군 군대 앞으로 운송되는모든 화물을 말하며 미합중국 정부의 타의 기관앞으로 운송되는 화물은 이와 구별되어야 한다.

바. 대한민국 세관당국이 필요하다고 인정하는 경우에는 미합중국 군대의 군인용 판매기관 등 앞으로 미합중군 정부의 선하증권에 의하여 운송되는 화물에 대하여 검사를 한다.

6. 관세면제물품의 양도의제한및 동물품양수시의관세징수

가. 미합중국 군대 또는 미합중국 정부의 세출외 자금에 의하여 운영되는 군인용 판매기관 등 과 미합중국군대의 구성원군속 및 그가족이 본 협정에 의하여 관세및기타의 과징금을 면제받고 수입한 물품은

(1) 재 수출할수 있으며

(2) 한미 양당국의 합의한 조건하에 처분을 인정하는 경우를 제외

0046

하고는 본 협정 기타 대한민국 법령에 의거 관세및국징금의 면제특권이 부여된 이외의자에게 한국내에서 매각 증여 등 형식으로 처분하지 못한다.

나. 미합중국 군대의 구성원 군속 및그가족인 자가 제대 사직 이혼등 이유로 일반인이 되었을때에는 본인이 구성원 군속 및그가족으로 있을 당시에 소유하든 면세물품을 계속 소유하고있는한 본 협정의 표범이 있다.

다. 본 협정에 의하여 면세 수입된 물품에 대한 양도의 제한이나 소정절차의 이행을 요하는 미합중국 군대의 구성원 군속 및 그가족 등이 직접 수입한 물품에 한정되는것이 아니고 미합중국 군대로부터 지급된 물품 군인용 판매기관 등에서 구입한 면세물품 등을 양도하는경우에도 적용된다.

마. 본 협정에 의하여 면세된 물품을 무단 양도하였을 때에는 한국 관세법에 의하여 처벌된다.

7. 미합중국군 당국의 협조

가. 미합중국군 당국은 대한민국 당국과 협력하여 본 협정에서 미합중국 군대 그 구성원 군속및 그가족에게 허여한 특권의 남용을 방지하는데 필요한 조치를 취하여야 한다.

나. 미합중국군 당국은 관세및 기진법령에 관한 위반행위를 대한민국 당국이 조사실시 및 증거의수집을 하는데 대하여 원조하여야 한다.

양당국은 본항의 위반행위를 방지하는데 필요한 계속적인 정보의 교환은 물론 법위반의 잠재적 요소가 농후한 군인용판매기관 등에 대한 수시적인 조사를 실시하고 제반 증거 수집에 상호 협조한다.

다. 미합중국 군당국은 대한민국 세관당국에 의하여 또는 기타 대한민국

0047

관헌에 의하여 압수된 물품이 한국 세관당국으로 인도되도록 가능한 모든 원조를 하여야 한다.

라. 미합중국군 당국은 미합중국 군대 구성원 군속 또는 그가족이 납부하여야할 관세조세 및 벌금의 납부를 확보하기 위하여 가능한 모든 원조를 제공 하여야 한다.

마. 미합중국 군 당국은 세관검사의 목적을 위하여 군대가 관리하는 부두와 비행장에 파견된 세관공무원에게 모든 실제적 원조를 제공하여야한다.

AGREED MINUTES TO ARTICLE (Customs)

1. The quantity of goods imported under paragraph 2 by non-appropriated fund organizations of the United States armed forces for the use of the members of the United States armed forces, the civilian component, and their dependents shall be limited to the extent reasonably required for such use. Non-appropriated fund organizations referred to in paragraph 2 shall be permitted to import such materials, supplies and equipment only with non-appropriated fund.

2. Paragraph 3 (a) does not require concurrent shipment of goods with travel of owner nor does it require single loading or shipment. In this connection, members of the United States armed forces or civilian component and their dependents may import free of duty their personal and household effects during a period of ~~three~~ 6 mo months ~~from~~ the date of their first arrival. The quantity of such personal and household effects shall be limited to reasonable amount.

3. The term "military cargo" as used in paragraph 5 (c) is not confined to arms and equipment but refers to all cargo consigned to the United

0049

States armed forces. (deleted)

4. The United States armed forces will take every practicable measure to ensure that goods will not be imported into the Republic of Korea by or for the members of the United States armed forces, the civilian component, or their dependents, the entry of which would be in violation of Korean customs laws and regulations. The United States armed forces will promptly notify the Korean customs authorities whenever the entry of such goods is discovered.

5. The Korean customs authorities may, if they consider that there has been an abuse or infringement in connection with the entry of goods under Article , take up the matter with the appropriate authorities of the United States armed forces.

6. The words "The United States armed forces shall render all assistance within their power," etc., in paragraph 9 (b) and (c) refer to reasonable and practicable measures by the United States armed forces. (deleted)

0050

第二次에 對한 美側修正案

ARTICLE (Customs)

2. All materials, supplies and equipment imported by the United States armed forces in cluding their authorized procurement agencies and their non-appropriated fund organizations provided for in Article , for the official use of the United States armed forces or for the use of forces logistically supported by the United States armed forces or for the use of the members of the United States armed forces, the civilian component, or their dependents shall be permitted entry into the Republic of Korea free from customs cuties and other such charges. Similarly, materials, supplies and equipment which are imported by others than the United States armed forces but are to be used exclusively by the United States armed forces and or forces logistically supported by the United States amred forces or are ultimately to be incorporated into articles of facilities to be used by such forces shall be permitted entry into the Republic of Korea free from customs duties and other such charges. Appropriate certification shall be made by the United States armed forces with respect to the importation of materials, supplies and equipment for the foregoing specified purposes.

0051

美日側案 (Ori) OK by ROK

ARTICLE (Customs)

OK 1. Save as provided in this Agreement, members of the United States armed forces, the civilian component, and their dependents shall be subject to the laws and regulations administered by the customs authorities of the Republic of Korea.

合意

OK 2. All materials, supplies and equipment imported by the United States armed forces, (including their authorized procurement agencies and their non-appropriated fund ~~organizations~~ activities provided for in Article), for the official use of the United States armed forces or for the use of the members of the United States armed forces, the civilian component, and their dependents, and materials, supplies and equipment which are to be used exclusively by the United States armed forces or are ultimately to be incorporated into articles or facilities used by such forces, shall be permitted entry into the Republic of Korea; such entry shall be free from customs duties and other such charges. Appropriate certification shall be made that such materials, supplies and equipment are being imported by the United States armed forces, (including their authorized procurement agencies and their non-

Sports Activities, Officers club

0052

appropriated fund ~~organizations~~ activities provided for in Article

), or, in the case of materials, supplies and equipment to be used exclusively by the United States armed forces or ultimately to be incorporated into articles or facilities used by such forces, that delivery thereof is to be taken by the United States armed forces for the purposes specified above. The exemptions provided in this paragraph shall extend to materials, supplies and equipment imported by the United States armed forces for the use of other armed forces (under the Unified Command) in Korea which receive logistical support from the United States armed forces.

3. Property consigned to and for the personal use of members of the United States armed forces, the civilian component, and their dependents, shall be subject to customs duties and other such charges, except that no duties or charges shall be paid with respect to:

(a) Furniture, household goods, and personal effects for their private use imported by the members of the United States armed forces or civilian component when they first arrive to serve in the Republic of Korea or by their dependents when they first arrive for reunion with members of such forces or civilian component;

0053

(b) Vehicles and parts imported by members of the United States armed forces or civilian component ~~within [illegible] months after their first arrival in Korea~~ for the private use of themselves or their dependents;

OK (c) Reasonable quantities of personal effects and household goods of a type which would ordinarily be purchased in the United States for the private use of members of the United States armed forces, civilian component, and their dependents, which are mailed into the Republic of Korea through United States military post offices.

OK. 4. The exemption granted in paragraphs 2 and 3 shall apply only to cases of importation of goods and shall not be interpreted as refunding customs duties and domestic excises collected by the customs authorities at the time of entry in cases of purchase of goods on which such duties and excises have already been collected.

5. Customs examination shall not be made in the following cases:

(a) Members of the United States armed forces under orders entering or leaving the Republic of Korea; for official duty purpose, but not for leave or recreation purpose.

0054

(b) Official documents under official seal and mail in United States military postal channels;

(c) Military cargo consigned to the United States armed forces, ~~including their authorized procurement agencies, and their non-appropriated fund organizations provided for in Article~~ activities

6. Except as such disposal may be authorized by the United States and Korean authorities in accordance with mutually agreed conditions, goods imported into the Republic of Korea free of duty shall not be disposed of in the Republic of Korea to persons not entitled to import such goods free of duty.

7. Goods imported into the Republic of Korea free from customs duties and other such charges pursuant to paragraphs 2 and 3, may be re-exported free from customs duties and other such charges.

8. The United States armed forces, in cooperation with Korean authorities, shall take such steps as are necessary to prevent abuse of privileges granted to the United States armed forces, members of such forces, the civilian component, and their dependents in accordance with this Article.

0055

9. (a) In order to prevent offense against laws and regulations administered by the customs authorities of the Government of the Republic of Korea, the Korean authorities and the United States armed forces shall assist each other in the conduct of inquiries and the collection of evidence.

(b) The United States armed forces shall render all assistance within their power to ensure that articles liable to seizure by, or on behalf of, the customs authorities of the Government of the Republic of Korea are handed to those authorities.

(c) The United States armed forces shall render all assistance within their power to ensure the payment of duties, taxes, and penalties payable by members of such forces or of the civilian component, or their dependents.

(d) (e) Vehicles and articles belonging to the United States armed forces seized by the customs authorities of the Government of the Republic of Korea in connection with an offense against its customs or fiscal laws or regulations shall be handed over to the appropriate authorities of the forces concerned.

0056

C

AGREED MINUTES TO ARTICLE (Customs)

OK 1. The quantity of goods imported under paragraph 2 by non-appropriated fund ~~organizations~~ activities of the United States armed forces for the use of ~~the members of the United States armed forces, the civilian component, and their dependents~~ persons authorized by Article 13, and its Agreed Minutes shall be limited to the extent reasonably required for such use.

2. Paragraph 3(a) does not require concurrent shipment of goods with travel of owner nor does it require single loading or shipment. In this connection, members of the United States armed forces or civilian component and their dependents may import free of duty (reasonable quantities of) their personal and household effects during a period of six months from the date of their first arrival.

3. The term "military cargo" as used in paragraph 5(c) is not confined to arms and equipment but refers to all cargo consigned to the United States armed forces, (including their authorized procurement agencies, ~~and their~~ ~~but excluding~~ non-appropriated fund ~~organizations~~ activities provided for in Article.)

A.M.

OK 4. The United States armed forces will take every practicable measure to ensure that goods will not be

ROK 제시안 1/9. 38차

0057

imported into the Republic of Korea by or for the members of the United States armed forces, the civilian component, or their dependents, the entry of which would be in violation of Korean customs laws and regulations. The United States armed forces will promptly notify the Korean customs authorities whenever the entry of such goods is discovered.

5. The Korean customs authorities may, if they consider that there has been an abuse or infringement in connection with the entry of goods under Article , take up the matter with the appropriate authorities of the United States armed forces.

6. The words "The United States armed forces shall render all assistance within their power", etc., in paragraph 9(b) and (c) refer to reasonable and practicable measures by the United States armed forces. ~~authorized by United States law and service regulations.~~

0058

CONFIDENTIAL

Agreed Minute

7. It is understood that the duty free treatment provided in paragraph 2 shall apply to materials, supplies, and equipment imported for sale (through commissaries ~~and non-appropriated fund organizations,~~) under such regulations as the United States armed forces may promulgate, to those individuals and organizations referred to in Article PX and its Agreed Minute. — 削除 (但回範囲)

① (commissary — dependents — no
PX — dependents — yes.

② Regulation 265 에서 사기시을 쓰게하느냐?

③ PX. A.M. 5.. 範囲 如何 에 따라 Commissary 의 ...

이때 {dependents 가 問題.
총각}

[redacted]

0059

ARTICLE (Access by Aircraft and Vessel)

I. United States and foreign vessels and aircraft operated by, for, or under the control of the Government of the United States for the purpose of this Agreement shall be accorded access to any port or airport of the Republic of Korea free from toll or landing charges. When cargo or passengers not accorded the exemption of this Agreement are carried on such vessels and aircraft notification shall be given to the appropriate Korean authorities, and their entry into and departure from the Republic of Korea shall be according to the laws and regulations of the Republic of Korea.

2. When the vessels mentioned in paragraph I enter Korean ports, appropriate notification shall be made to the appropriate Korean authorities. Such vessels shall have freedom from c compulsory pilotage. If, however, a pilot is taken, pilotage shall be paid fo at appropriate rates.

0060

AGREED MINUTES TO ARTICLE (Access by Aircraft and Vessel)

I. The Vessels mentioned in paragraph I include chartered vessels (bare boat charter, voyage charter and time charter), except space chartered vessels.

0061

Vehicle, Vessel & Aircraft Access

ARTICLE

1. United States and foreign vessels and aircraft operated by, for, or under the control of the United States for official purposes shall be accorded access to any port or airport of Korea free from toll or landing charges. When cargo or passengers not accorded the exemptions of this Agreement are carried on such vessels and aircraft, notification shall be given to the appropriate Korean authorities, and their entry into and departure from Korea shall be according to the laws and regulations of Korea.

2. The vessels and aircraft mentioned in paragraph 1, United States Government-owned vehicles including armor, and members of the United States armed forces, the civilian component, and their dependents shall be accorded access to and movement between facilities and areas in use by the United States armed forces and between such facilities and areas and the ports or airports of Korea. Such access to and movement between facilities and areas by United States military vehicles shall be free from toll and other charges.

3. When the vessels mentioned in paragraph 1 enter Korean ports appropriate notification shall, under normal conditions, be made to the proper Korean authorities. Such vessels shall have freedom from compulsory pilotage, but if a pilot is taken pilotage shall be paid for at appropriate rates.

0062

AGREED MINUTES TO ARTICLE

1. "United States and foreign vessels...operated by, for, or under the control of the United States for official purposes" mean United States public vessels and chartered vessels (bare boat charter, voyage charter and time charter). Space charter is not included. Commercial cargo and private passengers are carried by them only in exceptional cases.

2. The Korean ports mentioned herein will ordinarily mean "open ports".

3. An exception from making the "appropriate notification" referred to in paragraph 3 will apply only in unusual cases where such is required for security of the United States armed forces or similar reasons.

4. The laws and regulations of Korea will be applicable except as specifically provided otherwise in this Article.

0063

ARTICLE (Control of Navigations and Meteorological Services)

1. All civil and military air traffic control and communications systems shall be developed in close coordination between the two Governments and shall be integrated to the extent necessary for mutual security interests. Procedures, and any subsequent changes thereto, necessary to effect this coordination and integration will be established by arrangements between the appropriate authorities of the two Governments.

2. Lights and other aids to navigation of vessels and aircraft places or established in the facilities and areas in use by the United States and in territorial waters adjacent thereto or in the vicinity thereof shall confirm to the system in use in the Republic of Korea. The Republic of Korea and United States authorities which have established such navigation aids shall notify each other of their positions and characteristics and shall give advance notification before making any changes in them or establishing additional navigation aids.

3. The Governments of the Republic of Korea and the United States shall cooperate in meteorological services through exchanges of meteorological observations, climatological information and seismographic data in accordance with arrangements between the appropriate authorities of the two Governments.

0064

Agreed Minute to Article ____

The establishment and construction of aids to navigation for vessels and aircrafts referred to in Paragraph 2 shall be effected in accordance with arrangements between the two Governments through the Joint Committee provided for in Article ____.

Joint Committee

0065

Airtraffic Control + Navigational Aids

대외비 CONFIDENTIAL

ARTICLE (~~Control of Navigations and Meteorological Services~~)

1. All civil and military air traffic control and communications systems shall be developed in close coordination between the two Governments and shall be integrated to the extent necessary for mutual security interests. Procedures, and any subsequent changes thereto, necessary to effect this coordination and integration will be established by arrangements between the appropriate authorities of the two Governments.

2. Lights and other aids to navigation of vessels and aircraft placed or established in the facilities and areas in use by the United States and in territorial waters adjacent thereto or in the vicinity thereof shall confirm to the system in use in the Republic of Korea. The Republic of Korea and United States authorities which have established such navigation aids shall notify each other of their positions and characteristics and shall give advance notification before making any changes in them or establishing additional navigation aids.

3. The Governments of the Republic of Korea and the United States shall cooperate in meteorological services through exchanges of meteorological observations, climatological information and seismographic data in accordance with arrangements between the appropriate authorities of the two Governments.

0066

CONFIDENTIAL

A

Air traffic Control & Navigational Aids

ARTICLE

完全合意 38차 ⌗ 60

1. All civil and military air traffic control shall be developed in close coordination and shall be integrated to the extent necessary for the operation of this Agreement. Procedures, and any subsequent changes thereto, necessary to effect this coordination and integration will be established by arrangement between the appropriate authorities of the two Governments.

2. The United States is authorized to establish, construct and maintain aids to navigation ~~for vessels~~ and aircraft, both visual and electronic as required, throughout the Republic of Korea and in the territorial waters thereof. Such navigation aids shall conform generally to the system in use in Korea. The United States and Korean authorities which have established navigation aids shall duly notify each other of their positions and characteristics and shall give advance notification where practicable before making any changes in them or establishing additional navigation aids.

挿入字句: through agreement between appropriate authorities of the two governments.

in accordance with procedures and ~~[illegible]~~ arrangements agreed upon between the two Governments through the Joint Committee.

②

0067

Agreement between ROK and U.S.

ARTICLE X

1. United States and foreign vessels and aircraft operated by, for, or under the control of the Government of the United States for the purpose of this Agreement shall be accorded access to any port or airport of the Republic of Korea free from toll or landing charges.

2. The vessels mentioned in paragraph 1 of this Article include chartered vessels (bare boat charter, voyage charter and time charter,), except space chartered vessels.

3. When the vessels menioned in paragraph 1 enter Korean ports, appropriate notification shall be made to the appropriate Korean authorities. Such vessels shall have freedom from compulsory pilotage. If, however, a pilot is taken, pilotage shall be paid for at appropriate rates.

Joint

0068

ARTICLE XI

1. All civil and military air traffic control and communications systems shall be developed in close coordination between the two Governments and shall be integrated to the extent necessary for mutual security interests. Procedures, and any subsequent changes thereto, necessary to effect this coordination and integration will be established by arrangements between the appropriate authorities of the two Governments.

2. Lights and other aids to navigation of vessels and aircraft placed or established in the facilities and areas in use by the United States and in territiorial waters adjacent thereto or in the vicinity thereof shall conform to the system in use in the Republic of Korea. The Republic of Korea and United States authorities which have established such navigation aids shall notify each other of their positions and characteristics and shall give advance notification before making any changes in them or establishing additional navigations aids.

0069

Agreement between U.S. and Japan

ARTICLE V

1. United States and foreign vessels and aircraft operated by, for, or under the control of the United States for official purposes shall be accorded access to any port or airport of Japan free from toll or landing charges. When cargo or passengers not accorded the exemptions of this Agreement are carried on such vessels and aircraft notification shall be given to the appropriate Japanese authorities, and their entry into and departure from Japan shall be according to the laws and regulations of Japan.

2. The vessels and aircraft mentioned in paragraph 1, United States Government-owned vehicles including armor, and members of the United States armed forces, the civilian component, and their dependents shall be accorded access to and movement between facilities and areas in use by the United States armed forces and between such facilities and areas and the ports or airports of Japan. Such access

0070

to and movement between facilities and areas by United States military vehicles shall be free from toll and other charges.

3. When the vessels mentioned in paragraph 1 enter Japanese ports, appropriate notification shall, under normal conditions, be made to the proper Japanese authorities. Such vessels shall have freedom from compulsory pilotage, but if a pilot is taken pilotage shall be paid for at appropriate rates.

ARTICLE VI

1. All civil and military air traffic control and communications systems shall be developed in close coordination and shall be integrated to the extent necessary for fulfillment of collective security interests. Procedures, and any subsequent changes thereto, necessary to effect this coordination and integration will be established by arrangement between the appropriate authorities of the two Governments.

2. Lights and other aids to navigation of vessels and aircraft placed or established in the facilities and areas in use by United States armed

0071

3. The Governments of the Republic of Korea and the United States shall cooperate in meteorological services through exchanges of meteorological observations, climatological information and seismographic data in accordance with arrangements between the appropriate authorities of the two Governments.

0072

forces and in territorial waters adjacent thereto or in the vicinity thereof shall conform to the system in use in Japan. The United States and Japanese authorities which have established such navigation aids shall notify each other of their positions and characteristics and shall give advance notification before making any changes in them or establishing additional navigation aids.

ARTICLE VII

The United States armed forces shall have the use of all public utilities and services belonging to, or controlled or regulated by the Government of Japan, and shall enjoy priorities in such use, under conditions no less favorable than those that may be applicable from time to time to the ministries and agencies of the Government of Japan.

ARTICLE VIII

The Government of Japan undertakes to furnish the United States armed forces with the following meteorological services in accordance with arrangements

0073

between the appropriate authorities of the two Governments:

(a) Meteorological observations from land and ocean areas including observations from weather ships.

(b) Climatological information including periodic summaries and the historical date of the Meteorological Agency.

(c) Telecommunications service to disseminate meteorological information required for the safe and regular operation of aircraft.

(d) Seismographic data including forecasts of the estimated size of tidal waves resulting from earthquakes and areas that might be affected thereby.

0074

U.S.-ETHIOPIA, 1953

ARTICLE VI

The Imperial Ethiopian Government grants to the Government of the United States the right to employ and use public and commercial utilities, services, transportation and communication facilities in Ethiopia in connection with operations under this Agreement. The Government of the United States shall pay for any employment or usage of such facilities at the most favorable rates obtained by other public users who employ and use such facilities.

0075

U.S.-LIBYA, 1954

ARTICLE V

PUBLIC SERVICES AND FACILITIES

Upon the request of the Government of the United States of America and provided that the Government of the United Kingdom of Libya is assured that the public and private interests in Libya will be duly safeguarded, the public services and facilities in Libya shall be made available as far as practicable for the use of the Government of the United States of America and members of the United States forces. The charges therefor shall be the same as those paid by other users, unless otherwise agreed.

0076

U.S.-PHILIPPINES, 1947

Article VII

Use of Public Services

It is mutually agreed that the United States may employ and use for United States military forces any and all public utilities, other services and facilities, airfields, ports, harbors, reads, highways, railreads, bridges, viaducts, cannals, lakes, rivers and streams in the Philippnines under conditions no less favorable than those that may be applicable from time to time to the military forces of the Philippines.

0077

Article (Facilities and Areas)

1. The Government of the Republic of Korea grants, under Article IV of the Mutual Defense Treaty between the Republic of Korea and the United States of America, to the United States the use of the facilities and areas in the Republic of Korea as provided for in this Agreement. Arrangements as to the specific facilities and areas shall be ~~made~~ concluded by the two Governments through the Joint Committee.

2. Facilities and areas referred to in this Agreement include existing furnishings, equipment and fixtures wherever located and used in necessary to the operation of such facilities and areas.

3. The facilities and areas of which the United States has the use at the time of entry into force of this Agreement, shall be regarded, for the purpose of this Agreement, as facilities and areas granted to the United States under this Agreement. For the purpose of this paragraph, all facilities and areas of which the United States has the use at the time.

재산관계 알기 위해서?

0078

of entry into force of this Agreement shall be surveyed and determined by the two Governments through the Joint Committee.

4. With regard to the private property used as facilities and areas by the United States armed forces under this Agreement, the United States shall make reasonable compensation through the Government of the Republic of Korea to the owners of such facilities and areas with a view to alleviating their losses. Detailed arrangements, including the amounts of compensation, shall be made between the two Governments through the Joint Committee.

5. The Governments of the United States bears without cost to the Republic of Korea all expenditures incident to the maintenance of the facilities and areas granted under this Agreement.

6. At the request of either Government, the Government of the Republic of Korea and the Government of the United States shall review such arrangements referred to in paragraph 1 and may agree that such

0079

facilities and areas shall be returned to the Republic of Korea or that additional facilities and areas may be provided.

7. The facilities and areas used by the United States shall be promptly returned to the Government of the Republic of Korea whenever they are no longer needed for the purpose of this Agreement, and the Government of the United States agrees to keep the needs for facilities and areas under continual observation with a view toward such return.

8. When facilities and areas are temporarily not being used by the United States, interim use by the authorities of the Republic of Korea or nationals may be arranged through the Joint Committee.

9. With respect to facilities and areas which are to be used by the United States for limited period of time, the Joint Committee shall specify in the agreements covering such facilities and areas the extent to which the provisions of this Agreement shall apply.

0080

10. Within the facilities and areas, the Government of the United States may take all the measures necessary for their establishment, operation, safeguarding and control. In order to provide access for the United States forces to the facilities and areas for their support, safeguarding and control, the Government of the Republic of Korea shall, at the request of the Government of the United States and upon consultation between the two Governments through the Joint Committee, take necessary measures within the scope of applicable laws and regulations over land, territorial waters and airspace adjacent to, or in the vicinities of the facilities and areas. The Government of the United States may also take necessary measures for such purposes upon consultation between the two Governments through the Joint Committee.

11. The Government of the United States agrees not to take the measures referred to in paragraph 1 in such a manner as to interfere unnecessarily with

0081

navigation, aviation, communication, or land travel to or from or within the territories of the Republic of Korea. All questions relating to frequencies, power and like matters used by apparatus employed by the Government of the United States designed to emit electric radiation shall be settled by arrangement between the appropriate authorities of the two Governments.

12. Operations in the facilities and areas in use by the Government of the United States shall be carried on with due regard to the public safety.

13. The Government of the United States is not obliged, when it returns facilities and areas to the Government of the Republic of Korea on the expiration of this Agreement or at an earlier date, to restore the facilities and areas to the conditions in which they were at the time they became available to the United States, or to compensate the Government of the Republic of Korea in lieu of such restoration.

0082

However, in case of private property extremely demolished by the use of the United States, the Government of the United States shall, upon the request of the Government of the Republic of Korea, pay due consideration to its restoration or compensation in lieu thereof.

14. The Government of the Republic of Korea is not obliged to make any compensation to the Government of the the United States for any improvements made in the facilities and areas or for the buildings, structures, supply or any other materials left thereon on the expiration of this Agreement or the earlier return of the facilities and areas.

0083

I. —

Article II - Facilities and Areas (Grant of and Return)

018

1. .....

(b) The facilities and areas of which the United States armed forces have the use at the effective date of this agreement together with those areas and facilities which the United States armed forces have returned to the Republic of Korea with the reserved right of re-entry, when these facilities and areas have been re-entered by U.S. forces, shall be considered as the facilities and areas agreed upon between the two Governments in accordance with subparagraph (a) above. Records of facilities and areas of which the United States armed forces have the use or right of re-entry shall be maintained through the Joint Committee after this Agreement comes into force.

Survey

95%

US ROK

1964.10

0084

85-86

F (A) 4

CONFIDENTIAL

ARTICLE

1. (a) The United States is granted, under Article IV of the Mutual Defense Treaty, the use of facilities and areas in the Republic of Korea. Agreements as to specific facilities and areas shall be concluded by the two Governments through the Joint Committee provided for in Article of this Agreement. "Facilities and Areas" include existing furnishings, equipment and fixtures, wherever located used in the operation of such facilites and areas.

(b) The facilities and areas of which the United States has the use at the effective date of this agreement shall be considered as facilities and areas agreed upon between the two Governments in accordance with sub-paragraph (a) above.

2. At the request of either Government, the Governments of the United States and the Republic of Korea shall review such ~~Arrangements~~ agreements and may agree that such facilities and areas or portions thereof shall be returned to the Republic of Korea or that additional facilities and areas may be provided.

3. The facilities and areas used by the United States shall be returned to the Republic of Korea under such conditions as may be agreed through the Joint Committee whenever they are no longer needed for the purposes of this Agreement and the United States agrees to keep the needs for

0085

1. The Government of the Republic o
under Article IV of the Mutual Defense Tr
the Republic of Korea and the United Stat
America, to the United States the use of
facilities and areas in the Republic of K
provided for in this Agreement. Arrangem
the specific facilities and areas shall b
two Governments through the Joint Committ

2. Facilities and areas referred t
Agreement include existing furnishings,
and fixtures necessary to the operation
facilities and areas.

3. The facilities and areas of whic
States has the use at the time of entry i
of this Agreement, shall be regarded
, as facilities and area
the United States under this Agreement.
purpose of this paragraph, all facilities
of which the United States has the use at
of entry into force of this Agreement sh
and determined by the two Governments th
Joint Committee.

5. At the request of either Governm
Government of the Republic of Korea and t
of the United States shall review such ar
referred to in paragraph 1 and may agree
facilities and areas shall be returned to
of Korea or that additional facilities an
be provided.

7. The facilities and areas used b
States shall be promptly returned to the
of the Republic of Korea whenever they a
needed for the purpose of this Agreement
Government of the United States agrees t
needs for facilities and areas under con
observation with a view toward such ret

8 A

CONFIDENTIAL

ARTICLE

(a) The United States is granted, under Article
Mutual Defense Treaty, the use of facilities and
the Republic of Korea. Agreements as to specific
s and areas shall be concluded by the two Govern-
ough the Joint Committee provided for in Article
greement. "Facilities and Areas" include existing
gs, equipment and fixtures, wherever located, used
eration of such facilites and areas.

(b) The facilities and areas of which the United
s the use at the effective date of this agreement
considered as facilities and areas agreed upon
he two Governments in accordance with sub-paragraph

At the request of either Government, the Governments
ited States and the Republic of Korea shall review
gements and may agree that such facilities and
ortions thereof shall be returned to the Republic
r that additional facilities and areas may be

he facilities and areas used by the United
l be returned to the Republic of Korea under
tions as may be agreed through the Joint Committee
ey are no longer needed for the purposes of this
nd the United States agrees to keep the needs for

0085

1. The Government of the Republic of Korea grants, under Article IV of the Mutual Defense Treaty between the Republic of Korea and the United States of America, to the United States the use of the facilities and areas in the Republic of Korea as provided for in this Agreement. Arrangements as to the specific facilities and areas shall be made by the two Governments through the Joint Committee.

2. Facilities and areas referred to in this Agreement include existing furnishings, equipment and fixtures necessary to the operation of such facilities and areas.

3. The facilities and areas of which the United States has the use at the time of entry into force of this Agreement, shall be regarded for the purpose of this Agreement, as facilities and areas granted to the United States under this Agreement. For the purpose of this paragraph, all facilities and areas of which the United States has the use at the time of entry into force of this Agreement shall be surveyed and determined by the two Governments through the Joint Committee.

6. At the request of either Government, the Government of the Republic of Korea and the Government of the United States shall review such arrangements referred to in paragraph 1 and may agree that such facilities and areas shall be returned to the Republic of Korea or that additional facilities and areas may be provided.

OK

7. The facilities and areas used by the United States shall be promptly returned to the Government of the Republic of Korea whenever they are no longer needed for the purpose of this Agreement, and the Government of the United States agrees to keep the needs for facilities and areas under continual observation with a view toward such return.

0086

facilities and areas under continual observation with a view toward such return.

4. (a) When facilifies and areas are temporarily not being used and the Government of the Republic of Korea is so advised, the Government of the Republic of Korea may make, or permit Korean nationals to make, interim use of such facilities and areas provided that it is agreed between the two Governments through the Joint Committee that such use would not be harmful to the purposes for which the facilities and areas are normally used by the United States armed forces.

(b) With respect to facilities and areas which are to be used by United States armed forces for limited periods of time, the Joint Committee shall specify in ~~the~~ agreements covering such facilities and areas the extent to which the provisions of this Agreement shall apply.

8. When fa
not being used by
the authorities
may be arranged

9. With resp
are to be used by
of time, the Joint
agreements coverin
extent to which th
apply.

0087

SECRET

s and areas under continual observation with
ward such return.

(a) When facilities and areas are temporarily used and the Government of the Republic of so advised, the Government of the Republic of make, or permit Korean nationals to make, se of such facilities and areas provided that it between the two Governments through the Joint that such use would not be harmful to the for which the facilities and areas are normally he United States armed forces.

(b) With respect to facilities and areas which used by United States armed forces for limited f time, the Joint Committee shall specify in ments covering such facilities and areas the which the provisions of this Agreement shall not

[redacted]

8. When facilities and areas are temporarily not being used by the United States, interim use by the authorities of the Republic of Korea or nationals may be arranged through the Joint Committee.

[redacted]

9. With respect to facilities and areas which are to be used by the United States armed forces for limited periods of time, the Joint Committee shall specify in the agreements covering such facilities and areas the extent to which the provisions of this Agreement shall apply.

OK

0088

[redacted]

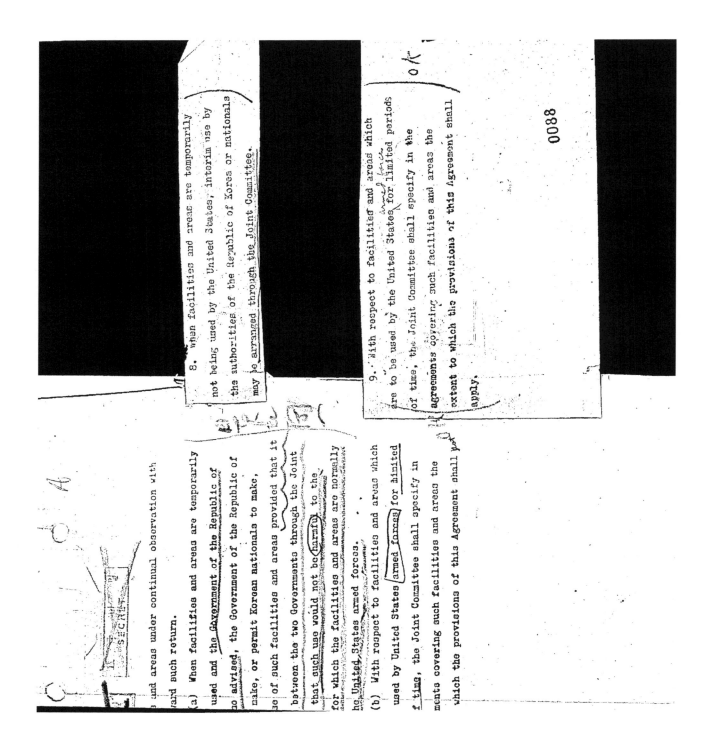

ARTICLE III - Facilities and Areas
(Security Measures In)

AGREED MINUTE

It is agreed that in the event of an emergency, the United States armed forces shall be authorized to take such measures in the vicinity of the areas and facilities as may be necessary to provide for their safeguarding and control.

Record에 unduly impair 가지않도록 하고 있음

0089

89-90

(B)

CONFIDENTIAL

ARTICLE

1. Within the facilities and areas, the United States may take all the measures necessary for their establishment, operation, safeguarding and control. In an emergency, measures necessary for their safeguarding and control may also be taken in the vicinity thereof. In order to provide access for the United States armed forces to the facilites and areas for their support, safeguarding and control, the Government of the Republic of Korea shall, at the request of the United States armed forces and upon consultation between the two Governments through the Joint Committee, take necessary measures within the scope of applicable laws and regulations over land, territorial waters and airspace adjacent to, or in the vicinities of the facilites and areas. The United States may also take necessary measures for such purposes upon consultation between the two Governments through the Joint Committee.

2. (a) The United States agrees not to take the measures referred to in paragraph 1 in such a manner as to interfere unnecessarily with navigation, aviation, communication, or land travel to or from or within the territories of the Republic of Korea.

(b) All questions relating to telecommunication including radio frequencies for electromagnetic radiating devices, or like matters, shall continue to be resolved

10. Within the facil
ment of the United States
necessary for their estab
safeguarding and control.
for the United States for
areas for their support,
the Government of the Rep
the request of the Govern
and upon consultation bet
through the Joint Committ
within the scope of appli
over land, territorial wa
to, or in the vicinities
The Government of the Uni
necessary measures for su
tion between the two Gove
Committee.

11. (a) The Government
not to take the measures
in such a manner as to in
navigation, aviation, co
to or from or within the
of Korea. (b) All questions
power and like matters u
the Government of the Un
electric radiation shall
between the appropriate
Governments.

0090

B

X within the extent that the Korean nationals and their properties are not unduly impaired.

Record only

and areas, the United
res necessary for their
eguarding and control. In
ary for their safeguarding
in the vicinity thereof,
r the United States armed
reas for their support,
Government of the Republic
t of the United States (armed)
between the two Governments
take necessary measures within
and regulations over land,
ace adjacent to, or in the
and areas. The United States
ures for such purposes upon
Governments through the

es agrees not to take the
agraph 1 in such a manner as
with navigation, aviation,
el to or from or within the
of Korea.
relating to telecommunication
for electromagnetic radiating
hall continue to be resolved

0090

10. Within the facilities and areas, the Government of the United States may take all the measures necessary for their establishment, operation, safeguarding and control. In order to provide access for the United States forces to the facilities and areas for their support, safeguarding and control, the Government of the Republic of Korea shall, at the request of the Government of the United States armed forces and upon consultation between the two Governments through the Joint Committee, take necessary measures within the scope of applicable laws and regulations over land, territorial waters and airspace adjacent to, or in the vicinities of the facilities and areas. The Government of the United States may also take necessary measures for such purposes upon consultation between the two Governments through the Joint Committee.

11. (a) The Government of the United States agrees not to take the measures referred to in paragraph 1 in such a manner as to interfere unnecessarily with navigation, aviation, communication, or land travel to or from or within the territories of the Republic of Korea. (b) All questions relating to frequencies, power and like matters used by apparatus employed by the Government of the United States designed to emit electric radiation shall be settled by arrangement between the appropriate authorities of the two Governments.

0091

CONFIDENTIAL

expeditiously in the utmost spirit of coordination and cooperation by arrangement between the designated communications authorities of the two Governments.

(c) The Government of the Republic of Korea shall, within the scope of applicable laws, regulations and agreements, take all reasonable measures to avoid or eliminate interference with electromagnetic radiation sensitive devices, telecommunications devices, or other apparatus required by the United States armed forces.

3. Operations in the facilities and areas in use by the United States armed forces shall be carried on with due regard for the public safety.

J.C. article 9 "except where otherwise provided."

12. Operations in the facilities and areas in use by the Government of the United States shall be carried on with due regard to the public safety.

0092

CONFIDENTIAL

ARTICLE

1. The United States is not obliged, when it returns facilites and areas to the Republic of Korea on the expiration of this Agreement or at an earlier date, to restore the facilities and areas to the condition in which they were at the time they became available to the United States armed forces, or to compensate the Republic of Korea in lieu of such restoration.

2. All removable facilities erected or constructed by or on behalf of the United States at its expense and all equipment, materials and supplies brought into or procured inthe Republic of Korea by or on behalf of the United States in connection with the construction, development, operation, maintenance, safeguarding and control of the facilities and areas will remain the property of the United States Government and may be removed from the Republic of Korea.

3. The foregoing provisions shall not apply to any construction which the Government of the United States may undertake under special arrangements with the Government of the Republic of Korea.

CONFIDENTIAL

0093

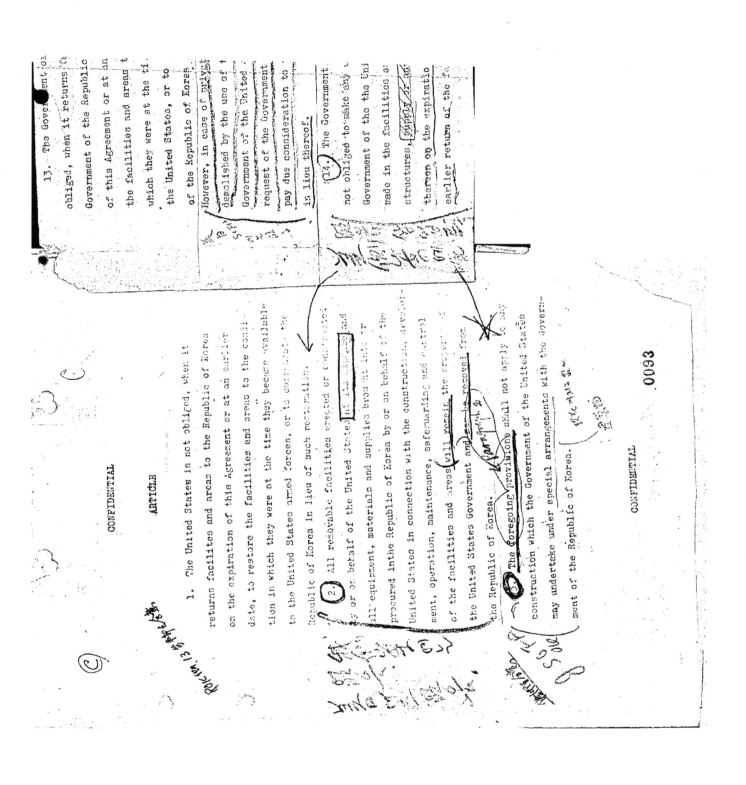

13. The Government [illegible] obliged, when it returns fa[cilities] ... Government of the Republic ... of this Agreement or at an ... the facilities and areas t[o] ... which they were at the ti[me] ... the United States, or to ... of the Republic of Korea. However, in case of privat[e] ... demolished by the use of t[he] ... Government of the United ... request of the Government ... pay due consideration to ... in lieu thereof.

14. The Government ... not obliged to make any ... Government of the the Uni[ted] ... made in the facilities a[nd] ... structures, supply or an[y] ... thereon on the expiratio[n] ... earlier return of the fa[cilities] ...

FIDENTIAL

ARTICLE

States is not obliged, when it
nd areas to the Republic of Korea
f this Agreement or at an earlier
e facilities and areas to the condi-
were at the time they became available
armed forces, or to compensate the
in lieu of such restoration.
able facilities erected or constructed
the United States at its expense and
erials and supplies brought into or
ublic of Korea by or on behalf of the
onnection with the construction, develop-
aintenance, safeguarding and control
and areas will remain the property of
Government and may be removed from
orea.
going provisions shall not apply to any
h the Government of the United States
er special arrangements with the Govern-
lic of Korea.

CONFIDENTIAL

0093

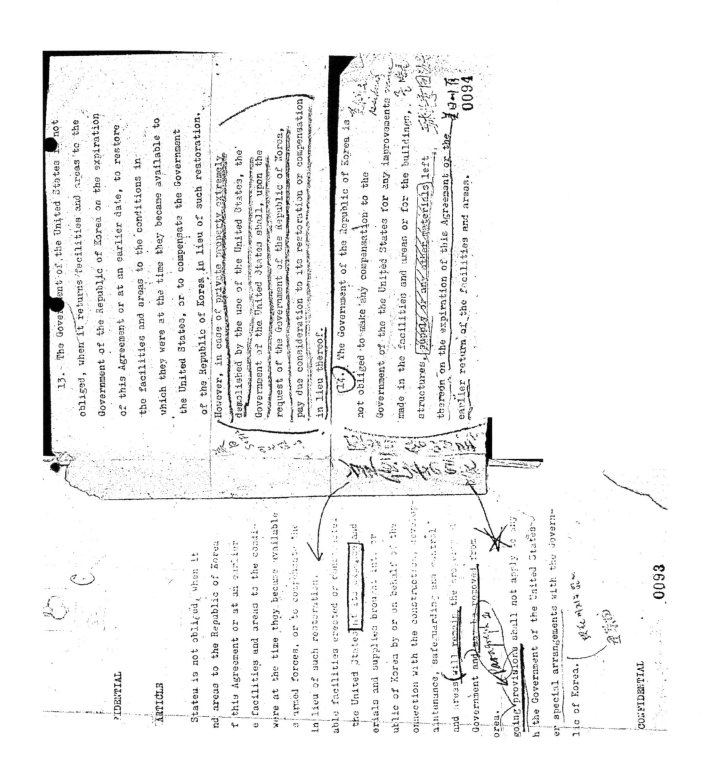

13. The Government of the United States is not obliged, when it returns facilities and areas to the Government of the Republic of Korea on the expiration of this Agreement or at an earlier date, to restore the facilities and areas to the conditions in which they were at the time they became available to the United States, or to compensate the Government of the Republic of Korea in lieu of such restoration. However, in case of private property extremely demolished by the use of the United States, the Government of the United States shall, upon the request of the Government of the Republic of Korea, pay due consideration to its restoration or compensation in lieu thereof.

14. The Government of the Republic of Korea is not obliged to make any compensation to the Government of the the United States for any improvements made in the facilities and areas or for the buildings, structures, supply or any other materials left thereon on the expiration of this Agreement or the earlier return of the facilities and areas.

0094

CONFIDENTIAL

ARTICLE

5. 1. It is agreed that the United States will bear for the duration of the Agreement without cost to the Republic of Korea all expenditures incident to the maintenance of the United States armed forces in the Republic of Korea, ~~except those to be borne by the Republic of Korea as provided in paragraph 2.~~

2. It is agreed that the Republic of Korea will furnish for the duration of this Agreement without cost to the United States and make compensation where appropriate to the owners and suppliers threof all facilities and areas and rights of way, including facilities and areas jointly used such as those at airfields and ports as provided in Articles II and III. The Government of the Republic of Korea assures the sue of such facilities and areas to the United States Government and will hold the United States Government as well as its agencies and employees harmless from any third party claims which may be advanced in connection with such use.

3. (Use of public utilities and services to be inserted later.)

Study Congressional intent on the Mutual Security Act

US; of the Defense Mutual Security Act

CONFIDENTIAL

0095

5. The Governments of t[...] without cost to the Republic [...] incident to the maintenance o[...] areas granted under this Agree[...]

[redacted]

4. With regard to the p[...] facilities and areas by the U[...] under this Agreement, the Uni[...] reasonable compensation throu[...] Republic of Korea to the owner[...] and areas with a view to allev[...] Detailed arrangements, includi[...] compensation, shall be made be[...] through the Joint Committee.

126

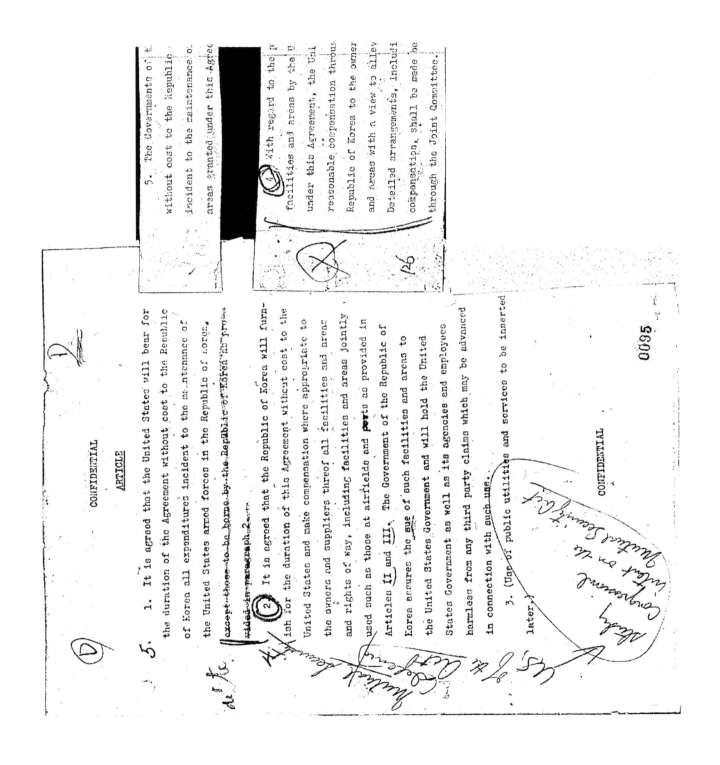

CONFIDENTIAL

ARTICLE

d that the United States will bear for
Agreement without cost to the Republic
tures incident to the maintenance of
ed forces in the Republic of Korea.
orne by the Republic of Korea as pro-

d that the Republic of Korea will furn-
of this Agreement without cost to the
ke compensation where appropriate to
iers threof all facilities and areas
including facilities and areas jointly
at airfields and ports as provided in
The Government of the Republic of
ue of such facilities and areas to
overnment and will hold the United
s well as its agencies and employees
hird party claims which may be advanced
such use.
lic utilities and services to be inserted

CONFIDENTIAL

0095

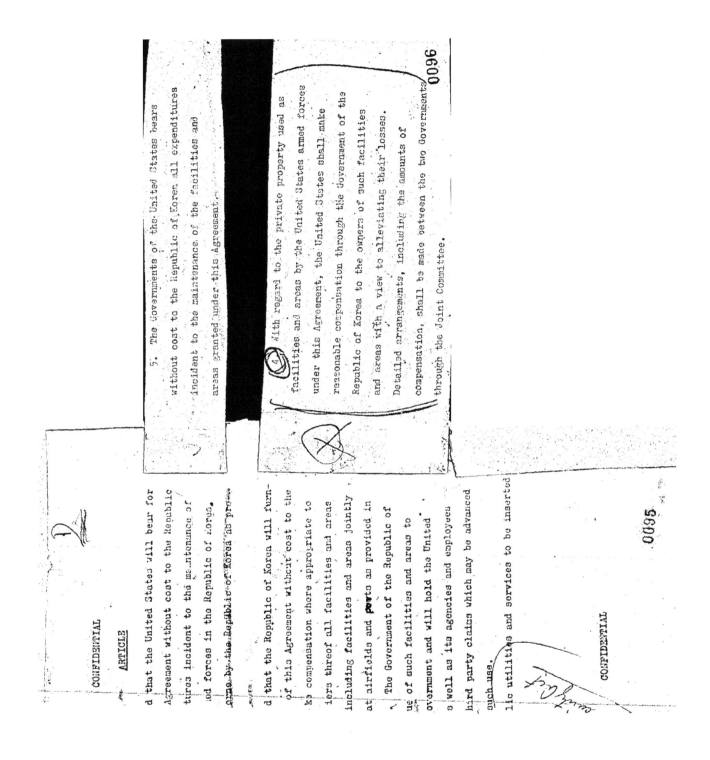

5. The Governments of the United States bears without cost to the Republic of Korea all expenditures incident to the maintenance of the facilities and areas granted under this Agreement.

4. With regard to the private property used as facilities and areas by the United States armed forces under this Agreement, the United States shall make reasonable compensation through the Government of the Republic of Korea to the owners of such facilities and areas with a view to alleviating their losses. Detailed arrangements, including the amounts of compensation, shall be made between the two Governments through the Joint Committee.

0096

AREAS AND FACILITIES ARTICLE

PROPOSED ADDITIONAL PARAGRAPH TO

AREAS AND FACILITIES ARTICLE PERTAINING

TO RETURN OF FACILITIES AND AREAS

韓國側 14
이 첨한 代案

The Republic of Korea is not obligated to compensate the United States for improvements made in United States facilities and areas or for the buildings or structures, supplies or any other materials remaining thereon upon the return of the facilities and areas.

Proposed New Draft of Utilities and Services Provisions

3. (a) The United States armed forces shall have the use of all utilities and services which are owned, controlled or regulated by the Government of the Republic of Korea or local administrative subdivisions thereof. The term "utilities and services" shall include, but not be limited to, transportation and communications facilities and systems, electricity, gas, water, steam, heat, light, power, and sewage disposal. The use of utilities and services as provided herein shall not prejudice the right of the United States to operate military transportation, communication, power and such other utilities and services deemed necessary for the operations of the United States armed forces. This right shall not be exercised in a manner inconsistent with the operation by the Government of the Republic of Korea of its utilities and services.

(b) The use of such utilities and services by the United States shall be in accordance with priorities, conditions, and rates or tariffs no less favorable than those accorded any other user.

(4. Removed from this article; to be placed elsewhere in SOFA.)

0098

Agreed Minutes

1. The Joint Committee shall be given the opportunity of discussing any changes (determined by the Korean authorities of) priority or rates applicable to the United States armed forces prior to their effective date.

2. Paragraph 3 of Article ______ will not be construed as in any way abrogating the Utilities and Claims Settlement Agreement of December 18, 1958, which continues in full force and effect unless otherwise agreed by the two governments.

3. Should the emergency operating needs of the United States armed forces so require, the Republic of Korea shall, after consultation thereon, take appropriate measures to assure provision of utilities and services necessary to meet these needs.

0099

OK.
45th
3/6

with understanding [redacted]

<u>Agreed Minute #1</u>

It is understood that (the application of) any changes determined by the Korean authorities in priorities, conditions, and rates or tariffs, applicable to the United States armed forces shall be the subject of consultation in the Joint Committee prior to their effective date.

遞信部 — 事前協議
交通部 — 通告 beyond 30 days
韓電 — 通告 within 15 days
서울市 — 事前協議

0100

Agreed Minute #3

In an emergency the Republic of Korea agrees to take appropriate measures to assure provision of utilities and services necessary to meet the needs of the United States armed forces.

0101

CONFIDENTIAL

Proposed New Draft of Utilities and Services Provisions

(Changes requiring Washington approval underlined)

3. (a) The United States armed forces shall have the use of all utilities and services which are owned, controlled or regulated by the Government of the Republic of Korea or local administrative subdivisions thereof. The term "utilities and services" shall include, but not be limited to, transportation and communications facilities and systems, electricity, gas, water, steam, heat, light, power, however produced, and sewage disposal. The use of utilities and services as provided herein shall not prejudice the right of the United States to operate military transportation, communication, power and such other utilities and services deemed necessary for the operations of the United States armed forces. This right shall not be exercised in a manner inconsistent with the operation by the Government of the Republic of Korea of its utilities and services.

(b) The use of such utilities and services by the United States shall be in accordance with priorities, conditions, and rates or tariffs no less favorable than those accorded any other user. (Final sentence converted to Agreed Minute #3)

(4. Removed from this article; to be placed elsewhere in SOFA.)

Agreed Minutes

1. The Joint Committee shall be given the opportunity of discussing any changes in priority or rates applicable to the United States armed forces prior to their effective date.

2. Paragraph 3 of Article ____ will not be construed as in any way abrogating the Utilities and Claims Settlement Agreement of December 18, 1958, which continues in full force and effect unless otherwise agreed by the two governments. Existing arrangements under that Agreement for the use of utilities

0102

and services by the United States armed forces and the payment therefor continue in effect, unless otherwise agreed upon by the Governments.

3. Should the emergency operating needs of the United States armed forces so require, the Republic of Korea shall, after consultation thereon, take appropriate measures to assure provision of utilities and services necessary to meet these needs.

0103

CONFIDENTIAL

D

Facilities and Areas

Article ____ Utilities & Services

3. (a) The United States armed forces shall have the use of all utilities and services, ~~whether publicly or privately owned~~ which are owned, controlled or regulated by the Government of the Republic of Korea or ~~political~~ local administrative subdivisions thereof. The term "utilities and services" shall include, but not be limited to, transportation and communications facilities and systems, electricity, gas, water, steam, heat, light, power, ~~however produced~~, and sewage disposal. The use of utilities and services as provided herein shall not prejudice the right of the United States to operate military transportation, communication, power and such other services and facilities deemed necessary for the operations of the United States armed forces.

(b) The use of such utilities and services by the United States shall be in accordance with priorities, conditions, and rates or tariffs no less favorable than those accorded any other user, ~~governmental or private~~. ~~The Republic of Korea shall insure that, by reason of legislation or otherwise, there shall be no discrimination against the United States armed forces in the procurement of such utilities and services.~~ Should the emergency operating needs of the United States armed forces so require, the Republic of Korea shall, upon notification thereof, take all measures to assure provision of utilities and services necessary to meet these needs.

삭제 제의 OK

삭제 제의

삭제 제의

OK

Omit

reasonable & justifiable

삭제 제의

this right shall not be exercised in a manner inconsistent with the operation by the Government of the Republic of Korea of its utilities and services

ROK AM:

0104

4. It is agreed that arrangements will be effected between the Governments of the United States and the Republic of Korea for accounting applicable to financial transactions arising out of this Agreement.

0105

CONFIDENTIAL

Agreed Minutes to Article______

1. It is understood that any change in priority ~~or~~ rates ~~increase in utility or service rates~~ applicable to the United States armed forces shall be the subject of prior consultation in the Joint Committee.

2. Paragraph 3 of Article____ will not be construed as in any way abrogating the Utilities and Claims Settlement Agreement of December 18, 1958 which continues in full force and effect.

ROK, 제4 (24차)
shall, at the Joint Committee, be notified within 15 days after the effective date of such a change.

US. — suitable language

0106

35차
11/14

UTILITIES AND SERVICES

Proposed new third and fourth sentences, Paragraph 3 (a)

Article "D"

The use of utilities and services as provided herein shall not prejudice the right of the United States to operate military transportation, communication, power and such other utilities and services deemed necessary for the operations of the United States armed forces. This right shall not be exercised in a manner inconsistent with the operation by the Government of the Republic of Korea of its utilities and services.

0107

METHOD OF ACCOUNTING CURRENTLY USED BY USFK

1. The appropriate Technical Service has specifications prepared for the type of services or purchases desired and processes these specifications along with fund citations to the US Army Korea Procurement Agency.

2. The US Army Korea Procurement Agency analyzes the specifications, determines the type of action required, and then either advertises for bids from private Korean contractors or arranges for contract negotiations with Korean government agencies, as in the case of nationalized utility systems. Bids or negotiations are usually on the basis of unit price for the utility or service furnished. Contracts normally specify what is to be shown on billings so that a proper basis of making payments can be established.

3. Upon completion of successful bidding or negotiations the US Army Korea Procurement Agency awards the contract for the specified services or purchases. Normally service contracts run for one year and indicate that the contractor or Korean government agency will present a bill for the services every 30 days or at least once each quarter. A Contracting Officer Representative from the Technical Service concerned accomplishes inspection duties for the US armed forces and insures that the services rendered are of the quality and amount required by specifications. The appropriate Technical Service certifies to the correctness of the billing received and forwards the certified billing to the US Army Korean Procurement Agency.

4. The Army Procurement Agency processes the billing and prepares appropriate payment documents and processes these to the US Army Finance and Accounting Office.

0108

5. US Army Finance and Accounting Office makes payment by check to the contractor or Korean agency involved.

METHOD OF ACCOUNTING CURRENTLY USED BY USFK

1. The appropriate Technical Service has specifications prepared for the type of services or purchases desired and processes these specifications along with fund citations to the US Army Korea Procurement Agency.

2. The US Army Korea Procurement Agency analyzes the specifications, determines the type of action required, and then either advertises for bids from private Korean contractors or arranges for contract negotiations with Korean government agencies, as in the case of nationalized utility systems. Bids or negotiations are usually on the basis of unit price for the utility or service furnished. Contracts normally specify what is to be shown on billings so that a proper basis of making payments can be established.

3. Upon completion of successful bidding or negotiations the US Army Korea Procurement Agency awards the contract for the specified services or purchases. Normally service contracts run for one year and indicate that the contractor or Korean government agency will present a bill for the services every 30 days or at least once each quarter. A Contracting Officer Representative from the Technical Service concerned accomplishes inspection duties for the US armed forces and insures that the services rendered are of the quality and amount required by specifications . The appropriate Technical Service certifies to the correctness of the billing received and forwards

0109

the certified billing to the US Army Korean Procurement Agency.

4. The Army Procurement Agency processes the billing and prepares appropriate payment documents and processes these to the US Army Finance and Accounting Office.

5. US Army Finance and Accounting Office makes payment by check to the contractor or Korean agency involved.

0110

Article _____ (Utilities and Servises)

1. The United States armed forces shall have the use of all public utilities and services belonging to, or controlled or regulated by the Government of the Republic of Korea. The term "utilities and services" shall include, but not be limited to, transportation and communications facilities and systems, electricity, gas, water, steam, heat, light, power, however produced and sewage disposal. In the use of such utilities and services the United States armed forces shall enjoy priorities under conditions no less favorable that those that may be applicable from time to time to the ministries and agencies of the Government of the Republic of Korea.

2. (a) Specific arrangements as to the use of such public utilities and services by the United States armed forces and the payment therefor shall be made between the appropriate authorities of the two Governments or their agencies.

(b) The existing arrangements concerning the use of such public utilities and services by the United States armed forces at the effective date of this Agreement shall be regarded as the arrangements referred to in the foregoing paragraph.

3. (a) The operation by the United States armed forces of the military transportation, communication, power, and other utilities and services shall be to the extent which is deemed necessary for the operation of the United States armed forces and which is not inconsistent with the operation by the Republic of Korea of such utilities and Services.

0111

The United States armed forces may operate its owned military transportation, communication, power, and other utilities and services deemed necessary for the operations of the United States armed forces.

Training of Reservists .. Agreed minute

The term "eligible United States citizens residing in the Republic of Korea "includes the staff of the United States Embassy and the civilian component of the United States armed forces.

The Term "eligible United States citizens residing in the Repiblic of Korea" includes those who are present in Korea and obliged to comply with the alien entry, exit and registration law of Korea".

0112

Article ____ (Utilities and Services)

1. The United States armed forces shall have the use of all public utilities and services belonging to, or controlled or regulated by the Government of the Republic of Korea. The term "utilities and services" shall include, but not be limited to, transportation and communications facilities and systems, electricity, gas, water, steam, heat, light, power, however produced, and sewage disposal. In the use of such utilities and services the United States armed forces shall enjoy priorities under conditions no less favorable than those that may be applicable from time to time to the ministries and agencies of the Government of the Republic of Korea.

2 (a) Specific arrangements as to the use of such public utilities and services by the United States armed forces and the payment therefor shall be made between the appropriate authorities of

0113

the two Governments or their agencies.

(b) The existing arrangements concerning the use of such public utilities and services by the United States armed forces at the effective date of this Agreement shall be regarded as the arrangements referred to in the foregoing paragraph.

A.M. 2

may

include the utilities & claims Act. Agreement and other arrangements entered into between the U.S.A.F. and authorities operating various utilities & services

0114

Article (Utilities and Services)

The United States armed forces shall have the use of all public utilities and services belonging to, or controlled or regulated by the Government of the Republic of Korea. In the use of such utilities and services the United States armed forces shall enjoy priorities under conditions no less favorable than those that may be applicable from time to time to the ministries and agencies of the Government of the Republic of Korea.

0115

Additional Sentences to Utilities and Services Article

Specific arrangements as to the use of such public utilities and services by the United States armed forces shall be made between the appropriate authorities of the two Governments or their agencies.

The existing arrangements concerning the use of such public utilities and services by the United States armed forces at the effective date of this Agreement shall be regarded as the arrangements ~~made in accordance with~~ referred to in the foregoing paragraph.

0116

공익물 용역에 관한 미측안의 검토

1. 총체적으로 보아 미측안은 일방적인 자기 위주의 규정이라 아니할수 없음. 일별하여 이는 우리의 모든 공익물 시설이 미군을 위하여 봉사하여야 할 의무 규정으로 된것같은 감이 있음. 이와 같이 광범하고 일방적인 규정은 그 유형을 찾아보기 힘이 들 정도임. 따라서 하기에 언급한 구절을 삭제하도록 주장하든지 또는 우리측 안을 내어 절충하는 것이 좋은것임.

2. (a) 항의 " whether publicly or privately owned" 는 그 다음에 오는 "which are controlled or regulated by the Government of the Republic of Korea" 로서 충분함으로 이 구절의 삭제를 요망함. 그 다음에 공익물 용역을 구체적으로 예시한 것은 반대할 이유는 없다 하겠으나 그후의 " The use of utlities and services" 이라 끝 까지는 불필요한 규정임. 왜냐하면 공익물에 관한 규정은 미군직속의 공익물 용역에 부과적으로 우리들의 그것을 사용하도록 허용하고 협조하는데 그 취지가 있기때문이며 이러한 규정을 두면 필요이상으로 우리측의 공익물 용역 의무가 많을 우려가 있기 때문임.

(b) 항 첫단의 공익물 용역의 사용 우선권 및 조건등에 있어 "any other user, governmental or private" 는 우리측 안의 정부 부처 또는 정부기관의 그것과 동일한 대우를 한다는 규정으로 족하며 미측안대로 하면 그 우선적 대우에 있어 우리측의 의무가 광범하게 될것임. 그리고 (b) 항 후단의 규정도 역시 우리측의 의무 부담만을 규정한 것이며 이는 전단의 대우 및 우선순위 규정에 있어 우리 정부나 또는 그 기관의 그것보다 불리하지 않은 대우를 받는다는 규정으로 족하며 그와 같은 대우를 하면 자연히 차별이 있을수 없은것이므로 우리측으로선 불필요한 규정임.

0117

(b) 항의 최후단의 규정도 역시 같은 이유로 삭제할것이나 우리나라의 특수사정 즉 반 전시하에 있다는 이유를 고려한다면 이는 그냥 양보하여도 가할것임.

합의의사록의 1 항도 역시 우리측의 의무 부담만 불필요하게 많게하며 모순되는 규정이라 아니할수 없음. 왜냐하면 공익물 사용에 있어 대우나 조건은 이미 본문에서 우리 정부 기관의 그것과 동일하며 또 그 용역의 사용의 가격등은 계약에 의하여 별도 약정에서 규정되도록 되어 있기 때문임.

2 항의 규정은 우리측안과 동일한 취지임.

0118

공익물 및 용역의 사용

1. 입장

공익물 사용 및 용역에 관하여 주한 미군, 군대구성원, 군속, 또는 그 가족이 우리 정부 또는 정부 관리 기업체에서 제공하는 공익물과 용역을 사용할수 있도록 허용하고 그 대우에 있어서 주한 미국 군대는 우리 정부의 각 부처의 그것 보다 불리하지 않는 대우를 받을수 있도록 함. 그리고 구체적인 사용 약정은 양국 정부의 관계 당국 또는 그 대행기관간에 체결하도록 규정함.

11. 문제점

공익물 용역의 사용에 관하여는 1958 년 12 월 18 일자로 서명되고 1957 년 7 월 1 일자로 소급 발효한 "공익물에 관한 청구권 청산을 위한 한미간의 협정"이 있고 또 개별적 계약으로서는 수도 사용에 관하여 1957 년 7 월 3 일자로 내무부와 미합중국간에 "수도공급 계약"과 전기 사용에 관하여는 1957 년 7 월 3 일자로 경성전기회사와 미국간에 "전기 공급 계약"을 체결한바 있음. 따라서 군대지위 협정에 있어서 제 협정 또는 계약의 효력에 관하여는 구체적으로 규정함이 없이 다만 원칙 문제만을 규제하는 것이 좋다고 생각함. 이 문제에 관하여는 우선 상기 부처의 관계관의 의견을 타진하고 미국측의 태도를 타진 하여야 할것임.

본 문제에 관한 초안 제 2 항은 합의의사록에 규정하여도 무방할 것임.

0119

111. 안

1. The United States armed forces, members of such forces and of civilian components, and their dependents may use public utilities and services belonging to, or controlled or regulated by the Government of the Republic of Korea. In the use of such utilities and services the United States forces shall be accorded treatment no less favorable than that given from time to time to the ministries and agencies of the Government of the Republic of Korea.

2. Specific arrangements as to the use of such public utilities and services by the United States forces shall be concluded between the appropriate authorities of the two Governments or their agencies.

0120

기상 업무

I. 입장

기상 업무에 관하여 한미 양 정부는 각국의 관계 당국간의 합의에 따라서 기상 관측, 기상 자료 및 지진 관측자료의 교환을 통하여 기상 업무에 관하여 상호 협력함. 기상 업무에 관하여는 주한 미군도 군 작전의 필요상 우리나라에 있어서 광범한 기상 관측을 행하고 있는것으로 알려지고 있으므로 양 당사자간에 이에 관한 자료 교환등 협조를 증진한다면 양측의 이익을 위하여 좋으리라 생각됨.

II. 문제점

1. 일반 기상 업무에 관하여는 WMO 국제협약에 의하여 각국이 자국이 수집한 자료를 무전으로 모든 나라에 공개하게 되어 있으므로 현재 본 협정의 규정으로 인하여 직접적인 영향은 미치지 않으리라 생각되나 특수한 자료에 관하여는 현재 우리 공군과 미국 공군간에 상호간의 자료 교환이 있다고 사료됨으로 (중앙기상대 관계관의 말에 의하면) 특수자료 관계에 대하여는 관계관을 초치하여 문의하든가 또는 미측에 질의하여야 할것임.

2. 미일협정(1960) 제 3 조에 의하면 일본정부가 일방적으로 미군에게 (1) 육상 또는 해상으로 부터의 기상관측 자료 (2) 기상 관측소의 일기에 관한 정기 보고서 (3) 항공기의 안전과 정규 운영에 필요한 자료의 통신 전파 그리고 (4) 지진 관계자료를 제공할 의무를 지고 있으므로 이를 고려하여야 할것이나 우리나라는 일본과 사정이 달라 우리나라 전역에 걸쳐 미군이 주둔하고 이에 관한 업무를 실지 수행하고 있으므로 일본의 그것과 동일하게 우리 측만의 의무 부담이 필요 없으리라 생각되나 이는 미측의 태도가 밝혀 진후에 재검토 할 문제임.

0121

III. 안

The Governments of the Republic of Korea and the United States shall cooperate in meteorological services through exchanges of meteorological observations, climatological information and seismographic data in accordance with arrangements between the appropriate authorities of the two Governments.

0122

Article ____ (Meteorological Services)

The Governments of the Republic of Korea and the United States shall cooperate in mutually furnishing the relevant authorities of each Government with the following meteorological services in accordance with arrangements between the appropriate authorities of the two Governments:

(a) Meteorogogical observation,

(b) Climatological information, and

(c) Seismographic data.

0123

Jan 17, '64

CONFIDENTIAL

Proposed New Draft of Utilities and Services Provisions

3. (a) The United States armed forces shall have the use of all utilities and services which are owned, controlled or regulated by the Government of the Republic of Korea or local administrative subdivisions thereof. The term "utilities and services" shall include, but not be limited to, ~~transportation~~ and communications facilities and systems, electricity, gas, water, steam, heat, light, power, and sewage disposal. The use of utilities and services as provided herein shall not prejudice the right of the United States to operate military transportation, communication, power and such other utilities and services deemed necessary for the operations of the United States armed forces. This right shall not be exercised in a manner inconsistent with the operation by the Government of the Republic of Korea of its utilities and services.

(b) The use of such utilities and services by the United States shall be in accordance with priorities, conditions, and rates or tariffs no less favorable than those accorded any other user.

Agreed (4. Removed from this article; to be placed elsewhere in SOFA.)

0124

Jan 17 '64

Agreed Minutes

1. The Joint Committee shall be given the opportunity of discussing any changes determined by the Korean authorities of priority or rates applicable to the United States armed forces prior to their effective date.

agreed

2. Paragraph 3 of Article ______ will not be construed as in any way abrogating the Utilities and Claims Settlement Agreement of December 18, 1958, which continues in full force and effect unless otherwise agreed by the two governments.

3. Should the emergency operating needs of the United States armed forces so require, the Republic of Korea shall, after consultation thereon, take appropriate measures to assure provision of utilities and services necessary to meet these needs.

0125

Article____(Enrollment and Training of Reservists)

The United States may enroll and train eligible United States citizens residing in the Republic of Korea in the reserve organizations of the United States armed forces.

0126

ARTICLE (Enrollment and Training of Res.)

The United States may enroll in its reserve forces and train, in Korea, eligible United States citizens who are in the Republic of Korea.

(except for ordinary Tourists. — Mr. Chin 提案했으나 was not accepted)

① 15日 訪問者의 訓練 可能性은 거의 없다. — Col. Solf. 2/14

0127

Article___(Respect for Local Law)

It is the duty of the members of the United States armed forces, the civilian component, and their dependents to respect the law of the Republic of Korea, and to abstain from any activity inconsistent with the spirit of the present Agreement, and, in particular, from any political activity in the Republic of Korea.

0128

CONFIDENTIAL

(Respect for local Law) — OK

It is the duty of members of the United States Armed Forces, the civilian component, (the persons who are present in the Republic of Korea pursuant to Article __?__,) and their dependents, to respect the law of Korea and to abstain from any activity inconsistent with the spirit of this Agreement, and, in particular, from any political activity in Korea.

Full agreement . 1963. 6. 12

0129

Article ____

1. Members of the United States armed forces, the civilian component, and their dependents shall be subject to the foreign exchange controls of the Government of the Republic of Korea.

2. The preceding paragraph shall not be construed to preclude the transmission into or outside of the Republic of Korea of the United States dollars or dollar instruments representing the official funds of the United States or realized as a result of service or employment in connection with this Agreement by members of the United States armed forces and the civilian component, or realized by such persons and their dependents from sources outside of the Republic of Korea.

3. The United States authorities shall take suitable measures to preclude the abuse of the privileges stipulated in the preceding paragraph or circumvention of the Korean foreign exchange controls.

0130

Confidential

Agreed Minutes to Article Currency Control

Payment in Korea by the United States armed forces and by those organizations provided in Article PX to persons other than members of the United States armed forces, civilian component, their dependents and those persons referred to in Article Contractor shall be effected in accordance with the Korean Foreign Exchange Control Law and regulations. In these transactions the basic rate of exchange shall be used.

Official rate.

0131

CONFIDENTIAL

FOREIGN EXCHANGE CONTROLS

AGREED MINUTE

Payment in Korea by the United States armed forces including those activities provided in Article ______, to persons other than members of the United States armed forces, civilian component, their dependents and those persons referred to in Article ______ shall be effected in accordance with the Korean Foreign Exchange Control Law and regulations. The funds to be used for these transactions shall be convertible into currency of the Republic of Korea at the highest rate in terms of the number of Korean Won per United States dollar which, at the time the conversion is made, is not unlawful in the Republic of Korea.

effective official rate

Comprehensive aid agreement 에 근거한 것이라

1961. 12. 31 外換管理法

1961. 2. 1. — Uniform Rate 채택 130 : 1

0132

ARTICLE ______ currency control

1. Members of the United States armed forces, the civilian component and their dependents, shall be subject to the foreign exchange controls of the Government of the Republic of Korea.

2. The preceding paragraph shall not be construed to preclude the transmission into or out of Korea of United States dollars or dollar instruments representing the official funds of the United States or realized as a result of service or employment in connection with this Agreement by members of the United States armed forces and the civilian component, or realized by such persons and their dependents from sources outside Korea.

3. The United States authorities shall take suitable measures to preclude the abuse of the privileges stipulated in the preceding paragraphs or circumvention of the Korean foreign exchange controls.

ARTICLE

1. (a) United States military payment certificates denominated in dollars may be used by persons authorized by the United States for internal transaction within the facilities and areas in use by the United States forces.

(b) The United States Government will take appropriate action to ensure that authorized personnel are prohibited from engaging in transactions involving military payment certificates except as authorized by United States regulations.

(c) The Government of the Republic of Korea will take necessary action to prohibit unauthorized person from engaging in transactions involving military payment certificates and with the aid of United States authorities will undertake to apprehend and punish any person or persons under its jurisdiction involved in the counterfeiting or uttering of counterfeit military payment certificates.

(d) It is agreed that the United States authorities will apprehend and punish members of the United States forces, the civilian component, or their dependents, who tender military payment certificates to unauthorized persons and that no obligation will, after the date of coming into force of this Agreement, be due to such unauthorized persons or to the Government of the Republic of Korea or its agencies from the United States or any of its agencies as a result of any unauthorized use of military payment certificates within the Republic of Korea.

2. (a) In order to exercise control of military payment certificates the United States may designate certain American financial institutions to maintain and operate, under United States supervision, facilities for the use of persons authorized by the United States to use military payment certificates.

0134

(b) Institutions authorized to maintain military banking facilities will establish and maintain such facilities physically separated from their Korean commercial banking business, with personnel whose sole duty is to maintain and operate such facilities. Such facilities shall be permitted to maintain United States currency bank accounts and to perform all financial transactions in connection therewith including recipt and remission of funds to the extent provided by Article _____, paragraph 2, of this Agreement.

(c) The United States Government shall take proper measures necessary to ensure the implementation of the foregoing paragraph.

0135

MPC

ARTICLE

1. (a) United States military payment certificates denominated in dollars may be used by persons authorized by the United States for internal transaction [within the facilities and areas in use by the United States forces.]

(b) The United States Government will take appropriate action to ensure that authorized personnel are prohibited from engaging in transactions involving military payment certificates except as authorized by United States regulations.

(c) The Government of the Republic of Korea will take necessary action to prohibit unauthorized person from engaging in transactions involving military payment certificates and with the aid of United States authorities will undertake to apprehend and punish any person or persons under its jurisdiction involved in the counterfeiting or uttering of counterfeit military payment certificates.

0136

(d) It is agreed that the United States authorities will apprehend and punish members of the United States armed forces, the civilian component, or their dependents, who tender military payment certificates to unauthorized persons and that no obligation will, after the date of coming into force of this Agreement, be due to such unauthorized persons or to the Government of the Republic of Korea or its agencies from the United States or any of its agencies as a result of any unauthorized use of military payment certificates within the Republic of Korea.

2. (a) In order to exercise control of military payment certificates the United States may designate certain American financial institutions to maintain and operate, under United States supervision, facilities for the use of persons authorized by the United States to use military payment certificates.

0137

(b) Institutions authorized to maintain military banking facilities will establish and maintain such facilities physically separated from their Korean commercial banking business, with personnel whose sole duty is to maintain and operate such facilities. Such facilities shall be permitted to maintain United States currency bank accounts and to perform all financial transactions in connection therewith including receipt and remission of funds to the extent provided by Article ____, paragraph 2, of this Agreement.

withdrawn 17차

(c) The United States Government shall take proper measures necessary to ensure the implementation of the foregoing sub-paragraphs.

0138

Agreed Minute to Article ____

United States military payment certificates under custody of the Government of the Republic of Korea at the time of entry into force of this Agreement shall be disposed in accordance with the agreement between the two governments.

0139

APO

APO's Article

The United States may establish and operate, within the facilities and areas in use by the United States armed forces, United States military post offices for the use of members of the United States armef forces, the civilian component, and their dependents, for the transmission of mail between United States military post offices in the Republic of Korea and between such military post offices and other United States post offices.

0140

ARTICLE

MILITARY POST OFFICES

完全合意, 40次 1/24

1. The United States may establish and operate, within the facilities and areas in use by the U.S. armed forces, United States military post offices for the use of members of the United States armed forces, the civilian component, and their dependents, for the transmission of mail between United States military post offices in Korea and between such military post offices and other United States post offices.

2. United States military post offices may be used by other officers and personnel of the United States Government, and their dependents, ordinarily accorded such privileges abroad.

UPU Convention
Freedom of Transit

Dept.
Independent agency of U.S. gov. 의 officers
American Embassy
Retired personnel — 현직에서 특권을 인정받은 사람
civilian Crew members belonging to MSOT.
American Red Cross, 기타 사원.
} dependents.

宗教团体는 SOFA 登効時 使用不可.

0141

NAVIGATIONAL AIDS ARTICLE

Agreed Minute:

"Installation by the United States Armed Forces of permanent navigational aids for vessels and aircraft outside of areas and facilities in use by the United States Armed Forces will be effected in accordance with the procedures established under paragraph 1 of Article ."

0142

ARTICLE

1. Persons, including corporations organized under the laws of the United States, and their employees who are ordinarily resident in the United States and ~~those~~ whose presence in the Republic of Korea is solely for the purpose of executing contracts with the United States for the benefit of the United States armed forces, and who are designated by the Government of the United States in accordance with the provisions of the paragraph 2 below, shall, except as provided in this Article, be subject to the laws and regulations of the Republic of Korea.

2. The designation referred to in paragraph 1 above shall be made upon consultation with the Government of the Republic of Korea and shall be restricted to cases where open competitive bidding is not practicable due to security considerations, to the technical qualifications of the contracts involved, or to the unavailability of materials or services required by United States standards, or to the limitations of United States law.

The designation shall be withdrawn by the Government of the United States:

(a) upon completion of contracts with the United States for the United States armed forces;

(b) upon proof that such persons are engaged in business activities in the Republic of Korea other than those pertaining to the United States armed forces; or

(c) when such persons are engaged in practices illegal in the Republic of Korea.

3. Upon certification by the appropriate authorities of the United States as to their identity, such persons and their employees shall be accorded the following benefits

0143

of this Agreement:

(a) Entry into the Republic of Korea in accordance with the provisions of Article ___;

(b) the exemption fro customs duties, and other such charges provided for in Article _____, paragraph 3 for members of the United States forces, the civilian component, and their dependents;

(c) If authorized by the Government of the United States, the right to use the services of the organizations provided for in Article _____;

(d) Those provided for in Article _____, paragraph 2, for members of the United States armed forces, the civilian component, and their dependents;

(e) If authorized by the Government of the United States, the right to use military payment certificates, as provided for in Article _____;

(f) The use of postal facilities provided for in Article _____;

(g) Exemption from the laws and regulations of the Republic of Korea with respect to terms and conditions of employment.

4. Such persons and their employees shall be subject to the Korean passport and visa regulations and shall possess passport with their status described therein. Their arrival, departure and their residence while in the Republic of Korea shall be notified by the United States to the Government of the Republic of Korea.

5. Upon certification by an authorized officer of the United States armed forces, such contractors and their employees shall be exempt from taxation in the Republic of Korea on the holding, use, transfer by death, or transfer to

0144

persons or agencies entitled to tax exemption under this Agreement, of any movable property, the presence of which in the Republic of Korea is due solely to the temporary presence of these persons in the Republic of Korea, provided that such exemption shall not apply to property held for the purpose of investment or the conduct of other business than those executing contracts as described in paragraph 1 of this Article in the Republic of Korea.

6. The persons and their employees referred to in paragraph 1 shall not be liable to pay income tax to the Government of the Republic of Korea or to any other taxing agency in the Republic of Korea on any income derived under a contract made in the United States with the Government of the United States in connection with the construction, maintenance or operation of any of the facilities or areas covered by this Agreement. The provisions of this paragraph do not exempt such persons from payment of income or corporation taxes on income derived from other engagement than those mentioned in this paragraph.

7. The Korean authorities shall have the primary right to exercise jurisdiction over the contractors and their employees referred to in paragraph 1 of this Article in relation to offences committed in the Republic of Korea and punishable by the law of the Republic of Korea. In those cases in which the Korean authorities decide not to exercise such jurisdiction they shall notify the military authorities of the United States as soon as possible. Upon such notification the military authorities of the United States shall have the right to exercise such jurisdiction over the persons referred to as is conferred on them by the law of the United States.

0145

부 전 지

수 신 19 . . .

제 목
요 약

군계약자

우리측은 군계약자의 1)한국법에대한 복속원칙,
2)계약자의 지정 및 지정철회.
3)계약자가 향유할 이익.
4)계약자가 소지할 여권.
5.6)조세의 면제.
7)군계약자에대한 재판관할권 등 규제.

관계부처
협 조 처
전화번호 주부

발 신

공인양식 1—24 (1112-040-032-023) (130mm×190mm 32절지)

0146

Koo

ARTICLE Contractors

1. Persons, including corporations (organized under the laws of the United States,) and their employees (who are ordinarily resident in the United States) and whose presence in the Republic of Korea is solely for the purpose of executing contracts with the United States for the benefit of the United States armed forces, and who are designated by the Government of the United States in accordance with the provisions of the paragraph 2 below, shall, except as provided in this Article, be subject to the laws and regulations of the Republic of Korea.

2. The designation referred to in paragraph 1 above shall be made upon consultation with the Government of the Republic of Korea and shall be restricted to cases where open competitive bidding is not practicable due to security considerations, to the technical qualifications of the contractors involved, or to the unavailability of materials or services required by United States standards, or to the limitations of United States law.

0147

The designation shall be withdrawn by the Government of the United States.

(a) upon completion of contracts with the United States for the United States armed forces;

(b) upon proof that such persons are engaged in business activities in the Republic of Korea other than those pertaining to the United States armed forces; or

(c) when such persons are engaged in practices illegal in the Republic of Korea.

3. Upon certification by the appropriate authorities of the United States as to their identity, such persons and their employees shall be accorded the following benefits of this Agreement:

(a) Entry into the Republic of Korea in accordance with the provisions of Article Entry & Exit ___;

(b) The exemption from customs duties. and other such charges provided for in Article Customs duty ___, paragraph 3 for members of the United States armed forces, the civilian component, and their dependents;

(c) If authorized by the Government of the United States, the right to use the services of the organizations provided for in Article NAFO (PX) ___;

0148

ok (d) Those provided for in Article Currency Controls, paragraph 2, for members of the United States armed forces, the civilian component, and their dependents;

ok (e) If authorized by the Government of the United States, the right to use military payment certificates, as provided for in Article MPC;

ok (f) The use of postal facilities provided for in Article MPO;

(g) Exemption from the laws and regulations of the Republic of Korea with respect to terms and conditions of employment.

4. (Such persons and their employees shall be subject to the Korean passport and visa regulations and shall possess passports with their status described therein.) Their arrival, departure and their residence while in the Republic of Korea shall be notified by the United States to the Government of the Republic of Korea.

5. Upon certification by an authorized officer of the United States armed forces, such contractors and their employees shall be exempt from taxation

0149

in the Republic of Korea on the holding, use, transfer by death, or transfer to persons or agencies entitled to tax exemption under this Agreement, of any movable property, the presence of which in the Republic of Korea is due solely to the temporary presence of these persons in the Republic of Korea, provided that such exemption shall not apply to property held for the purpose of investment or the conduct of other business than those executing contracts as described in paragraph 1 of this Article in the Republic of Korea. 但書

6. The persons and their employees referred to in paragraph 1 shall not be liable to pay income or corporation taxes to the Government of the Republic of Korea or to any other taxing agency in the Republic of Korea on any income derived under a contract made in the United States with the Government of the United States in connection with the construction, maintenance or operation of any of the facilities or areas covered by this Agreement. The provisions of this paragraph do not exempt such persons from payment of income or corporation taxes on income derived from other engagement than those mentioned in this paragraph. 但.

0150

7. The Korean authorities shall have the primary right to exercise jurisdiction over the contractors and their employees such persons referred to in paragraph 1 of this Article in relation to offences committed in the Republic of Korea and punishable by the law of the Republic of Korea. In those cases in which the Korean authorities decide not to exercise such jurisdiction they shall notify the military authorities of the United States as soon as possible. Upon such notification the military authorities of the United States shall have the right to exercise such jurisdiction over the persons referred to as is conferred on them by the law of the United States.

0151

ARTICLE (Contractors)

6. The persons referred to in paragraph 1 shall not be liable to pay income or corporation texes to the Government of the Republic of Korea or to any other taxing agency in Korea on any income derived under a contract with the Government of the United States in connection with the construction, maintenance or operation of any of the facilities or areas covered by this Agreement. The provisions of this paragraph do not exempt such persons from payment of income or corporation taxes on income derived from Korean sources, other than those sources referred to in the first sentence of this paragraph, nor do they exempt such persons who claim Korean residence for United States income tax purposes from payment of Korean taxes on income. Periods during which such persons are in Korea solely in connection with the execution of a contract with the Government of the United States shall not be considered periods of residence or domicile in Korea for the purpose of such taxation.

Person – Time outside of Korea.

0152

ROK. 代案

Vinnel
1. Trans-Asia Engr.
2. Pacific Architecture Engr.
3. Trans-American Engr.
4. Trans-...
5. International Industrial

1. Persons, including corporations organized under the laws of the United States, and their employees, who are ordinarily resident in the United States and whose presence in the Republic of Korea is solely for the purpose of executing contracts with the United States for the benefit of the United States armed forces or other armed forces in Korea under the Unified Command receiving logistical support from the United States armed forces, ~~and~~ who are designated by the Government of the United States in accordance with the provisions of the paragraph 2 below, shall, except as provided in this Article, be subject to the laws and regulations of the Republic of Korea.

OK

2. The designation referred to in paragraph 1 above shall be made upon consultation with the Government of the Republic of Korea and shall be restricted to cases where open competitive bidding is not practicable due to security considerations, to the technical qualifications of the contractors involved, to the unavailability of materials or services required by United States standards, or to limitations of United States law. The designation shall be withdrawn by the Government of the United States:

0153

(a) Upon completion of contracts with the United States armed forces or other armed forces in Korea under the Unified Command receiving logistical support from the United States armed forces;

(b) Upon proof that such persons are engaged in business activities in Korea other than those pertaining to the United States armed forces or other armed forces in Korea under the Unified Command receiving logistical support from the United States armed forces;

(c) Upon proof that such persons are engaged in practices illegal in Korea.

3. Upon certification by appropriate United States authorities as to their identity, such persons shall be accorded the following benefits of this Agreement:

(a) Accession and movement, as provided for Article Vehicle, Aircraft and access, paragraph 2;

(b) Entry into Korea in accordance with the provisions of Article Entry & Exit;

(c) The exemption from customs duties, and other such charges provided for in Article Customs, paragraph 3, for members of the United States armed forces, the civilian component, and their dependents;

(d) If authorized by the Government of the United States, the use of the services of the organizations provided

0154

for in Article [PX]

(e) Those ~~provided in Article~~ [Currency Control], paragraph 2, for members of the United States armed forces, the civilian component, and their dependents;

(f) If authorized by the Government of the United States, the use of military payment certificates, as provided for in Article [MPC];

(g) The use of postal facilities provided for in Article [MPO];

(h) The use of utilities and services in accordance with those priorities, conditions, rates, or tariffs accorded the United States armed forces by Article paragraph 3, relating to utilities and services;

(i) Exemption from the laws and regulations of Korea with respect to [terms and conditions of employment] licensing and registration of business and corporations.

4. The arrival, departure, and place of residence in Korea of such persons shall from time to time be notified by the United States armed forces to the Korean authorities.

5. Upon certification by an authorized representative of the United States armed forces, depreciable assets, except houses, held, used or transferred by such persons exclusively for the execution of contracts referred to in paragraph 1 shall not be subject to taxes or similar

0155

charges of Korea.

6. Upon certification by an authorized representative of the United States armed forces, such persons shall be exempt from taxation in Korea on the holding, use, transfer by death, or transfer to persons or agencies entitled to tax exemption under this Agreement, of movable property, tangible or intangible, the presence of which in Korea is due solely to the temporary presence of these persons in Korea, provided that such exemption shall not apply to property held for the purpose of investment or the conduct of other business ~~than those executing contracts as described in paragraph 1 of this Article~~ in Korea or to any intangible property registered in Korea.

7. The persons referred to in paragraph 1 shall not be liable to pay income or corporation taxes to the Government of Korea or to any other taxing agency in Korea on any income derived under a contract with the Government of the United States in connection with the construction, maintenance or operation of any of the facilities or areas covered by this Agreement. Persons in Korea in connection with the execution of such a contract with the United States shall not be liable to pay any Korean taxes to the Government of Korea or to any taxing agency in Korea on income derived from sources

0156

outside of Korea nor shall periods during which such persons are in Korea be considered periods of residence or domicile in Korea for the purposes of Korean taxation. The provisions of this paragraph do not exempt such persons from payment of income or corporation taxes on income derived from Korean sources, other than those sources referred to in the first sentence of this paragraph, nor do they exempt such persons who claim Korean residence for United States income tax purposes from payment of Korean taxes on income.

8. The Korean authorities shall have the primary right to exercise jurisdiction over the contractors and their employees and dependents referred to in paragraph 1 of this Article in relation to offences committed in the Republic of Korea and punishable by the law of the Republic of Korea. In those cases in which the Korean authorities decide not to exercise such jurisdiction they shall notify the military authorities of the United States as soon as possible. Upon such notification the military authorities of the United States shall have the right to exercise such jurisdiction over the persons referred to as is conferred on them by the law of the United States.

0157

Agreed Minutes

1. This Article shall not prevent the persons referred to in paragraph 1 from employing third-country nationals who shall, except as provided in paragraph 2, and sub-paragraphs (a), (d), (e), (f), (g) of paragraph 3, be subject to the laws and regulations of the Republic of Korea.

2. The dependents of the persons and their employees, including third-country nationals, shall, except those benefits as provided in sub-paragraphs (d), (f) and (g), be subject to the laws and regulations of the Republic of Korea.

3. There is no obligation under this Article to grant exemption from taxes payable in respect of the use and ownership of private vehicles.

{ passenger car
Wagon type car
pleasure or Business car

0158

ARTICLE _____

CONTRACTORS

1. Persons, including corporations, their employees, and the dependents of such persons, present in Korea solely for the purpose of executing contracts with the United States for the benefit of the United States armed forces or other armed forces in Korea under the Unified Command receiving logistical support from the United States armed forces, who are designated by the Government of the United States in accordance with the provisions of paragraph 2 below, shall, except as provided in this Article, be subject to the laws and regulations of Korea.

2. The designation referred to in paragraph 1 above shall be made upon consultation with the Government of Korea and shall be restricted to cases where open competitive bidding is not practicable due to security considerations, to the technical qualifications of the contractors involved, to the unavailability of materials or services required by United States standards, or to limitations of United States law. The designation shall be withdrawn by the Government of the United States:

0159

(a) Upon completion of contracts with the United States for the United States armed forces or other armed forces in Korea under the Unified Command receiving logistical support from the United States armed forces; OK

(b) Upon proof that such persons are engaged in business activities in Korea other than those pertaining to the United States armed forces or other armed forces in Korea under the Unified Command receiving logistical support from the United States armed forces; OK

(c) Upon proof that such persons are engaged in practices illegal in Korea. OK

3. Upon certification by appropriate United States authorities as to their identity, such persons shall be accorded the following benefits of this Agreement:

? 美日에有 (a) Rights of accession and movement, as provided for in Article , paragraph 2; Vessels, Aircraft Access 불이 Condition?

(a) (b) Entry into Korea in accordance with the provisions of Article Entry & Exit OK

(b) (c) The exemption from customs duties, and other such charges provided for in Article Customs, paragraph 3, for members 修正後 OK

0160

of the United States armed forces, the civilian component, and their dependents;

(d) If authorized by the Government of the United States, the right to use the services of the activities provided for in Article ;

(e) Those rights provided in Article , paragraph 2, for members of the United States armed forces, the civilian component, and their dependents;

(f) If authorized by the Government of the United States, the right to use military payment certificates, as provided for in Article ;

(g) The use of postal facilities provided for in Article ;

(h) Those rights accorded the United States armed forces by Article , paragraph 3, relating to utilities and services;

(i) Those rights provided to members of the United States armed forces, the civilian component, and their dependents by Article , relating to driving permits and registration of vehicles;

(j) Exemption from the laws and regulations of Korea with respect to terms and conditions of employment, (and licensing and registration of businesses and corporations.)

4. The arrival, departure, and place of residence in Korea of such persons shall from time to time be notified by the United States armed

0161

forces to the Korean authorities.

5. Upon certification by an authorized representative of the United States armed forces, depreciable assets, except houses, held, used or transferred by such persons exclusively for the execution of contracts referred to in paragraph 1 shall not be subject to taxes or similar charges of Korea.

6. Upon certification by an authorized representative of the United States armed forces, such persons shall be exempt from taxation in Korea on the holding, use, transfer by death, or transfer to persons or agencies entitled to tax exemption under this Agreement, of movable property, tangible or intangible, the presence of which in Korea is due solely to the temporary presence of these persons in Korea, provided that such exemption shall not apply to property held for the purpose of investment or the conduct of other business in Korea or to any intangible property registered in Korea.

7. The persons referred to in paragraph 1 shall not be liable to pay income or corporation taxes to the Government of Korea or to any other taxing agency in Korea on any income derived under a contract with the Government of the United States in connection with the construction, maintenance or operation of any of the facilities or areas covered by this

0162

Agreement. Persons in Korea in connection with the execution of such a contract with the United States shall not be liable to pay any Korean taxes to the Government of Korea or to any taxing agency in Korea on income derived from sources outside of Korea, nor shall periods during which such persons are in Korea be considered periods of residence or domicile in Korea for the purposes of Korean taxation. The provisions of this paragraph do not exempt such persons from payment of income or corporation taxes on income derived from Korean sources, other than those sources referred to in the first sentence of this paragraph, nor do they exempt such persons who claim Korean residence for United States income tax purposes from payment of Korean taxes on income.

8.

Agreed Minute:

1. The execution of contracts with the United States in addition to those specified in paragraph 1 of Article Contractor shall not exclude the persons provided for in Article Contractor from the application of that Article.

USOM and its agencies

except paragraph 7

0163

Contractor

8. The persons referred to in paragraph 1 shall be subject to those provisions of Article C.J. and the Agreed Minutes thereto which pertain to members of the civilian component, and to dependents.

0104

Contractor

AGREED MINUTE

2. Contractor employees who are present in Korea on the effective date of this agreement and who would qualify for the privileges contained in Article _________ but for the fact that they are not ordinarily resident in the United States shall be entitled to enjoy such privileges so long as their presence is for the purpose stated in paragraph 1 of Article ________.

0165

ARTICLE

1. (a) Navy exchanges, post exchanges, messes, commissaries, social clubs, theaters and other non-appropriated fund organizations authorized and regulated by the authorities of the United States armed forces may be established within the facilities and areas in use by the United States armed forces for the exclusive use of the members of such forces, the civilian component, and their dependents. Except as otherwise provided in this Agreement, such organizations shall not be subject to Korean regulations, license, fees, taxes or similar controls.

(b) When a newspaper authorized and regulated by the authorities of the United States armed forces is sold to the general public, it shall be subject to Korean regulations, license, fees, taxes or similar controls so far as such circulation is concerned

2. No Korean tax shall be imposed on sales of merchandise and services by such organizations, except as provided in paragraph 1 (b) but purchase within the Republic of Korea of merchandise and supplies by such organizations shall be subject to Korean taxes unless otherwise agreed between the two Governments.

3. Goods which are sold by such organizations shall not be disposed of in the Republic of Korea to persons not authorized to make purchases from such organizations. Administrative measures shall be taken by the authorities of the United States to prevent such disposition.

4. The quantity of goods imported by such organizations for use of the members of the United States armed forces, the civilian component, and their dependents shall be

0166

limited to the extent reasonably required for such use.

5. The organizations referred to in this Article shall provide such information to the authorities of the Republic of Korea as is required by Korean legislations.

0167

Koo

Non-Appropriated fund Org

ARTICLE

NAFO 비非營.

1\. (a) Navy exchanges, post exchanges, messes, commissaries, social clubs, theaters and other non-appropriated fund organizations authorized and regulated by the authorities of the United States armed forces may be established within the facilities and areas in use by the United States armed forces for the exclusive use of the members of such forces, the civilian component, and their dependents. Except as otherwise provided in this Agreement, such organizations shall not be subject to Korean regulations, licenses, fees, taxes or similar controls.

Hotel Dance Hall

U.S. tourist Hotel

U.S. Contractors Article

Customs duties

(b) When a newspaper authorized and regulated by the authorities of the United States armed forces is sold to the general public, it shall be subject to Korean regulations, licenses, fees, taxes or similar controls so far as such circulation is concerned

OKed by US

2\. No Korean tax shall be imposed on sales of merchandise and services by such organizations, except as provided in paragraph 1 (b) but purchase within

0168

the Republic of Korea of merchandise and supplies by such organizations shall be subject to Korean taxes unless otherwise agreed between the two Governments.

3. Goods which are sold by such organizations shall not be disposed of in the Republic of Korea to persons not authorized to make purchases from such organizations. Administrative measures shall be taken by the authorities of the United States to prevent such disposition.

4. The quantity of goods imported by such organizations for use of the members of the United States armed forces, the civilian component, and their dependents shall be limited to the extent reasonably required for such use.

5. The organizations referred to in this Article shall provide such information to the authorities of the Republic of Korea as is required by Korean legislations.

0169

May 31, 1967

"CONFIDENTIAL"

Agreed Minutes (Claims Article)

1. The amount to be paid to each claimant, under the provisions of paragraph 5(b) of this Article, except the cases being determined by adjudication, shall be communicated to the authorities of the United States before the payment is made.

In case any reply in favour of the decision is received from the U.S. side, or in default of a reply within one month of receipt of the communication envisaged above, the amount decided by the Korean Claims Authorities shall be regarded as agreed upon between the both Governments.

If, however, the authorities of the United States disagree to the amount decided by the Korean Claims Authorities and reply to this effect within the one-month period, the Korean Claims Authorities shall re-examine the case concerned. The amount decided as a result of the re-examination shall be final and conclusive. The Korean Claims Authorities shall notify the authorities of the United States of the result of re-examination as early as practicable.

The amount agreed upon between the both Governments or decided through the re-examination shall be paid to the claimant concerned without delay.

"CONFIDNETIAL"

0170

2. The provisions of paragraph 5 of this Article will become effective after six months from the date of entry into force of this Agreement. Until such time the United States agrees to pay just and reasonable compensation in settlement of civil claims (other than contractual claims) arising out of acts or omissions of members of the United States armed forces done in the performance of official duty or out of any other act, omission or occurrence for which the United States armed forces are legally responsible. In making such payments United States authorities would exercise the authority provided under United States laws relating to Foreign Claims and regulations issued thereunder. In settling claims which are described as arising "..... out of any act, omission or occurrence for which the United States armed forces are legally responsible", United States authorities will take into consideration local law and practice.

3. For the purpose of paragraph 5 of this Article, members of the Korean Augmentation to the United States Army (KATUSA) and members of the Korean Service Corps (KSC) shall be considered respectively as members and employees of the United States armed forces.

CONFIDENTIAL

ARTICLE

Non-Appropriated Fund ~~Activities~~ Organization

1.(a) Military exchanges, messes, social clubs, theaters, newspapers and other non-appropriated fund ~~activities~~ authorized and regulated by the United States military authorities may be established by the United States armed forces for the use of members of such forces, the civilian component, and their dependents. Except as otherwise provided in this Agreement, such activities shall not be subject to Korean regulations, licenses, fees, taxes, or similar controls.

2. No Korean tax shall be imposed on sales of merchandise or services by such ~~activities~~ Organization except as provided in paragraph 1(b). Purchases within Korea of merchandise and supplies by such ~~activities~~ Org. shall be subject to the Korean taxes to which other purchasers of such merchandise and supplies are subject and at rates no less favorable than those imposed on other purchasers.

3. Except as such disposal may be permitted by the United States and Korean authorities in accordance with mutually agreed conditions, goods which are sold by such activities shall not be disposed of in Korea to persons not authorized to make purchases from such activities.

4. The activities referred to in this Article shall, ~~after~~ through consultation between the representatives of the two

0173

governments in the Joint Committee, provide such information to the Republic of Korea tax authorities as is required by Korean tax legislation.

5. The activities referred to in paragraph 1 may be used by other officers or personnel of the United States Government ordinarily accorded such privileges, by non-Korean persons whose presence in Korea is solely for the purpose of providing contract services financed by the United States Government, by the dependents of the foregoing, by organizations which are present in the Republic of Korea primarily for the benefit and service of the United States armed forces personnel, such as the American Red Cross and the United Service Organizations, and by the non-Korean personnel of such organizations and their dependents.

Revised a.m.

0174

AGREED MINUTE

5. The United States Armed Forces may grant the use of the organizations referred to in paragraph 1 of Article to: (a) other officers or personnel of the United States Government ordinarily accorded such privileges; (b) those other non-Korean Armed Forces in Korea under the Unified Command which receive logistical support from the United States Armed Forces, and their members; (c) those non-Korean persons whose presence in the Republic of Korea is solely for the purpose of providing contract services financed by the United States Government; (d) those organizations which are present in the Republic of Korea primarily for the benefit and service of the United States Armed Forces, such as the American Red Cross and the United Service Organizations, and their non-Korean personnel; (e) dependents of the foregoing; and (f) other persons and organizations with the express consent of the Government of the Republic of Korea.

Contractor

a) non-Korean Employees of USOM. USIS. Embassy, military attaches, MAG Personnel.

d) USO의 分駐隊

f). AKF. ~~Int'l Social Service~~ Int'l Lutheran. Scandinavian UNCURK, UNTDD. Diplomatic Corps.

c). USOM contractor

0175

38차 1/9 수교

OK (41차) ROK understanding US 가 accept.

2. No Korean tax shall be imposed on sales of merchandise or services by such organizations, except as provided in paragraph 1 (b) of this article. Purchases within the Republic of Korea of merchandise and supplies by such organizations shall be subject to the Korean taxes to which other purchasers of such merchandise and supplies are subject unless otherwise agreed between the two Governments.

0176

CONFIDENTIAL

Non-Appropriated Fund Activities Article

OKed

Suggested Paragraph 1 (b):

(b) When a newspaper authorized and regulated by the United States military authorities is sold to the general public, it shall be subject to Korean regulations, licenses, fees, taxes or similar controls so far as such circulation is concerned.

0177

ARTICLE ____ (Taxation)

1. The United States armed forces shall not be subject to taxes or similar charges on property held, used or transferred by such forces in the Republic of Korea.

2. Members of the United States armed forces, the civilian component, and their dependents shall not be liable to pay Korean taxes to the Government of the Republic of Korea or to any other taxing agency in the Republic of Korea on income received as a result of their service with or employment by the United States armed forces, or by the organizations provided for in Article ____. The provisions of this Article do not exempt such persons from payment of Korean taxes on income derived from sources other than those provided for in this paragraph.

3. Members of the United States armed forces, the civilian component, and their dependnets shall be exempt from taxation in the Republic of Korea on the holding, use, transfer <u>inter se</u>, or transer by death of any movable property, the presence of which in the Republic of Korea is due solely to the temporary presence of these persons in the Republic of Korea provided that such exemption shall not apply to property held for the purpose of investment or the conduct of business in the Republic of Korea.

4. Periods during which the persons referred to in the preceding paragraph are in the Republic of Korea solely by reason of being members of the United States armed forces or of the civilian component, or their dependents shall not be considered as periods of residence or comicile in the Republic of Korea for the purpose of Korean taxation.

ARTICLE ____

TAXATION 合意(33차)

1. The United States armed forces shall not be subject to taxes or similar charges on property held, used or transferred by such forces in Korea. OK

2. Members of the United States armed forces, the civilian component, and their dependents shall not be liable to pay any Korean taxes to the Government of Korea or to any other taxing agency in Korea on income received as a result of their service with or employment by the United States armed forces, including the activities (Organization) provided for in Article NAFO. Persons in Korea solely by reason of being members of the United States armed forces, the civilian component, or their dependents shall not be liable to pay any Korean taxes to the Government of Korea or to any taxing agency in Korea on income derived from sources outside of Korea, nor shall periods during which such persons are in Korea be considered as periods of residence or domicile in Korea for the purpose of Korean taxation. The provisions of this Article do not exempt such persons from payment of Korean taxes on income derived from Korean sources, other than those sources referred to in the first sentence of this paragraph, nor do they exempt United States citizens who claim Korean residence for United States income tax purposes from

0179

payment of Korean taxes on income.

3. Members of the United States armed forces, the civilian component, and their dependents shall be exempt from taxation in Korea on the holding, use, transfer inter se, or transfer by death of movable property, tangible or intangible, the presence of which in Korea is due solely to the temporary presence of these persons in Korea, provided that such exemption shall not apply to property held for the purpose of investment or the conduct of business in Korea or to any intangible property registered in Korea.

0180

ARTICLE

VEHICLE AND DRIVER LICENSES

1. The Republic of Korea shall accept as valid, without a driving test or fee, the driving permit or license or military driving permit issued by the United States to a member of the United States armed forces, the civilian component, and their dependents.

2. (a) Official vehicles of the United States armed forces and the civilian component shall carry a distinctive numbered plate or individual marking which will readily identify them.

(b) Privately owned vehicles of the members of the United States armed forces, the civilian component, and their dependents shall carry Korean number plates to be acquired under the same conditions as those applicable to the nationals of the Republic of Korea.

0181

ARTICLE

VEHICLE AND DRIVER LICENSES

I. The Republic of Korea shall accept as valid, without a driving test or fee, the driving permit or license or military driving permit issued by the United States to a member of the United States armed forces, the civilian component, and their dependents.

2. (a) Official vehicles of the United States armed forces and the civilian component shall carry a distinctive numbered plates or individual marking which will readily identify them.

(b) Privately owned vehicles of the members of the United States armed forces, the civilian component, and their dependents shall carry Korean number plates to be acquired under the same conditions as those applicable to the nationals of the Republic of Korea.

手數料
登錄稅
法令上의 諸措置
免除

0182

Agreed Minute to Article ____ (Definitions)

The expression "except for those for whom status has otherwise been provided" in Paragraph (a) refers only to personnel on active duty belonging to the United States land, sea or air armed services for whom status is provided in the Military Advisory Group Agreement signed on January 26, 1950, and personnel of service attache offices in the Embassy of the United States of America.

0183

ARTICLE

LICENSING OF MOTOR VEHICLES

1. Korea shall accept as valid, without a driving test or fee, the driving permit or license or military driving permit issued by the United States, ~~or political subdivision thereof,~~ to a member of the United States armed forces, the civilian component, and their dependents.

2. Official vehicles of the United States armed forces and the civilian component shall carry distinctive numbered plates or individual markings which will readily identify them.

3. Privately owned vehicles of members of the United States armed forces, the civilian component and their dependents may be licensed or registered, and shall be provided with license plate or other identification as appropriate, by the United States. The authorities of the United States shall take adequate safety measures for, and shall assure the technical supervision of, the vehicles licensed by them and shall, where necessary, and at the request of the Government of the Republic of Korea, furnish the name and address of the owner of a vehicle licensed by them.

0184

ARTICLE

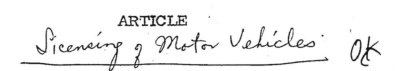

Licensing of Motor Vehicles OK

3. The Government of the Republic of Korea will license and register those vehicles privately owned by members of the United States armed forces, the civilian component, or dependents. The names of the owners of such vehicles and such other pertinent information as is required by Korean law to effect the licensing and registration of such vehicles, shall be furnished to the Government of the Republic of Korea by officials of the United States Government through the Joint Committee. Except for the actual cost of the issuance of license plates, members of the United States armed forces, the civilian component, and their dependents shall be exempt from the payment of all fees and charges relating to the licensing, registration, or operation of vehicles in the Republic of Korea and, in accordance with the provisions of Article ____, from the payment of all taxes relating thereto.

0185

D

OK

DEFINITIONS ARTICLE

PROPOSED ADDITIONAL SENTENCE TO SUBPARAGRAPH (b)

For the purposes of the Agreement only, dual nationals, i.e. persons having both United States and Korean nationality, who are brought into the Republic of Korea by the United States shall be considered as United States nationals.

0186

D

DEFINITIONS ARTICLE

AGREED MINUTE 7

With regard to subparagraph (b), it is recognized that persons possessing certain skills, not readily available from United States or Korean sources, who are nationals of third states may be brought into Korea by the United States armed forces solely for employment by the United States armed forces. Such persons, and third state nationals who are employed by, serving with, or accompanying the United States armed forces in Korea when this agreement becomes effective, shall be considered as members of the civilian component.

0187

DEFINITIONS ARTICLE

Agreed Minute:

"The personnel referred to in subparagraph (a) for whom status has otherwise been provided include personnel of the United States armed forces attached to the United States Embassy and personnel for whom status has been provided in the Military Advisory [redacted] Group Agreement of January 26, 1950 as amended."

means only

refers only to

을 article 중의 except 다음에 부치고 이 A.M.을 없앰

0188

CONFIDENTIAL

DEFINITIONS ARTICLE

AGREED MINUTE

With regard to Article 1(a), the expression "members of the United States armed forces" does not include personnel on active duty belonging ~~to~~ the United States land, sea or air armed services ~~for whom status has otherwise been provided such as personnel~~ for whom status is provided in the Military Advisory Group Agreement signd on January 26, 1950, and personnel of service attache officers in the Embassy of the United States of America.

0189

D. 1.

合 3/27 (17차)

ARTICLE I

In this Agreement the expression

(a) "members of the United States armed forces" means the personnel on active duty belonging to the land, sea or air armed services of the United States of America when in the territory of the Republic of Korea (except for those for whom status has otherwise been provided) ← 불미~곳

(b) "civilian component" means the civilian persons of U.S. nationality who are in the employ of, serving with, or accompanying the United States armed forces in the Republic of Korea, but excludes persons who are ordinarily resident in the Republic of Korea or who are mentioned in paragraph __ of Article (army contractor)

→ additional Sentence 挿入

(c) "dependents" means

(1) Spouse and children under 21;

(2) Parents, and children over 21, other relatives dependent for over half their support upon a member of the United States armed forces or civilian component.

0190

Article _____ (Local Procurement)

1. The United States may contract for any supplies or construction work to be furnished or undertaken in the Republic of Korea for purposes of, or authorized by, this Agreement, without restriction as to choice of supplier or person who does the constriction work. Such supplies or construction work may, upon agreement between the appropriate authorities of the two Governments, also be procured through the Government of the Republic of Korea.

2. Materials, supplies, equipment and services which are required from local sources for the maintenance of the United States armed forces and the procurement of which may have an adverse effect on the economy of the Republic of Korea shall be procured in coordination with, and, when desirable, through or with the assistance of, the competent authorities of the Republic of Korea.

3. Materials, supplies, equipment and services procured for official purposes in the Republic of Korea by the United States armed forces, or by authorized procurement agencies of the United States armed forces upon appropriate certification shall be exempt from the following Korean taxes:

(a) Commodity tax

(b) Gasoline tax

(c) Electricity and gas tax

Materials, supplies, equipment and services procured for ultimate use by the United States armed forces shall be exempt from commodity and gasoline taxes upon appropriate certification by the United States armed forces. With respect to any present or future Korean taxes not specifically referred to in this Article which might be found to constitute

0191

a significant and readily identifiable part of the gross purchase price of materials, supplies, equipment and services procured by the United States armed forces, or for ultimate use by such forces, the two Governments will agree upon a procedure for granting such exemption or relief therefrom as is consistent with the purpose of this Article.

4. Neither members of the United States armed forces, civilian component, nor their dependents, shall by reason of this Article enjoy any exemption from taxes or similar charges relating to personal purchases of goods and services in the Republic of Korea chargeable under Korean legislation.

5. Except as such disposal may be authorized by the Korean and United States authorities in accordance with mutually agreed conditions, goods purchased in the Republic of Korea exempt from the taxes referred to in paragraph 3, shall not be disposed of in the Republic of Korea to persons not entitled to purchase such goods exempt from such tax.

0192

Submitted by Korean Side on March 13, '64

CONFIDENTIAL

"4. Regarding para 3, it is understood that "materials, supplies, equipment and services procured for official purposes" refers to direct procurement by the United States armed forces or its authorized procurement agencies from Korean suppliers. "Materials, supplies, equipment and services procured for ultimate use" refers to procurement by contractors of the United States armed forces from Korean suppliers of items to be incorporated into or necessary for the production of the end product of their contracts with the United States Armed Forces".

0193

CONFIDENTIAL

Article ____ (Safety and Security Measures for U.S. Armed Forces, Its Members, Dependents, and Property)

The Republic of Korea and the United States will cooperate in taking such steps as may from time to time be necessary to ensure the security of the United States armed forces, the members thereof, the civilian component, their dependents, and their property. The Government of the Republic of Korea agrees to seek such legislation and to take such other action as may be necessary to ensure the adequate security and protection within its territory of installations, equipment, property, records and official information of the United States, and for the punishment of offenders under the applicable laws of the Republic of Korea.

0194

ARTICLE

SECURITY MEASURES

"The United States and the Republic of Korea will cooperate in taking such steps as may from time to time be necessary to ensure the security of the United States armed forces, the members thereof, the civilian component, the persons who are present in the Republic of Korea pursuant to Article [illegible], their dependents and their property. The Government of the Republic of Korea agrees to seek such legislation and to take such other action as may be necessary to ensure the adequate security and protection within its territory of installations, equipment, property, records, and official information of the United States, of the persons referred to in this paragraph, and their property and consistent with Article ___ to ensure the punishment of offenders under the applicable laws of the Republic of Korea."

③ Respect for Local Law.

0195

CONFIDENTIAL

1963. 7. 25

ARTICLE

Health and Sanitation

Consistent with the right of the United States to furnish medical support for its armed forces, civilian component and their dependents, matters of mutual concern pertaining to the control and prevention of diseases and the coordination of other public health, medical, sanitation, and veterinary services shall be resolved by the authorities of the two Governments in the Joint Committee established under Article ______ .

CONFIDENTIAL

CONFIDENTIAL

0196

9.5 9. 20 2 P.

1. Each Party waives all its claims against the other Party for damage to any property owned by it and used by its armed services, if such damage -

(a) was caused by a member or an employee of the armed services of the other Party, in execution of his official duties; or

(b) arose from the use of any vehicle, vessel or aircraft owned by the other Party and used by its armed services, provided either that the vehicle, vessel or aircraft causing the damage was being used in the execution of its official duty or that the damage was caused to property being so used.

Claims for maritime salvage by one Party against the other Party shall be waived, provided that the vessel or cargo salved was owned by the other Party and being used by its armed services for official purposes.

2. (a) In the case of damage caused or arising as stated in paragraph 1 to other property owned by either Party and located in the Republic of Korea, the issue of liability of the other Party shall be determined and the amount of damage shall be assessed, unless the two Governments agree otherwise, by a sole arbitrator selected in accordance with subparagraph (b) of this paragraph. The arbitrator shall also decide any countermeasures arising out of the same incidents.

(b) The arbitrator referred to in subparagraph (a) above shall be selected by agreement between the two Governments from amongst the nationals of the Republic of Korea who hold or have held high judicial office.

0197

(c) Any decision taken by the arbitrator shall be binding and conclusive upon the Parties.

(d) The amount of any compensation awarded by the arbitrator shall be distributed in accordance with the provisions of paragraph 5 (e) (i), (ii) and (iii) of this Article.

(e) The compensation of the arbitrator shall be fixed by agreement between the two Governments and shall, together with the necessary expenses incidental to the performance of his duties, be defrayed in equal proportions by them.

(f) Each Party waives its claim in any such case up to the amount equivalent to 800 United States dollars or 104,000 won. In the case of considerable variation in the rate of exchange between these currencies the two Governments shall agree on the appropriate adjustments of these amounts.

3. For the purpose of paragraph 1 and 2 of this Article the expression "owned by a Party" in the case of a vessel includes a vessel on bare boat charter to that Party or requisitioned by it on bare boat terms or seized by it in prize (except to the extent that the risk of loss or liability is borne by some person other than such Party).

4. Each Party waives all its claims against the other Party for injury or death suffered by any member of its armed services while such member was engaged in the performance of his official duties.

5. Claims (other than contractual claims and those to which paragraph 6 or 7 of this Article apply) arising out of acts or omissions of members or employees of the United States armed forces, including those employees who are nationals of or

0198

ordinarily resident in the Republic of Korea, done in the performance of official duty, or out of any other act, omission or occurence for which the United States armed forces are legally responsible, and causing damage in the Republic of Korea to third Parties, other than the Government of the Republic of Korea, shall be dealt with by the Republic of Korea in accordance with the following provisions:

(a) Claims shall be filed, considered and settled or adjudicated in accordance with the laws and regulations of the Republic of Korea with respect to the claims arising from the activities of its own armed forces.

(b) The Republic of Korea may settle any such claims, and payment of the amount agreed upon or determined by adjudication shall be made by the Republic of Korea in won.

(c) Such payment, whether made pursuant to a settlement or to adjudication of the case by a competent tribunal of the Republic of Korea, or the final adjudication by such a tribunal denying payment, shall be binding and conclusive upon the Parties.

(d) Every claim paid by the Republic of Korea shall be communicated to the appropriate United States authorities together with full particulars and a proposed distribution in conformity with sub-paragraph (e) (i) and (ii) below.

In default of a reply within two months, the proposed distribution shall be regarded as accepted.

(e) The cost incurred in satisfying claims pursuant to the preceding subparagraph and paragraph 2 of this Article shall be distributed between the Parties

0199

as follows:

(i) Where the United States alone is responsible, the amount awarded or adjudged shall be distributed in the proportion of 15 per cent chargeable to the Republic of Korea and 85 per cent chargeable to the United States.

(ii) Where the Republic of Korea and the United States are responsible for the damage, the amount awarded or adjudged shall be distributed equally between them. Where the damage was caused by the armed forces of the Republic of Korea and the United States and it is not possible to attribute it specifically to one or both of those armed services, the amount awarded or adjudged shall be distributed equally between the Republic of Korea and the United States.

(iii) Every half-year, a statement of the sums paid by the Republic of Korea in the course of the half-yearly period in respect of every case regarding which the proposed distribution on a percentage basis has been accepted, shall be sent to the appropriate authorities of the United States, together with a request for reimbursement. Such reimbursement shall be made, in won, within the shortest possible time.

(f) Members or employees of the United States armed forces, excluding those employees who are nationals of or ordinarily resident in the Republic of Korea, shall

0200

not be subject to any proceedings for the enforcement of any judgement given against them in the Republic of Korea in a matter arising from the performance of their official duties.

(g) Except in so far as subparagraph (e) of this paragraph applies to claims covered by paragraph 2 of this Article, the provisions of this paragraph shall not apply to any claims arising out of or in connection with the navigation or operation of a ship or the loading, carriage, or discharge of a cargo, other than claims for death or personal injury to which paragraph 4 of this Article does not apply.

6. Claims against members or employees of the United States armed forces (except employees who are nationals of or ordinarily resident in the Republic of Korea) arising out of tortious acts or omissions in the Republic of Korea not done in the performance of official duty shall be dealt with in the following manner:

(a) The authorities of the Republic of Korea shall consider the claim and access compensation to the claimant in a fair and just manner, taking into account all the circumstances of the case, including the conduct of the injured person, and shall prepare a report on the matter.

(b) The report shall be delivered to the appropriate United States authorities, who shall then decide without delay whether they will offer an ex gratia payment, and if so, of what amount.

0201

(c) If an offer of ex gratia payment is made, and accepted by the claimant in full satisfaction of his claim, the United States authorities shall make the payment themselves and inform the authorities of the Republic of Korea of their decision and of the sum paid.

(d) Nothing in this paragraph shall affect the jurisdiction of the courts of the Republic of Korea to entertain an action against a member or an employee of the United States armed forces unless and until there has been payment in full satisfaction of the claim.

7. Claims arising out of the unauthorized use of any vehicle of the United States forces shall be dealt with in accordance with paragraph 6 of this Article, except in so far as the United States forces are legally responsible.

8. If a dispute arises as to whether a tortious act or omission of a member or an employee of the United States armed forces was done in the performance of official duty or as to whether the use of any vehicle of the United States armed forces was unauthorized, the question shall be submitted to an arbitrator appointed in accordance with paragraph 2 (b) of this Article, whose decision on this point shall be final and conclusive.

9. (a) The United States shall not claim immunity from the jurisdiction of the courts of the Republic of Korea for members or employees of the United States armed forces in respect of the civil jurisdiction of the courts of the Republic of Korea except to the extent provided in paragraph 5 (f) of this Article.

0202

(b) In case any private movable property, excluding that in use by the United States armed forces, which is subject to compulsory execution under the Korean law, is within the facilities and areas in use by the United States armed forces, the United States authorities shall, upon the request of the courts of the Republic of Korea, possess and turn over such property to the authorities of the Republic of Korea.

(c) The authorities of the Republic of Korea and the United States shall cooperate in the procurement of evidence for a fair hearing and disposal of claims under this Article.

10. Disputes arising out of contracts concerning the procurement of materials, supplies, equipment, services by or for the United States armed forces, which are not resolved by the Parties to the contract concerned, may be submitted to the Joint Committee for conciliation, provided that the provisions of this paragraph shall not prejudice any right, which Parties to the contract may have, to file a civil suit.

11. Paragraphs 2 and 5 of this Article shall apply only to claims arising incident to non-combat activities.

0203

May 5, 1964

CONFIDENTIAL

1. The United States may contract for any materials, supplies, equipment and services (including construction work) to be furnished or undertaken in the Republic of Korea for purposes of, or authorized by, this Agreement, without restriction as to choice of contractor, supplier or person who provides such services. Such materials, supplies, equipment and services may, upon agreement between the appropriate authorities of the two Governments, also be procured through the Government of the Republic of Korea.

0204

Article (Revision)

Either Government may at any time request ~~the revision of~~ any article of this Agreement, in which case the two Governments shall enter into negotiation through diplomatic channels.

改正

0205

ARTICLE (Revision) 完合意 36次 11/5

Either Government may at any time request the revision of any Article of this Agreement, in which case the two Governments shall enter into negotiations through appropriate channels.

0206

CONFIDENTIAL

Article

1. The United States armed forces and the organizations provided for in Article ____ may employ civilian personnel under this Agreement. Such civilian personnel shall be nationals of the Republic of Korea.

2. Local labour requirements of the United States armed forces and of the said organizations shall be satisfied with the assistance of the Korean authorities. The obligations for the withholding and payment of income tax and social security contributions, and unless otherwise agreed upon in this article, the conditions of employment and work, such as those relating to wages and supplementary payments, the conditions for the protection of workers, and the rights of workers concerning labour relations shall be those laid down by the legislation of the Republic of Korea.

5. Should the United States armed forces dismiss a worker and a decision of a court or a Labour Commission of the Republic of Korea to the effect that the contract of employment has not terminated become final, the following procedures shall apply:

(a) The United States armed forces shall be informed by the Government of the Republic of Korea of

CONFIDENTIAL

0207

the decision of the court or Commission;

(b) Should the United States armed forces not desire to return the worker to duty, they shall so notify the Government of the Republic of Korea within ten days after being informed by the latter of the decision of the court or Commission, and may temporarily withhold the worker from duty;

(c) Upon such notification, the Government of the Republic of Korea and the United States armed forces shall consult together without delay with a view to finding a practical solution of the case;

(d) Should such a solution not be reached within a period of thirty days from the date of commencement of the consultations under (c) above, the worker will not be entitled to return to duty. In such case, the Government of the United States shall pay to the Government of the Republic of Korea an amount equal to the cost of employment of the worker for a period of time to be agreed between the two Governments through the Joint Committee.

4. The United States Government shall ensure that the contractors referred to in Article ______ employ the Korean personnel to the maximum extent practicable in connection with their activities under this Agreement.

The provisions of paragraph 2 of this Article shall be applied to the employment by the contractors of the said Korean personnel.

AGREED MINUTES

1. It is understood that the Government of the Republic of Korea shall be reimbursed for costs incurred under relevant contracts between appropriate authorities of the Korean Government and the United States armed forces or the organizations provided for in Article ____ in connection with the employment of workers to be provided for the United States armed forces or such organizations.

2. It is understood that the term "the legislation of the Republic of Korea" mentioned in Paragraph 2, Article ____ includes decisions of the courts and the Labour Commissions of the Republic of Korea, subject to the provisions of Paragraph 3, Article ______.

3. It is understood that the provisions of Article____, Paragraph 3 shall only apply to discharges for security reasons including disturbing the maintenance of military discipline within the facilities and areas used by the United States armed forces.

ARTICLE_____

Labor Procurement

1. In this Article the expression:

(a) "employer" refers to the United States armed forces (including nonappropriated fund ~~activities~~ Organization) and the persons referred to in the first paragraph of Article________.

(b) "employee" refers to any civilian (other than a member of the civilian component) employed by an employer, except (1) a member of the Korean Service Corps ~~who is an employee of the Government of Korea,~~ and (2) a domestic employed by an individual member of the United States armed forces, civilian component or dependent thereof.

2. Employers may accomplish the recruitment, employment and management of employees directly, and upon request by the employer, with the assistance of the authorities of the Republic of Korea.

3. The condition of employment, the compensation, and the labor-management practices shall be established by the United States armed forces for their employees in general conformity with the labor laws, customs and practices of the Republic of Korea; ~~provided however, that an employer may terminate employment whenever the continuation of such employment would materially impair the accomplishment of the mission of the United States armed forces.~~

4. (a) An employee shall have the same right to strike as an employee in a comparable position in the employment of the armed forces of the Republic of Korea. Such an employee may voluntarily organize and join a union or other employee group whose objectives are not inimical to the interests of the United States. Membership or nonmembership in such groups shall not be a cause for discharge or non-employment.

0210

(b) Employers will maintain procedures designed to assure the just and timely resolution of employee grievances.

5. (a) Should the Republic of Korea adopt measures allocating labor, the United States armed forces shall be accorded employment privileges no less favorable than those enjoyed by the armed forces of the Republic of Korea.

(b) In the event of a national emergency, employees who have acquired skills essential to the mission of the United States armed forces shall (may) be exempt from Republic of Korea military service or other compulsory service. The United States armed forces shall furnish to the Republic of Korea lists of those employees deemed essential.

6. Members of the civilian component shall not be subject to Korean laws or regulations with respect to their terms and conditions of employment.

AM. 3. It is understood that the government of the Republic of Korea shall be reimbursed for direct costs incurred in providing assistance requested pursuant to paragraph 2.

AGREED MINUTES

1. The Republic of Korea will make available, at designated induction points, qualified personnel for Korean Service Corps units in numbers sufficient to meet the requirements of United States armed forces. The employment of a domestic by an individual member of the United States armed forces, civilian component or dependent thereof shall be governed by applicable Korean law and in addition by wage scales and control measures promulgated by the United States armed forces.

2. The undertaking of the United States Government to conform to Korean labor laws, customs, and practices, does not imply any waiver by the United States Government of its immunities under international law. Moreover the United States government may terminate employment whenever the continuation of such employment would materially impair the accomplishment of the mission of the United States armed forces.

Article

Local Procurement

1. The United States may contract for any supplies or construction work to be furnished or undertaken in the Republic of Korea for purposes of, or authorized by, this Agreement, without restriction as to choice of supplier or person who does the construction work. Such supplies or construction work may, upon agreement between the appropriate authorities of the two Governments, also be procured through the Government of the Republic of Korea.

2. Materials, supplies, equipment and services which are required from local sources for the maintenance of the United States armed forces and the procurement of which may have an adverse effect on the economy of the Republic of Korea shall be procured in coordination with, and, when desirable, through or with the assistance of, the competent authorities of the Republic of Korea.

3. Materials, supplies, equipment and services procured for official purposes in the Republic of Korea by the United States armed forces, including their authorized procurement agencies, or procured for ultimate use by the United States armed forces shall be exempt from the following Korean taxes upon appropriate certification by the United States armed forces:

(a) Commodity tax;

(b) Traffic tax;

(c) Petroleum tax;

(d) Electricity and gas tax;

(e) Business tax.

0212

With respect to any present or future Korean taxes not specifically referred to in this Article which might be found to constitute a significant and readily identifiable part of the gross purchase price of materials, supplies, equipment and services procured by the United States armed forces, or for ultimate use by such forces, the two Governments will agree upon a procedure for granting such exemption or relief therefrom as is consistent with the purpose of this Article. OK

4. Neither members of the United States armed forces, civilian component, nor their dependents, shall by reason of this Article enjoy any exemption from taxes or similar charges relating to personal purchases of goods and services in the Republic of Korea chargeable under Korean legislation. OK

5. Except as such disposal may be authorized by the United States and Korean authorities in accordance with mutually agreed conditions, goods purchased in the Republic of Korea exempt from the? taxes referred to in paragraph 3, shall not be disposed of in the Republic of Korea to persons not entitled to purchase such goods exempt from such tax. final editing OK

AGREED MINUTES

1. The United States armed forces will furnish the Korean authorities with appropriate information as far in advance as practicable on anticipated major changes in their procurement program in the Republic of Korea.

2. The problem of a satisfactory settlement of difficulties with respect to procurement contracts arising out of differences between Korean and United States economic laws and business practices will be studied by the Joint Committee or other appropriate ~~persons~~ representatives. OK

Joint Committee에서 choose

0213

OK 46차 3/13 64.

3. The procedures for securing exemptions from taxation on purchases of goods for ultimate use by the United States armed forces will be as follows:

(a) Upon appropriate certification by the United States armed forces that materials, supplies and equipment consigned to or destined for such forces, are to be used, or wholly or partially used up, under the supervision of such forces, exclusively in the execution of contracts for the construction, maintenance or operation of the facilities and areas referred to in Article D&A or for the support of the forces therein, or are ultimately to be incorporated into articles or facilities used by such forces, an authorized representative of such forces shall take delivery of such materials, supplies and equipment directly from manufacturers thereof. In such circumstances the collection of (commodity & gasoline) taxes referred to in Article Local Pro, paragraph 3, shall be held in abeyance.

(b) The receipt of such materials, supplies and equipment in the facilities and areas shall be confirmed by an authorized officer representatives of the United States armed forces to the Korean authorities.

(c) Collection of the (commodity & gasoline) taxes on such materials, supplies and equipment shall be held in abeyance until

(1) The United States armed forces confirm and certify the quantity or degree of consumption of the above referred to materials, supplies and equipment, or

(2) The United States armed forces confirm and certify the amount of the above referred to materials, supplies, and equipment which have been incorporated into articles or facilities used by the United States armed forces.

0214

(d) Materials, supplies, and equipment certified under (c) (1) or (2) shall be exempt from taxes (referred to in Article 로.P. , paragraph 3,) insofar as the price thereof is paid out of United States Government appropriations or out of funds contributed by the Government of the ~~the~~ Republic of Korea for disbursement by the United States.

4. 挿入

AFAK 援助 포함

assistance

Regarding Paragraph 3, it is understood that "materials, supplies, equipment and services procured for official purposes" refers to direct procurement by the United States armed forces or their authorized procurement agencies from Korean suppliers. "Materials, supplies, equipment and services procured for ultimate use" refers to procurement by contractors of the United States armed forces from Korean suppliers of items to be incorporated into or necessary for the production of the end product of their contracts with the United States Armed Forces."

0215

CONFIDENTIAL

ARTICLE

MILITARY PAYMENT CERTIFICATES

1. (a) United States military payment certificates denominated in dollars may be used by persons authorized by the United States for internal transactions. The Government of the United States will take appropriate action to insure that authorized personnel are prohibited from engaging in transactions involving military payment certificates except as authorized by United States regulations. The Government of Korea will take necessary action to prohibit unauthorized persons from engaging in transactions involving military payment certificates and with the aid of United States authorities will undertake to apprehend and punish any person or persons under its jurisdiction involved in the counterfeiting or uttering of counterfeit military payment certificates.

(b) It is agreed that the United States authorities will to the extent authorized by United States law apprehend and punish members of the United States armed forces, the civilian component, or their dependents, who tender military payment certificates to unauthorized persons and that no obligation will be due to such unauthorized persons or to the Government of Korea or its agencies from the United States or any of its agencies as a result of any unauthorized use of military payment certificates within Korea.

0216

合意

2. (a) In order to exercise control of military payment certificates the United States may designate certain American financial institutions to maintain and operate, under United States supervision, facilities for the use of persons authorized by the United States to use military payments certificates.]

合意

(b) Institutions authorized to maintain military banking facilities will establish and maintain such facilities physically separated from their Korean commercial banking business, with personnel whose sole duty is to maintain and operate such facilities Such facilities shall be permitted to maintain United States currency bank accounts and to perform all financial transactions in connection therewith including receipt and remission of funds to the extent provided by Article .... paragraph 2, of this Agreement.

0217

ARTICLE XIX - Military Payment Certificates

AGREED MINUTE

(2)

Inasmuch as United States Military Payment Certificates are property of the United States Government, any Military Payment Certificates which are in, or come into, the possession of the Government of the Republic of Korea shall be returned without compensation to the authorities of the United States armed forces as expeditiously as practicable.

0218

Meteorological Services

Article____

The Government of the Republic of Korea undertakes to furnish the United States armed forces with the following meteorological services in accordance with arrangements between the appropriate authorities of the two Governments:

(a) Meteorological observations from land and ocean areas including observations from ships;

(b) Climatological information including periodic summaries and historical data wherever available;

(c) Telecommunications service to disseminate meteorological information;

(d) Seismographic data.

0219

55차 April 28/1965
Korean side

CONFIDENTIAL

LABOR ARTICLE

(Underlining indicates modifications from Korean draft of the Labor Article tabled at 69th session)

1. In this Article the expression:

(a) "employer" refers to the United States Armed Forces (including non-appropriated fund activities).

(b) "employee" refers to any civilian (other than a member of the civilian component of the United States Armed Forces) employed by an employer. Such civilian personnel shall be nationals of the Republic of Korea.

2. Employers may recruit, employ and administer their personnel. Recruitment services of the Government of the Republic of Korea shall be utilized to the maximum extent practicable. In case employers accomplish direct recruitment of employees, The United States Armed Forces shall provide such relevant information as may be required for labor administration to the Office of Labor Affairs of the Republic of Korea.

3. To the extent not inconsistent with the provisions of this Article or except as may otherwise be mutually agreed, the conditions of employment and work, such as those relating to wages and supplementary payments, the conditions for the protection and welfare of employees, compensations, and the rights of employees, concerning labor relations shall conform with those laid down by the labor legislation of the Republic of Korea.

4. (a) With regard to any dispute between employers and any employees or labor unions which cannot be settled through the use of existing procedures of the United States Armed Forces, settlement shall be accomplished in the following manner:

0220

CONFIDENTIAL

(1) The dispute shall be referred to the Office of Labor Affairs of the Republic of Korea for conciliation.

(2) In the event that the dispute is not settled by the procedures described in (1) above, the dispute shall be referred to a special committee designated by the Joint Committee for further conciliation efforts.

(3) In the event that the dispute is not settled by the procedures outlined above, the Joint Committee will resolve the dispute. The decisions of the Joint Committee shall be binding.

(4) Neither employee organizations nor employees shall engage in any practices disruptive of normal work requirements unless the cooling-off period set forth in Article 14 of the Korean Labor Dispute Law has elapsed after the dispute is referred to the specially-designated committee mentioned in (2) above.

(5) Failure of any employee organization or employee to abide by the decision of the Joint Committee on any dispute, or engaging in practices disruptive of normal work requirements in violation of the provisions laid down in (4) above, shall be considered cause for the depriviation of the rights and protection accorded by the relevant labor legislation of the Republic of Korea.

(b) The right concerning strike shall be accorded to employees except those whose exercise of the right is prohibited by the Joint Committee.

5. In the event of a national emergency, such as war, hostilities or situations where war or hostilities is imminent, the application of this Article shall be limited in accordance with the emergency measures taken by the Government of the Republic of Korea, and, in addition, the following arrangements will be made:

(a) Should the Government of the Republic of Korea adopt measures allocating labor, the United States Armed Forces shall be accorded allocation privileges no less favorable than those enjoyed by the Armed Forces of the Republic of Korea.

(b) Employees who have acquired skills essential to the mission of the United States Armed Forces will, upon request of the United States Armed Forces and through mutual agreement, be deferred from Republic of Korea military service or other compulsory services. The United States Armed Forces shall in advance furnish to the Government of the Republic of Korea lists of those employees deemed necessary.

6. Members of the civilian component of the United States Armed Forces shall not be subject to Korean laws or regulations with respect to their terms and conditions of employment.

AGREED MINUTES

1. The undertaking of the United States to conform to the labor legislation of the Republic of Korea does not imply any waiver by the United States Government of its immunitiss under international law.

2. It is understood that the Government of the Republic of Korea shall be reimbursed for direct costs incurred in providing assistance pursuant to Paragraph 2.

3. **Employers will withhold from the pay of their employees, and pay over to the Government of the Republic of Korea withholdings required by the income tax legislation of the Republic of Korea.**

4. In case where it is impossible for employers to conform to the labor legislations of the Republic of Korea applicable under Paragraph 3 on account of the military requirements of the United States Armed Forces, the matter shall be referred, in advance, to the Joint Committee for mutual agreement. The Government of the Republic of Korea will give due consideration to the military requirements of the United States Armed Forces.

February 14. 1964
submitted by
U. S. Side

CONFIDENTIAL

ARTICLE

Criminal Jurisdcition

1. Subject to the provisions of this Article:

(a) the military authorities of the United States shall have the right to exercise within the Republic of Korea criminal and disciplinary jurisdiction conferred on them by the law of the United States over the members of the United States armed forces and the civilian components.

(b) the authorities of the Republic of Korea shall have jurisdiction over the members of the United States armed forces, the civilian component, and their dependents with respect to offenses committed within the territory of the Republic of Korea and punishable by the law of the Republic of Korea.

2. (a) The military authorities of the United States shall have the right to exercise exclusive jurisdiction over members of the United States armed forces and the civilian components with respect to offenses, including offenses relating to its security, punishable by the law of the United States, but not by the law of the Republic of Korea.

(b) The authorities of the Republic of Korea shall have the right to exercise exclusive jurisdiction over members

0224

of the United States armed forces, the civilian component, and their dependents with respect to offenses, including offenses relating to the security of the Republic of Korea, punishable by its law but not by the law of the United States.

(c) For the purpose of this paragraph and of paragraph 3 of this Article a security offense against a State shall include:

(i) treason against the State;

(ii) sabotage, espionage or violation of any law relating to official secrets of that State, or secrets relating to the national defense of that State.

제12條

3. In cases where the right to exercise jurisdiction is concurrent the following rules shall apply;

(a) The military authorities of the United States shall have the primary right to exercise jurisdiction over members of the United States armed forces or the civilian component in relation to:

(i) offenses solely against the property or security of the United States, or offenses solely against the person or property of another member of the United States armed forces or the civilian component or of a dependent;

(ii) offenses arising out of any act or omission done in the performance of official duty provid that such act or omission is directly related to the duty. The question as to whether offenses were committed in the performance of official duty shall be decided by a competent district public prosecutor of the Republic of Korea.

In case the offender's commanding officer finds otherwise, he may appeal from the prosecutor's decision to the Minister of Justice within ten days from the receipt of the decision of the prosecutor, and the decision of the Minister of Justice shall be final.

(b) In the case of any other offenses the authorities of the Republic of Korea shall have the primary right to exercise jurisdiction.

(c) If the State having the primary right decides not to exercise jurisdiction, it shall notify the authorities of the other State as soon as practicable. The authorities of the State having the primary right shall give sympathetic consideration to a request from the authorities of the other

State for a waiver of its right in cases where that other State considers such waiver to be of particular importance.

4. The foregoing provisions of this Article shall not imply any right for the military authorities of the United States to exercise jurisdiction over persons who are nationals of or ordinarily resident in the Republic of Korea, unless they are members of the United States forces.

5. (a) The military authorities of the United States and the authorities of the Republic of Korea shall assist each other in the arrest of members of the United States armed forces, the civilian component, or their dependents in the territory of the Republic of Korea and in handing them over to the authorities which is to exercise jurisdiction in accordance with the above provisions.

(b) The authorities of the Republic of Korea shall notify the military authorities of the United States of the arrest of any member of the United States armed forces, the civilian component, or their dependents.

(c) The military authority of the United States shall immediately notify the authority of the Republic of Korea of the arrest of a member of the United States armed forces, the civilian component, or a dependent, unless the United States authority has the right to exercise exclusive jurisdiction over such a person.

(d) An accused member of the United States armed for the civilian component or a dependent over whom the Republic Korea is to exercise jurisdiction shall, if he is in the hand of the United States, be under the custody of the United State Upon presentation of a warrant issued by a judge of the Republ Korea he shall be handed over immediately to the Korean Authorities.

6. (a) The authorities of the Republic of Korea and the military authorities of the United States shall assist each other in the carrying out of all necessary investigations into offenses, and in the collection and production of evidence including the seizure and, in proper case, the handing over of objects connected with an offense. The handing over of such objects may, however, be made subject to their return within the time specified by the authority delivering them.

(b) The authorities of the Republic of Korea and the military authorities of the United States shall notify each other of the disposition of all cases in which there are concurr rights to exercise jurisdiction.

7. (a) A death sentence shall not be carried out in the Republic of Korea by the military authorities of the United States if the legislation of the Republic of Korea does not provide for such punishment in a similar case.

(b) The authorities of the Republic of Korea shall give sympathetic consideration to a request from the military authorities of the United States for assistance in carrying out a sentence of imprisonment pronounced by the military authorities of the United States under the provisions of this Article within the territory of the Republic of Korea.

8. Where an accused has been tried in accordance with the provisions of this Article either by the authorities of the Republic of Korea or the military authorities of the United States and has been acquitted, or has been convicted and is serving, or has served, his sentence or has been pardoned, he may not be tried again for the same offense within the territory of the Republic of Korea by the authorities of the other State. However, nothing in this paragraph shall prevent the military authorities of the United States from trying a member of its forces for any violation of rules of discipline arising from an act or omission which constituted an offense for which he was tried by the authorities of the Republic of Korea.

9. Whenever a member of the United States armed forces, the civilian component or a dependent is prosecuted under the jurisdiction of the Republic of Korea he shall be entitled:

(a) to a prompt and speedy trial;

0229

(b) to be informed, in advance of trial, of the specific charge or charges made against him;

(c) to be confronted with the witnesses against him;

(d) to have compulsory process for obtaining witnesses in his favor, if they are within the jurisdiction of the Republic of Korea;

(e) to have legal representation of his own choice for his defense or to have free or assisted legal representation under the conditions prevailing in the Republic of Korea;

(f) If he considers it necessary, to be provided with the services of a competent interpreter; and

(g) to communicate with a representative of the Government of the United States and to have such a representative present at his trial.

10. (a) Regularly constituted military units or formation of the United States armed forces shall have the right to police any facilities or areas which they use under Article IV of this Agreement. The military police of such forces may take all appropriate measures to ensure the maintenance of order and security within such facilities and areas.

(b) Outside these facilities and areas such military police shall be employed only subject to arrangements with the authorities of the Republic of Korea and in liaison with those authorities and in so far as such employment is necessary to maintain discipline and order among the members of the United States armed forces.

0231

Feb. 28, 1964 submitted by Korean side

CONFIDENTIAL

Agreed Minutes

RE Paragraph 2(c)

Both Governments shall inform each other of the details of all ~~the security~~ offenses mentioned in this subparagraph and the provisions governing such offenses in the existing laws of their respective countries.

RE Paragraph 3(a) (ii)

The term "official duty" is not meant to include all acts by members of the United States armed forces or the civilian component during periods while they are on duty. Any departure from acts which are duly required to be done as a normal function of a particular duty shall be deemed as an act outside of his "official duty."

RE Paragraph 3(c)

Mutual procedures relating to waivers of the primary right to exercise jurisdiction shall be determined by the Joint Committee.

Trials of cases in which the authorities of the Republic of Korea waived the primary right to exercise jurisdiction, and trials of cases involving offenses described in paragraph 3(a) (ii) committed against the State or nationals of the Republic of Korea shall be held promptly in the Republic of Korea within a reasonable distance from the places where the offenses are alleged to have taken place unless other arrangements are mutually agreed upon. Representatives of the authorities of the Republic of Korea may be present at such trials.

RE Paragraph 4

Dual nationals, the Republic of Korea and United States, who are the members of the United States armed forces or the civilian component and are brought to the Republic of Korea shall not be considered as nationals of the Republic of Korea, but shall be considered as United States nationals for the purposes of this paragraph.

0232

RE Paragraph 5(b)

In case the authorities of the Republic of Korea have arrested an offender who is a member of the United States armed forces, the civilian component or a dependent with respect to a case over which the Republic of Korea has the primary right to exercise jurisdiction, the authorities of the Republic of Korea will, unless they deem that there is adequate cause and necessity to retain such offender, release him to the custody of the United States military authorities provided that he shall, on request, be made available to the authorities of the Republic of Korea, if such be the condition of his release. The United States authorities shall, on request, transfer his custody to the authorities of the Republic of Korea at the time he is indicted by the latter.

RE Paragraph 6

1. A member of the United States armed forces or the civilian component shall, if sommoned by the authorities of the Republic of Korea as a witness in the course of investigations and trials, make himself available to the authorities of the Republic of Korea.

2. If any person sommoned as witness did not make himself available to the authorities of the Republic of Korea, they may take necessary measures in accordance with the provisions of the law of the Republic of Korea. Subject to the foregoing, the military authorities of the United States shall, upon presentation of a warrant issued by a judge of the Republic of Korea, immediately take all appropriate measures to ensure the execution of the warrant by the authorities of the Republic of Korea.

RE Paragraph 9

1. The rights enumerated in this paragraph are guaranteed to all persons on trial in the Korean courts by the provisions of the Constitu- 0233

tion of the Republic of Korea. In addition to these rights, a member of the United States armed forces, the civilian component or a dependent who is prosecuted under the jurisdiction of the Republic of Korea shall have such other rights as are guaranteed under the Constitution and laws of the Republic of Korea to all persons on trial in the Korean courts.

2. Nothing in the provisions of paragraph 9(g) concerning the presence of a representative of the United States Government at the trial of a member of the United States armed forces, the civilian component or a dependent prosecuted under the jurisdiction of the Republic of Korea, shall be so construed as to prejudice the provisions of the Constitution of the Republic of Korea with respect to public trials.

RE Paragraph 10(a) and 10(b)

1. The United States military authorities will normally make arrests of the members of the United States armed forces and the civilian component within facilities and areas in use by and guarded under the authority of the United States armed forces. The authorities of the Republic of Korea may arrest all persons who are subject to the jurisdiction of the Republic of Korea within facilities and areas in cases where the authorities of the United States armed forces have given consent, or in cases of pursuit of a flagrant offender who has committed a serious crime.

Where persons whose arrest is desired by the authorities of the Republic of Korea and who are not subject to the jurisdiction of the United States armed forces are within facilities and areas in use by the United States armed forces, the United States military authorities shall, upon request, promptly arrest such persons. All persons arrested 0234 by the United States military authorities, who are not subject to the jurisdiction of the United States armed forces, shall immediately be turned over to the authorities of the Republic of Korea.

The United States military authorities may, under due process of law, arrest within or in the vicinity of a facility or area any person in the commission of an offense against the security of that facility or area. Any such person not subject to the jurisdiction of the United States armed forces shall immediately be turned over to the authorities of the Republic of Korea.

2. The authorities of the Republic of Korea will normally not exercise the right of seizure, search, or inspection with respect to any person or property within facilities and areas in use by and guarded under the authorities of the United States armed forces or with respect to property of the United States armed forces wherever situated except in cases where the authorities of the United States armed forces consent to such seizure, search, or inspection by the authorities of the Republic of Korea of such persons or property.

Where seizure, search, or inspection with respect to persons or property within facilities and areas in use by the United States armed forces or with respect to property of the United States armed forces in the Republic of Korea is desired by the authorities of the Republic of Korea, the United States military authorities shall, upon request, make such seizure, search, or inspection. In the event of a judgement concerning such property, except property owned or utilized by the United States Government or its instrumentalities, the United States shall turn over such property to the authorities of the Republic of Korea for disposition in accordance with the judgement.

0235

May 20, '64

CONFIDENTIAL

Agreed Minute

Re Paragraph 3(a) (ii)

Where a member of the United States armed forces or civilian component is charged with an offense, a certificate issued by a staff judge advocate on behalf of his commanding officer stating that the alleged offense, if committed by him, arose out of an act or omission done in the performance of official duty, shall be sufficient evidence of the fact for the purpose of determining primary jurisdiction, unless the contrary is proved.

If the chief prosecutor of the Republic of Korea considers that there is proof contrary to the certificate of official duty, he will refer the matter to the Joint Committee for decision.

The above statements shall not be interpreted to prejudice in any way Article 308 of the Korean Code of Criminal Procedure.

0236

May 20, '64

CONFIDENTIAL

Agreed Minute

Re Paragraph 3(c)

The authorities of the Republic of Korea will, upon the notification of individual cases falling under the waiver provided in Article ____ paragraph 3(c) from the military authorities of the United States, waive its primary right to exercise jurisdiction under Article ____ except where they determine that it is of particular importance that jurisdiction be exercised by the authorities of the Republic of Korea.

CONFIDENTIAL

0237

May 20, '64

CONFIDENTIAL

Paragraph 5(d)

An accused member of the United States Armed Forces or civilian component over whom the Republic of Korea is to exercise jurisdiction will, if he is in the hand of the United States, be under the custody of the United States during all judicial proceedings and until custody is requested by the authorities of the Republic of Korea.

The military authorities of the United States may transfer custody to the Korean authorities at any time and shall give sympathetic consideration to any request for the transfer of custody which may be made by the Korean authorities in specific cases.

Paragraph 5(e)

In respect of offenses solely against the security of the Republic of Korea provided in Paragraph 2(c), custody shall remain with the authorities of the Republic of Korea.

CONFIDENTIAL 0238

10/15

제 70 차

주둔군지위협정 체결 교섭 실무자회의에 임할

우리측 입장

제67차 한·미간 실무자회의에서 미측이 제시한 포괄적 제안은 우리측 대표가 제50차 및 동52차회의 석상에서 제안한 우리의 입장과는 아직 상당한 거리가 있으므로 우리는 제50차 및 동52차 회의이래 우리측이 주장하여 온 입장, 특히 경합적 관할권의 포기에 관한 종전의 입장을 최대한 반영시키는 한편 미측이 제67차 회의시 제안한 주장을 참작하여 다음과 같은 역시 포괄적인 대안을 제시하여 미측으로 하여금 이를 일괄적으로 수락할 것을 촉구한다.

1. 경합적 관할권의 포기

가. 합의의사록 제3항초안

대한민국은 미군법에 복하는 자에 관하여 질서와 규률을 유지함이 미국당국의 주된 책임임을 인정하여 본조 3(c)항의 규정에 따른 미군당국의 요청을 받으면 (대한민국당국이 관할권을 행사함이 특히 중대하다고 인정하는 경우를 제외하고) 제3(b)항의 규정하에서 관할권을 행사하는 제1차적 권리를 미군당국에 포기한다. 만약에 어느편이 관할권을 행사하느냐에 관하여 의문이 생길 경우에는 주한미국외교사절은 대한민국당국과 협의할수 있는 기회가 부여되어야 한다. 대한민국당국은 ~~한·미양국의 이해관계를 충분히 고려하여 그 문제를 해결하여야 한다.~~

대한민국이 관할권을 행사할 제1차적 권리를 포기하는 사건의 재판과 제3(a)(ii)항에 규정된 범죄(공무집행중 범죄)로서 대한민국 또는 대한민국 국민에 대하여 범하여진 범죄에 관련된 사건의

— 1 —

0239

재판은 별도의 조치가 상호 합의되지 않는한 범죄가 행하여 졌다는 장소로부터 적당한 거리내에서 행하여 진다. 대한민국의 대표는 그러한 재판에 입회할수 있다.
범죄의 신속한 처리를 촉진하기 위하여 미국 및 대한민국당국간에 통고없이 처리하기 위한 ~~조치를~~ 약정을 할수 있다.

나. 상기 초안을 제안함에 있어서 실지운영상의 논난의 여지를 제거하기 위하여 다음과 같은 양해사항을 기록에 남긴다.

"특정한 사건에 있어서 특수한 사정을 이유로 대한민국이 관할권을 행사함이 특히 중대하다고 인정하는 경우에 해당되는 사건이라 함은 특정사건에 대한 상세한 조사결과에 달려 있지만 특히 다음과 같은 경우를 칭한다: (ㄱ) 대한민국의 안전에 대한 범죄, (ㄴ) 사람을 죽이거나 또는 치사케한 범죄, (ㄷ) 강도죄, (ㄹ) 강간죄, (ㅁ) 기타 한·미양국이 특히 중대하다고 인정하는 범죄, 및 (ㅂ) 상기 범죄의 미수 또는 공범죄."

다. 문제점

(1) 우리측이 과거 제1차관할권의 포기문제에서 주장하여 온바와 같이 한국당국이 특히 중대하다고 인정하는 사건을 한국법정에서 재판할 수 있는 재량권이 확보된다면,

(2) 기타 미측이 제67차회의에서 제의한바와 같이 미국당국에 미국법에 복하는 자들에 대한 질서와 규율을 유지하는 주된 책임이 있음을 인정하고,

(3) 재판권 행사당국 결정에 관하여 한·미간에 이의가 있을 경우에 외교교섭을 통하여 해결하려는 미측제안을 수락하는 것은 무방할 것이다.

(4) 미측이 한국측이 관할권을 행사할수 있는 범죄의 종류를 예시한정한 대한민국의 안전에 대한 범죄, 강간죄, 또는 고의적 살인에 관련된 범죄에 국한하고 있는바 실지운영상의 필요성을 고려하여 강도죄, 기타 한·미양국의 중대하다고 인정하는 범죄 및 상기 각종 범죄의 미수 또는 공범죄를 추가삽입하여 양해사항으로 규정함도 가할 것이다.

2. <u>공무집행중 범죄</u>

가. <u>합의의사록제3 (a) (ii) 항 초안</u>

(1) 미측안을 수락한다. 즉,

"미국군대구성원, 또는 군속이 범죄의 혐의를 받았을 때에, 그자가 범하였다면 혐의된 범죄가 공무집행중에 행한 작위 또는 부작위에 기인한 것임을 진술한 미국군대의 권한있는 당국이 발행한 증명서는 제1차 관할권을 결정하기 위한 사실의 충분한 증거가 된다.

"대한민국의 검찰청장은 공무집행증명서에 대한 반증이 있다고 사료하는 예외적인 경우에는 공무집행증명서는 대한민국관계관과 주한외교사절간의 협의를 통한 재심의 대상이 될수 있다."

(2) 미측이 제시한 2개의 양해사항을 다음과 같이 일부 수정하여 수락한다.

(ㄱ) 미군당국이 발행한 공무집행증명서는 미측이 수정하지 않는한 구속력을 갖는다. 그러나 미군당국은 대한민국이 제시한 이의에 대하여 정당한 고려를 하여야 한다.

(ㄴ) 공무집행증명서에 대한 재심의 지연으로 피의자의 신속한 재판을 받을 권리가 박탈되어서는 아니된다.

나. 미측이 제49차 회의에서 양해사항으로 제안한 공무집행의 정의를 합의의사록에 규정할 것을 제안한다.

"공무라 함은 미군대구성원 및 군속이 공무중 행한 모든 행위를 포함하는 것을 의미하는 것이 아니며 개인이 집행하는 공무의 기능으로서 행하여 질것이 요구되는 행위에만 적용되는 것을 의미한다. 그러므로 어떤자가 특정 공무에 있어서 행할 것이 요구되는 행위로 부터 이탈된 행위는 통상 그의 공무밖의 행위이다."

다. 문제점

(1) 미측이 제67차회의에서 제안한 공무집행중 범죄에 관한 대안은 대체적으로 독일보충협정의 내용과 유사하며

(2) 그내용중 미군당국이 발행한 공무집행증명서의 효력을 일단 충분한 것으로 인정한 점과,

(3) 반증이 있는 경우 외교교섭을 통하여 재심토록 한점은 협정안으로서 하나의 발전이라고 사료됨.

(4) 다만 미측이 지금까지 주장하여 온바와 같이 검찰총장이 이의를 제기한 경우에 합의되지 않는한 이미 발행된 증명서는 계속 유효하여야 한다는 것은 미측의 기본적 방침인 것으로 사료됨으로 우리측은 이를 양해사항으로 수락하되 그대신 우리측도 한국당국이 이의를 제기한 경우에는 미국당국도 이를 신중히 고려하여야 한다는 점을 미측에 주장할 필요가 있으며,

(5) 무엇이 공무집행중 행위인가를 명확히 하기 위하여 미극동군이 1956년도에 예하부대에 시달한 일이 있는 공무집행중 행위에 관한 정의를 합의의사록에 규정하기 위하여 노력할 필요가 있다.

3. 피의자의 재판전 구금

우리측이 제 52 차회의에서 미측에 제안한 초안과 그후의 미측 주장을 참작하여 다음과 같은 우리측 수정안을 제안한다.

가. 본문제 5 항 초안

5(c) 미군당국이 대한민국이 관할권을 행사할 제 1 차적 권리를 갖는 사건에 관련된 미군인, 군속 또는 가족을 체포하였을 경우에는 즉시 대한민국에 통고하여야 한다.

5(d) 대한민국이 관할권을 행사할 미군인, 군속 또는 가족이 미군당국의 수중에 있을 경우에는 모든 재판절차 진행중 그리고 대한민국당국이 신병을 요청할때까지 미군당국이 구금한다.

5(e) 피의자의 신병이 대한민국의 수중에 있을 경우에 대한민국당국이 그러한 피의자의 신병을 구금할 정당한 사유와 필요성이 있다고 사료하지 않는 한 미군당국이 요청하면 미국당국에 신병 구금을 이양하며 모든 사법절차 진행중 그리고 대한민국당국이 신병 인도를 요청할때 까지 미군당국이 구금한다.

5(f) 제 2 (c) 항에 규정된바 대한민국의 안전에 대한 범죄에 관련된 피의자의 신병은 대한민국당국이 구금한다.

제 5 (d) 항 및 5 (e) 항의 규정에 따라 피의자의 신병이 미군당국의 수중에 있을 경우에 미군당국은 언제던지 신병을 한국당국에 인도할수 있으며 특별한 사건에 있어서 대한민국당국이 신병의 인도를 요청하면 호의적인 고려를 한다.

미군당국은 한국당국이 요청하면 즉시 대한민국당국이 피의자에 대한 수사 또는 재판을 할수 있게 하여야 한다.

대한민국당국은 미군당국이 군인, 군속 또는 가족의 신병을 구금함에 있어서 조력을 요청하면 호의적인 고려를 한다.

나. 본문제 5 (e) 항 및 제 5 (f) 에 관한 양해사항

미측 양해사항을 다음과 같이 수정 채택한다.

(가) "제 5 (e) 항 및 제 5 (f) 항에 규정된 한국당국의 신병구금사정의 적당여부에 대하여 한.미양국간의 상호 협의가 있어야 한다."

(나) 한국의 구금시설은 미국수준으로 보아 적당하여야 한다.

다. 문제점

(1) 대한민국이 피의자를 체포하였을 때에 그러한 피의자의 신병을 계속 구금할 필요가 있다고 인정되는 경우에 그렇게 할수있는 근거를 마련하려는 것이 우리측의 기본적 입장임으로 이입장을 관철하기 위하여 미측의 입장을 참작하여

(2) 한국당국이 구금할 사정의 적당여부에 관하여 미국당국과 협의내지는 합의할수 있는 방법도 고려된다.

(3) 한.미양국당국중 어느편이 체포하였건 간에 일단 미국당국이 구금하게된 피의자의 신병을 재판후 한국당국에 인도하는 시기는 동일함이 타당하며,

(4) 다만 피의자의 신병이 미국당국 수중에 있을 때에 한국당국이 수사상 또는 재판상 필요할 경우 신속하고도 용의하게 피의자를 신문

또는 소환할수 있는 편의가 보장되어야 할 것이다.

4. 피의자의 권리

가. 합의의사록 제9항초안

우리측은 미측이 주장하고 있는 피의자의 권리중 우리나라 형사소송제도에 위배되는 규정을 다음과 같이 수정할 것을 주건으로 미측이 제안한 피의자의 권리를 합의의사록에 열거할 것을 수락한다.

(1) 미측 합의의사록 제9(a)항 후단에 규정된 한국군법회의에 관한 사항은 협정본문 제1(b)항에 규정될 한국의 관할권 행사당국의 문제의 해결을 기다려 해결하기 위하여 보류한다.

(2) 합의의사록 제9(a)항에 규정된 미국정부대표가 결석중에 행한 피의자의 진술은 유죄의 증거로 사용할수 없다는 미측초안에 다음과 같은 단서를 추가한다.

(ㄱ) "다만 미국정부대표가 정당한 이유없이 출석하지 아니한 경우에는 그러하지 아니한다."

(3) 합의의사록 제9항의 제2(e)항 및 제4항에 규정된 상소제도에 관한 미측초안에 관하여는 다음과 같이 주장한다.

(ㄱ) 합의의사록 제9항의 제2(e)항에 대하여는 우리측이 제20차회의에서 제안한 다음과 같은 대안을 계속 주장한다.

"피고인이 상소한 사건과 피고인을 위하여 상소한 사건에 있어서는 원심판결의 형보다 중한 형을 선고받지 아니하는 권리.

(ㄴ) 합의의사록 제9항의 제4항의 상소이유에 관한 규정은 우리나라 상소제도의 취지와 상반되는 것임으로 삭제할 것을 계속

주장한다.

(4) 합의의사록 제9항의 제3항에 규정된 위법 부당한 방법으로 수집된 증거의 증명능력에 관한 미측 제안에 대하여는 우리측 종전제안대로 "부당한"이라는 용어를 삭제하고 수락한다.

나. 미측이 제안한 다음과 같은 권리는 이를 수락한다.

(1) 합의의사록 제9(b)항의 규정중 피의자에게 불리하게 사용될 증거의 성질을 사전에 통고받을 권리.

(2) 합의의사록 제9(e)항에 규정된 피고인이 변호인과 비밀히 상의할 권리.

(3) 합의의사록 제9항의 제2(f)항에 규정된 범죄의 범행후 피고인에게 불리하게 변경된 증거법칙이나 증명요건에 의하여 소추받지 아니하는 권리.

(4) 합의의사록 제9항의 제2(i)항에 규정된 피고인이 재판에 회부됨이 없이 입법부 또는 행정부에 의하여 소추 또는 처벌되지 아니하는 권리.

(5) 합의의사록 제9항의 제2(k)항의 육체적 또는 정신적으로 부적당한 경우의 심판 불출두 권리.

다. 문제점

(1) 미측이 미초안의 피의자의 권리를 전부 합의의사록에 규정하려는 것은 미행정부가 미국의회 및 국민에 대하여 설사 미군관계 범법자를 한국의 재판관할권에 복하게 할지라도 미국법에 보장된 인권이 충분히 보장될 것임을 납득

시키려는데 그 근본적 의도가 있다고 사료 됨으로 미측의 권리열거원칙에 동의함으로써 미측에 대하여 우리나라의 성의를 표시하는 것은 교섭타결 촉구를 위하여 유의할 것으로 보며,

(2) 다만 우리나라 형사소송제도의 근본정신에 위배되는 권리만은 계속 수정 또는 삭제할 것을 미측에 요구하여 우리나라 소송제도 운영에 지장을 초래하지 않도록 노력함이 필요하다.

A. Waiver of the Primary Right to exercise Jurisdiction

1. Agreed Minute, Re Paragraph 3

"The Republic of Korea, recognizing that it is the primary responsibility of the United States authorities to maintain good order and discipline where persons subject to United States military law are concerned, will, upon the request of the military authorities of the United States pursuant to paragraph 3(c), waive its primary right to exercise jurisdiction under paragraph 3(b) except when it determines that it is of particular importance that jurisdiction be exercised by the authorities of the Republic of Korea. If any question arises concerning who is to exercise jurisdiction the United States diplomatic mission will be afforded an opportunity to confer with the proper authorities of the Republic of Korea. The authorities of the Republic of Korea, giving due consideration to the interests of the Republic of Korea and to the interests of the United States, shall resolve the matter.

Trials of cases in which the authorities of the Republic of Korea waive the primary right to exercise jurisdiction, and trials of cases involving offenses described in paragraph 3(a) (ii) committed against the state or nationals of the Republic of Korea will be held within a reasonable distance from the place where the offenses are alleged to have taken place unless other arrangements are mutually agreed upon. Representatives of the Republic of Korea may be present at such trials.

To facilitate the expeditious disposal of offenses of minor importance, arrangements may be made between the United States authorities and the competent authorities of the Republic of Korea to dispense with notification.

2. Understanding

"Subject to a careful examination of each specific cases and to the results of such examination, the authorities of the Republic of Korea shall, under the provisions of Re Paragraph 3, exercise jurisdiction in particular in the following cases:

a. An offense against the security of the Republic of Korea;
b. An offense causing the death of a human being;
c. Rape;
d. Robbery;
e. Any other offense which the authorities of both Governments consider to be of particular importance as the result of examination thereof;
f. An attempt to commit foregoing offenses or participation therein.

B. Official Duty Certificate

1. Agreed Minute 1, Re Paragraph 3(a) (ii)

"Where a member of the United States armed forces or civilian component is charged with an offense, a certificate issued by competent authorities of the United States armed forces stating that the alleged offense, if committed by him, arose out of an act or omission done in the performance of official duty shall be sufficient evidence of the fact for the purpose of determining primary jurisdiction.

In those exceptional cases where the chief district prosecutor for the Republic of Korea considers that there is proof contrary to a certificate of official duty, it may be made the subject of review through discussions between appropriate officials of the Government of the Republic of Korea and the diplomatic mission of the United States."

0249

2. Agreed Minute 2, Re Paragraph 3(a)(ii)

"The term 'official duty' as used in Article _____ and the Agreed Minute is not meant to include all acts by members of the armed forces and the civilian components during periods when they are on duty, but is meant to apply only to acts which are required to be done as functions of those duties the individuals are performing. Thus, any departure from the acts a person is required to perform in a particular duty usually will indicate an act outside of his official duty."

3. Understandings

a. "The certificate will be conclusive unless modification is agreed upon. The United States shall give due consideration to any objection which may be raised by the chief prosecutor for the Republic of Korea.

b. The accused should not be deprived of his entitlement to a prompt and speedy trial as a result of protracted reconsideration of the duty certificate."

C. Pre-Trial Custody

1. Text

5(c). The military authorities of the United States shall promptly notify the authorities of the Republic of Korea of the arrest of a member of the United States armed forces, the civilian component, or a dependent in any case in which the Republic of Korea has the primary right to exercise jurisdiction.

5(d). An accused member of the United States armed forces or civilian component or a dependent over whom the Republic of Korea is to exercise jurisdiction will, if he is in the hands of the military authorities of the United States, be under the custody of the military authorities of the United

States during all judicial proceedings and until custody is requested by the authorities of the Republic of Korea.

5(e). If an accused is in the hands of the Republic of Korea, he will, on request, be handed over to the military authorities of the United States, unless the authorities of the Republic of Korea consider that there is adequate cause and necessity to retain him, and be in their custody during all judicial proceedings and until custody is requested by the authorities of the Republic of Korea.

5(f). In respect of offenses solely against the security of the Republic of Korea provided in paragraph 2(c), an accused shall be under the custody of the authorities of the Republic of Korea.

Where an accused has been under the custody of the military authorities of the United States under paragraph 5(d) and (e), the military authorities of the United States may transfer custody to the authorities of the Republic of Korea at any time, and shall give sympathetic consideration to any request for the transfer of custody which may be made by the authorities of the Republic of Korea in specific cases.

The military authorities of the United States shall promptly make any such accused available to the authorities of the Republic of Korea upon their request for purposes of investigation and trial.

The authorities of the Republic of Korea will give sympathetic consideration to a request from the military authorities of the United States for assistance in maintaining custody of an accused member of the United States armed forces, the civilian component or a dependent.

2. Understandings

a. There must be mutual ROK-U.S. consultation as to the circumstances in which such custody of the authorities of the Republic of Korea as provided for in paragraph 5(e) and 5(f) is appropriate.

b. Korean confinement facilities must be adequate by U.S. standard.

D. Trial Safeguards

1. Re Paragraph 9(b)

He shall be informed a reasonable time prior to trial of the nature of the evidence that is to be used against him.

2. Re Paragraph 9(g)

And no statement of the accused taken in the absence of such a representative shall be admissible as evidence in support of the guilt of the accused except when such a representative fails to be present at a designated place on a fixed date without due cause.

3. Paragraph 2(e) and 4, Re Paragraph 9

(e). shall not be subject to a heavier penalty than the one that was applicable at the time the alleged criminal offense was committed or was adjudged by the court of the first instance as the original sentence when an appeal of a case is made by or on behalf of the accused.

Paragraph 4, Re Paragraph 9 --- To be deleted

4. Paragraph 2(k), Re Paragraph 9

(k). shall not be required to stand trial if he is physically or mentally unfit to stand trial and participate in his defense.

5. Paragraph 3, Re Paragraph 9

No confession, admission, or other statement, or real

evidence, obtained by illegal means will be considered by courts of the Republic of Korea in prosecutions under this Article.

6. Re Paragraph 9(e)

The right to legal representation shall exist from the moment of arrest or detention and shall include the right to have counsel present, and to consult confidentially with such counsel, at all preliminary investigations, examinations, pretrial hearings, the trial itself, and subsequent proceedings, at which the accused is present.

7. Paragraph 2(f), Re Paragraph 9

(f) shall not be held guilty of an offense on the basis of rules of evidence or requirements of proof which have been altered to his prejudice since the date of the commission of the offense.

8. Paragraph 2(i), Re Paragraph 9

(i) shall not be subject to prosecution or punishment by legislative or executive act.

CONFIDENTIAL

January 23, 1965

Revised Korean Draft of Labor Article
(The underlined parts are modification)

1. The United States Armed Forces and the organizations provided for in Article ____ (hereinafter referred to as "employer") may employ civilian personnel (hereinafter referred to as "employee") under this Agreement. Such civilian personnel shall be nationals of the Republic of Korea.

2. The employers may recruit, employ and administer their personnel. Recruitment services of the Government of the Republic of Korea shall be utilized to the maximum extent practicable. In case employers accomplish direct recruitment of employees, the United States Armed Forces shall provide such relevant information as may be required for labor administration to the Office of Labor Affairs of the Republic of Korea.

3. Except as may otherwise be mutually agreed, the conditions of employment and work, such as those relating to wages and supplementary payments, the conditions for the protection and welfare of employees, compensations, and the rights of employees, concerning labor relations shall conform with those laid down by the legislation of the Republic of Korea.

4. Employers shall insure the just and timely resolution of employee grievances.

5. (a) Should the Republic of Korea adopt measures allocating labor, the United States Armed Forces shall be accorded allocation privileges no less favorable than those enjoyed by the Armed Forces of the Republic of Korea.

0254

(b) In the event of a national emergency such as war, hostilities, or other imminent situations, the employees who have acquired skills essential to the mission of the United States Armed Forces may, upon request of the United States Armed Forces, be deferred from Republic of Korea military service or other compulsory services. The United States Armed Forces shall in advance furnish to the Republic of Korea lists of those employees deemed essential.

6. Members of the civilian component shall not be subject to Korean laws or regulations with respect to their terms and conditions of employment.

AGREED MINUTES

1. The undertaking of the United States to conform with those laid down by the legislation of the Republic of Korea does not imply any waiver by the United States Government of its immunities under international law.

2. Employers shall withhold from the pay of their employees, and pay over to the Government of the Republic of Korea, withholdings required by the income tax legislation of the Republic of Korea.

3. It is understood that the Government of the Republic of Korea shall be reimbursed for direct costs incurred in providing assistance pursuant to Paragraph 2.

4. In case where it is impossible for the employers to conform, on account of the military requirements of the United States Armed Forces, with the Korean labor legislation under the provisions of Paragraph 3, the matter shall in advance be referred to the Joint Committee for mutual agreement.

The Republic of Korea will give due consideration to the military requirements of the United States Armed Forces.

5. With regard to any dispute between the employers and any employees or labor unions which cannot be settled through the use of existing procedures of the United States Armed Forces, settlement shall be accomplished in the following manner:

(a) The dispute shall be referred to the Office of Labor Affairs of the Republic of Korea for conciliation.

(b) In the event that the dispute is not settled by the procedures described in (a) above, the dispute shall be referred to a special committee designated by the Joint Committee for further conciliation efforts.

(c) In the event that the dispute is not settled by the procedures outlined above, the Joint Committee will resolve the dispute. The decisions of the Joint Committee shall be binding.

(d) Neither employee organizations nor employees shall engage in any practices disruptive of normal work requirements unless the cooling-off period set forth in Article 14 of the Korean Labor Dispute Law has elapsed after the dispute is referred to the Office of Labor Affairs mentioned in (a) above.

(e) Failure of any employee organization or employee to abide by the decision of the Joint Committee on any dispute, or engaging in practices disruptive of normal work requirements in violation of the provisions of Paragraph (d) above, shall be considered cause for the depriviation of the rights and protection accorded by the relevant laws of the Republic of Korea.

형사재판관할권 한국측 초안 (가역)

1. 본조 규정에 따를것을 조건으로 하여

(a) 미합중국군당국은 미합중국군대구성원 및 군속에 대하여 미합중국 법령이 부여한 형사상 및 징계상의 재판권을 대한민국내에서 행사할 권리를 갖는다.

(b) 대한민국당국은 미합중국군대 구성원, 군속 및 그가족에 대하여 대한민국의 영역내에서 범한 범죄로서 대한민국 법령에 의하여 처벌할수 있는 범죄에 관하여 재판권을 갖는다.

2. (a) 미합중국군당국은 미합중국군대 구성원, 군속에 대하여, 미합중국의 안전에 관한 범죄를 포함하여, 미합중국 법령에 의하여는 처벌되지만 대한민국 법령에 의하여는 처벌할수 없는 범죄에 관하여 전속적재판권을 행사할 권리를 갖는다.

(b) 대한민국 당국은 미합중국 군대구성원, 군속 및 그가족에 대하여, 대한민국의 안전에 관한 범죄를 포함하여 대한민국 법령에 의하여는 처벌되지만 미합중국 법령에 의하여는 처벌할수 없는 범죄에 관하여 전속적 재판권을 행사할 권리를 갖는다.

(c) 본조 2항 및 3항에서 국가의 안전에 관한 범죄라 함은 다음의 것을 포함한다.

(i) 당해국에 대한 반역

(ii) 파괴, 간첩행위 또는 당해국의 공무상, 또는 국방상 비밀에 관한 법령의 위반.

3. 재판권을 행사할 권리가 경합하는 경우에는, 다음의 규정을 적용한다.

(a) 미합중국군당국은 미합중국군대구성원 및 군속에 대하여 다음의 범죄에 관하여 재판권을 행사할 제1차적 권리를 갖는다.

0257

(i) 전혀 미합중국의 재산 또는 안전에 대한 범죄 또는 전혀 미합중국군대 구성원, 군속 및 가족의 신체 또는 재산에 대한 범죄.

(ii) 공무의 집행중에 행하여진 작위 또는 부작위에 기인하는 범죄로써 그 작위 및 부작위가 공무와 직접 관련된 범죄. 범죄가 공무의 집행중에 행하여졌는지 여부의 문제는 대한민국의 관할 지방검찰청 검사가 결정한다. 당해범인의 지휘관이 견해를 달리할때에는 이러한 검사의 결정에 대하여 동결정을 접수한지 10일이내에 법무부장관에게 항변할수 있으며 동법무부장관의 결정은 최종적이다.

(b) 기타의 범죄에 관하여는, 대한민국 당국이 재판권을 행사할 제1차적 권리를 갖는다.

(c) 제1차적 권리를 갖는 국가가 재판권을 행사하지 않을것을 결정한 때에는, 가급적 속히 타방국가당국에 이를 통고한다. 제1차적 권리를 갖는 국가당국은 타방국가가 그 권리의 포기를 특히 중요하다고 인정한 경우에 그 타방국가당국으로부터 그 권리포기의 요청이 있으면 그요청에 대하여 호의적 고려를 하여야 한다.

4. 본조의 전기 제규정은 미합중국군당국이 대한민국의 국민인자 또는 대한민국에 통상적으로 거주하고 있는자에 대하여 재판권을 행사할 권리를 갖는다는 것을 뜻하지 않는다. 단, 이들이 미합중국군대의 구성원인 경우에는 이에서 제외된다.

0258

5. (a) 미합중국군당국과 대한민국 당국은 대한민국의 영역내에 있어서 미합중국군대 구성원, 군속 또는 그가족의 체포 및 전기규정에 따라서 재판권을 행사할 당국에 이들을 인도하는데 있어 상호 원조하여야 한다.

(b) 대한민국당국은 미합중국군당국에 미합중국군대 구성원, 군속 및 그가족의 체포를 통고하여야 한다.

(c) 미합중국군당국은, 동당국이 전속적재판권을 행사할 권리를 갖지 않는 모든 경우에 있어서, 대한민국 당국에 미합중국 군대 구성원, 군속 및 그가족의 체포를 즉시 통고하여야 한다.

(d) 대한민국이 재판권을 행사할 미합중국군대 구성원, 군속 또는 그가족인 피의자는, 그신변이 미합중국의 수중에 있는 경우에는 미합중국의 구금하에 있는다. 대한민국의 형사가 발부한 영장이 제시되면 동피의자를 즉시 한국당국에 인도하여야 한다.

6. (a) 대한민국당국과 미합중국군당국은, 범죄에 관련된 물건의 압수 및 합당한 경우에는 그인도도 포함하여, 범죄에 관하여 필요한 모든 수사의 실시 및 증거의 수집과 제출에 관하여 상호 원조한다. 단, 그러한 물건의 인도는 인도를 행하는 당국이 정하는 기간내에 반환할것을 조건으로 하여 행할수 있다.

(b) 대한민국 당국과 미합중국군당국은 재판권을 행사하는 권한이 경합하는 모든 사건의 처리에 관하여 상호 통고하여야 한다.

7. (a) 사형의 판결은 대한민국의 법제가 동일한 사건에 있어 사형을 규정하지 않는 경우에는 미합중국군당국이 대한민국내에서 이를 집행할수 없다.

0259

(b) 대한민국당국은 미합중국군당국이 본조의 규정에 따라서 대한민국 영역내에서 언도한 자유형의 집행에 관하여 미합중국군당국으로 부터 원조 요청이 있는 경우에는 이 요청에 대하여 호의적 고려를 하여야 한다.

8. 피고인이 본조의 규정에 따라서 대한민국당국이나 또는 미합중국군당국에 의하여 재판을 받은 경우에 있어서, 무죄가 된때, 또는 유죄의 판결을 받고 복역하고 있을때, 복역을 완료한때, 또는 사면을 받았을때에는 타방국 당국은 대한민국 영역내에 있어서 동일한 범죄에 대하여 다시 그를 재판할수 없다.

단, 본항의 규정은 미합중국군당국이 미합중국군대 구성원을 그가 대한민국당국에 의하여 재판을 받은 범죄를 구성하는 작위 또는 부작위에 기인하는 군기위반에 관하여 재판함을 방해하지 아니한다.

9. 미합중국군대 구성원, 군속 또는 가족은 대한민국의 재판관할하에서 기소된 경우에 언제든지 다음의 권리를 갖는다.

(a) 즉시 신속한 재판을 받을 권리.

(b) 재판전에 자신에 대한 구체적인 혐의사실을 통지 받을 권리.

(c) 자신에 불리한 증인과 대질심문할 권리.

(d) 증인이 대한민국의 관할권내에 있는 경우에는 자신을 위하여 강제적 절차에 의거 증인을 획득할 권리.

(e) 자신의 변호를 위하여 자신이 선택한 변호인을 가질권리, 또는 대한민국에서 행하여지는 조건하에 비용을 요하지 않거나 또는 비용의 보조를 받는 변호인을 가질 권리.

0260

(f) 필요하다고 인정한때에는 유능한 통역의 조력을 받을 권리.

(g) 미합중국정부의 대표자와 연락할 권리 및 자신의 재판에 그대표자를 입회시킬 권리.

10. (a) 미합중국군대의 정규편성부대 및 편성대는 본 협정 제 조에 따라서 사용하는 시설 또는 지역에서 경찰권을 행사할 권리를 갖는다. 미합중국 군대의 군사경찰은 동시설 및 지역내에서 질서 및 안전의 유지를 보장하기 위하여 모든 적절한 조치를 취할수 있다.

(b) 상기의 시설 및 지역의 외부에 있어서는, 전기한 군사경찰은 반드시 대한민국 당국과의 협의에 따를 것을 조건으로 하고 또한 대한민국 당국과 연락하에 사용되어야 하며, 그사용은 미합중국 군대 구성원간의 규율 및 질서의 유지를 위하여 필요한 범위내에 국한된다.

0261

합의의사록 (우리측 초안)

제 2 항 (c) 에 관하여

양국정부는 이세항에 규정된 안전에 관한 모든 범죄의 상세한 내용과 이러한 범죄에 관한 각기 자국의 현행법령상의 규정을 상호 통고하여야 한다.

제 3 항 (a) (ii) 에 관하여

"공무"라함은 미합중국군대 구성원 또는 군속이 공무를 행하는 기간중 그들에 의한 모든 행위를 포함하는 것은 아니다. 특정공무의 정상적 기능으로서 행할것이 마땅히 요구되는 그러한 행위로 부터의 이탈한 행위는 그의 "공무"밖의 행위이다.

제 3 항 (c) 에 관하여

재판권을 행사하는 제 1 차적권리의 모기에 관한 상호간의 절차는 합동위원회가 결정하여야 한다.

대한민국당국이 재판권을 행사하는 제일차적 권리를 모기한 사건의 재판 및 제 3 항 (a) (ii) 에서 규정된 범죄로서 대한민국 또는 대한민국 국민에 대하여 범한 범죄에 관한 사건의 재판은 별단의 협의에 상호 합의하지 않는한 대한민국내에서 범죄가 행하여졌다고 인정되는 장소로 부터 적당한 거리내에서 즉시 행하여야 한다.

대한민국 당국의 대표자는 그러한 재판에 입회할수 있다.

제 4 항에 관하여

미합중국군대 구성원 또는 군속인 대한민국 및 미합중국의 이중국적자로서 대한민국에 들어온 자는 제 4 항의 적용상 대한민국국민으로 간주하지 아니하고 미합중국국민으로 간주한다.

0262

제 5 항 (b) 에 관하여

대한민국당국은 대한민국이 재판권을 행사하는 제일차적 권리를 갖는 사건에 관하여 미합중국군대 구성원, 군속 또는 가족인 범인을 체포한 경우에는 대한민국당국은 그러한 범인을 구속할 정당한 이유 및 필요가 있다고 사료하는 경우를 제외하고 당해 범인을 석방하여 미합중국 군당국으로 하여금 구금케 한다.

단, 대한민국당국이 그범인을 수사할수 있다는 것을 그석방의 조건으로 한 경우에는 대한민국당국의 요청에 따라 대한민국당국이 그범인을 언제던지 수사할수 있도록 하여야 한다. 미합중국 당국은 대한민국당국의 요청이 있으면, 대한민국당국이 그범인을 기소한 때에는 그범인의 신병을 대한민국 당국에 인도하여야 한다.

제 6 항에 관하여

1. 미합중국군대구성원 또는 군속은 수사 및 재판에 있어서 대한민국당국에 의하여 증인으로서 출두,소환을 받을 때에는 대한민국당국에 출두하여야 한다.

2. 증인으로서 출두소환된 자가 대한민국당국에 출두하지 아니하는 경우에는 대한민국당국은 대한민국의 법령의 규정에 따라 필요한 조치를 취할수 있다. 전기한바를 조건으로 하여 미합중국군당국은 대한민국의 법관이 발급한 영장의 제시에 따라 대한민국당국이 영장을 집행할수 있는 모든 적절한 조치를 취하여야 한다.

제 9 항에 관하여

1. 본항에 열거된 권리는 대한민국 헌법의 규정에 의하여 대한민국 법정에서 재판을 받는 모든자에

0263

대하여 보장된다. 이들권리에 부과하여 미합중국 군대 구성원, 군속 또는 가족으로서 대한민국의 재판권에 의하여 소취된자는 대한민국 법정에서 재판을 받는 모든자에 대하여 대한민국의 헌법과 법률이 보장하는 기타의 권리를 갖는다.

2. 미합중국 군대구성원, 군속 또는 가족으로서 대한민국의 재판권에 의하여 소취된자의 재판에 미합중국정부의 대표자가 입회하는데 관한 제9항(g)의 여하한 규정도 재판의 공개에 관한 대한민국 헌법의 규정을 침해하는 것으로 해석하여서는 아니된다.

<u>제 10 항 (a) 및 제 10 항 (b) 에 관하여</u>

1. 미합중국군당국은 원칙적으로 미합중국군대가 사용하고 있으며 그권한에 의하여 경비하고 있는 시설과 지역내에서 체포를 할수 있다. 대한민국 당국은 미합중국당국이 동의하는 경우 또는 중대한 죄를 범한 현행범을 추적하는 경우에는 시설 및 지역내에서 대한민국의 재판권에 복하는 모든자를 체포할수 있다.

대한민국 당국이 체포할 것을 희망하는자로서 미합중국군대의 재판권에 복하지 아니하는 자가 미합중국군대가 사용하고 있는 시설 및 지역내에 있는 경우에는 미합중국군당국은 대한민국당국의 요청에 의하여 그러한 자를 즉시 체포하여야 한다. 미합중국군당국에 의하여 체포된자로서 미합중국군당국의 재판권에 복하지 아니하는 모든자는 즉시 대한민국당국에 인도하여야 한다.

미합중국군당국은 시설 또는 지역내 또는 그 주변에서, 당해시설 또는 지역의 안전에 대한 범죄의 기수현행범을 법의 정당한 절차에 따라 체포할수 있다. 미합중국군당국에 의하여 체포된자로서 미합중국군대의

0264

재판권에 복하지 아니하는 자는 즉시 대한민국 당국에 인도하여야 한다.

2. 대한민국당국은 미합중국군대가 사용하고 있으며 그권한에 의하여 경비하고 있는 시설 또는 지역내에 있는 자 또는 재산에 관하여 또는 소재 여하를 불문하고 미합중국군대의 재산에 관하여 압수, 수색, 검증을 행하는 권리를 원칙적으로 행사하지 아니한다. 단 미합중국군당국이 대한민국당국으로 하여금, 그러한 자 또는 재산에 대하여 그러한 압수, 수색, 검증을 하는 것에 동의할 때에는 그러하지 아니한다.

대한민국 당국이 미합중국이 사용하고 있는 시설과 지역내에 있는 자나 재산 또는 대한민국 내에 있는 미합중국 군대의 재산에 관하여 압수, 수색, 검증을 하고저 할때에는 미합중국군당국은 요청에 따라 압수, 수색, 검증을 하여야 한다.

미합중국 정부 또는 그 기관이 소유하거나, 사용하는 재산을 제외하고 상기 재산에 관한 판결의 경우에는 미합중국은 그 재산을 판결에 따른 처분을 위하여 대한민국 당국에 인도하여야 한다.

0265

형사재판관할권 미국측 초안 (가역)

1. 본조 규정에 따른것을 조건으로 하여,

(a) 미합중국당국은 미합중국군대구성원, 군속 및 그가족에 대하여 미합중국 법령이 부여한 모든 형사상 및 징계상의 재판권을 대한민국내에서 행사할 권리를 갖는다.

(b) 대한민국의 민사당국은 미합중국군대구성원, 군속 및 그가족에 대하여 대한민국 영역내에서 범한 범죄로서 대한민국 법령에 의하여 처벌할수 있는 범죄에 관하여 재판권을 행사할 권리를 갖는다.

2. (a) 미합중국 당국은 미합중국군대 구성원, 군속 및 그가족에 대하여 미합중국의 안전에 관한 범죄를 포함하여 미합중국 법령에 의하여는 처벌되지만 대한민국 법령에 의하여는 처벌할수 없는 범죄에 관하여 전속적 재판권을 행사할 권리를 갖는다.

(b) 대한민국 당국은 미합중국군대 구성원, 군속 및 그가족에 대하여 대한민국의 안전에 관한 범죄를 포함하여 대한민국 법령에 의하여는 처벌되지만 미합중국 법령에 의하여는 처벌할수 없는 범죄에 관하여 전속적 재판권을 행사할 권리를 갖는다.

(c) 본조 2항 및 3항에서 국가의 안전에 관한 범죄라 함은 다음의 것을 포함한다.

(i) 당해국에 대한 반역

(ii) 파괴, 간첩행위, 또는 당해국의 공무상 또는 국방상 비밀에 관한 법령의 위반.

3. 재판권을 행사할 권리가 경합하는 경우에는 다음의 규정을 적용한다.

0266

(a) 미합중국 당국은 미합중국군대 구성원, 군속 및 그가족에 대하여, 다음의 범죄에 관하여 재판권을 행사할 제1차적 권리를 갖는다.

(i) 전혀 미합중국의 재산 또는 안전에 대한 범죄, 또는 전혀 미합중국군대 구성원, 군속 및 가족의 신체 또는 재산에 대한 범죄.

(ii) 공무의 집행중에 행하여진 작위 또는 부작위에 기인하는 범죄.

(b) 기타의 범죄에 관하여는 대한민국당국이 재판권을 행사할 제1차적 권리를 갖는다.

(c) 제1차적 권리를 갖는 국가가 재판권을 행사하지 않을것을 결정한 때에는, 가급적 속히 타방국가 당국에 이를 통고한다. 제1차적 권리를 갖는 국가당국은 타방국가가 그권리의 포기를 특히 중요하다고 인정한 경우에 그타방국가 당국으로 부터 그권리포기의 요청이 있으면 그요청에 대하여 호의적 고려를 하여야 한다.

4. 본조의 전기 제규정은 미합중국 당국이 대한민국의 국민인자 또는 대한민국에 통상적으로 거주하고 있는자에 대하여 재판권을 행사할 권리를 갖는다는 것을 뜻하지 않는다. 단, 이들이 미합중국군대의 구성원인 경우에는 이에서 제외된다.

5. (a) 미합중국 당국과 대한민국당국은 대한민국의 영역내에 있어서 미합중국군대구성원, 군속 또는 그 가족의 체포 및 하기 규정에 따라서 구금하게 될 당국에 이들을 인도하는데 있어 상호 원조하여야 한다.

(b) 대한민국 당국은 미합중국당국에 미합중국군대 구성원, 군속 및 가족의 체포를 즉시 통고 하여야 한다.

0267

(c) 대한민국이 재판권을 행사할 미합중국 군대구성원, 군속 또는 가족인 피의자는, 그신병이 미합중국의 수중에 있는 경우에는, 모든 사법절차가 완료되고 대한민국 당국이 구금을 요청할때까지 미합중국이 계속 구금한다. 전기 피의자의 신병이 대한민국 수중에 있는 경우에는 이를 즉시 미국 당국에 인도하여야 하며, 모든 사법절차가 완료되고 대한민국 당국이 구금을 요청할때까지 미합중국이 계속 구금한다. 미합중국 당국은 대한민국당국이 수사 및 재판을 위하여 요청하는 경우에는 대한민국 당국이 전기 피의자를 이용토록 한다. 대한민국 당국은 미합중국 당국이 미합중국군대 구성원, 군속 또는 가족인 피의자의 구금을 계속하는데 있어 원조를 요청할 경우에는 그 요청에 대하여 호의적인 고려를 하여야 한다.

6. (a) 미합중국 당국과 대한민국당국은 범죄에 관련된 물건의 압수 및 합당한 경우에는 그인도도 포함하여 범죄에 관하여 필요한 모든 수사의 실시 및 증거의 수집과 제출에 관하여 상호 원조한다. 단, 그러한 물건의 인도는 인도를 행하는 당국이 정하는 기간내에 반환할것을 조건으로 하여 행할수 있다.

(b) 미합중국당국과 대한민국당국은 재판권을 행사하는 권한이 경합하는 모든 사건의 처리에 관하여 상호 통고하여야 한다.

7. (a) 사형의 판결은 대한민국의 법제가 동일한 사건에 있어 사형을 규정하지 않는 경우에는 미합중국당국이 대한민국내에서 이를 집행할수 없다.

(b) 대한민국당국은 미합중국당국이 본조의 규정에 따라서 대한민국 영역내에서 언도한 자유형의

0268

집행에 관하여 미합중국당국으로 부터 원조요청이 있는 경우에는 이요청에 대하여 호의적 고려를 하여야 한다.

대한민국당국도 대한민국 법정에 의하여 언도된 구류형의 판결에 복역하고 있는 미합중국군대 구성원, 군속 또는 가족의 신병인도를 위한 미합중국당국으로 부터의 요청이 있는 경우에는 이요청에 대하여 역시 호의적 고려를 하여야 한다. 그러한 신병이 미합중국당국에 인도되는 경우에는 미합중국은 당해 구류형을 완전히 복역하였거나 또는 구류형으로 부터의 석방이 관계 대한민국 당국에 의하여 승인될때까지 미합중국의 적절한 구류시설에서 그자에 대한 구류형을 계속할 책임을 져야 한다.

8. 피고인이 본조의 규정에 따라 미합중국 당국이나 또는 대한민국당국에 의하여 재판을 받는 경우에 있어서 무죄로 되거나 유죄의 판결을 받고 복역하고 있거나, 복역을 완료하였거나, 감형되었거나, 형의집행이 정지되었거나 또는 사면을 받았을 때에는 타방국 당국은 대한민국 영역내에 있어서 동일한 범죄에 대하여 다시 그를 재판할수 없다. 단, 본항의 규정은 미합중국당국이 미합중국 군대구성원을 그가 대한민국당국에 의하여 재판을 받은 범죄를 구성하는 작위 또는 부작위에 기인하는 군기 위반에 관하여 재판함을 저해하지 아니한다.

9. 미합중국군대 구성원, 군속 또는 가족은 대한민국의 재판권에 의하여 소취된 경우에는 언제든지 다음의 권리를 갖는다.

(a) 즉시 신속한 재판을 받을 권리

(b) 재판전에 자신에 대한 구체적인 혐의사실을 통지 받을 권리.

(c) 자신에 불리한 증인과 대질심문할 권리.

0269

(d) 증인이 대한민국의 재판관할권내에 있을 경우에는 자신을 위하여 강제적 절차에 의거 증인을 획득할 권리.

(e) 자신의 변호를 위하여 자신이 선택한 변호인을 가질권리 또는 대한민국에서 그때에 행하여지는 조건하에 비용을 요하지 않거나 또는 비용의 보조를 받는 변호인을 가질 권리.

(f) 필요하다고 인정하는 때에 유능한 통역의 조력을 받을 권리.

(g) 미합중국정부의 대표자와 연락할 권리 및 자신의 재판에 그대표자를 입회시킬권리.

10. (a) 미합중국군대의 정규편성부대 및 편성대는 본협정 제1조에 따라서 사용하는 시설 또는 지역에서 경찰권을 행사할 권리를 갖는다. 미합중국 군대의 군사경찰은 동시설 및 지역내에서 질서 및 안전의 유지를 보장하기 위하여 모든 적절한 조치를 취할수 있다.

(b) 상기의 시설 및 지역의 외부에 있어서는 전기한 군사경찰은 반드시 대한민국당국과의 협의에 따를것을 조건으로 하고 또한 대한민국당국과 연락하에 사용되어야 하며, 그사용은 미합중국군대 구성원간의 규율 및 질서의 유지 또는 그들의 안전을 확보하기 위하여 필요한 한도내에 국한된다.

11. 상호 방위조약 제2조의 규정이 적용되는 적대행위가 발생한 경우에는 형사재판관할권에 관한 본협정의 규정은 즉시 정지되어야 하며 미합중국당국은 미합중국군대 구성원, 군속 및 그의 가족에 대하여 전속적 재판권을 행사할 권리를 갖는다.

12. 본조의 규정은 본협정의 효력발생이전에 범한 여하한 범죄에도 적용되지 아니한다. 그러한 사건에

0270

대하여서는 1950년 7월 12일 대전에서 각서교환으로 효력을 발생한 미합중국 및 대한민국간의 협정의 규정을 적용한다.

보통문서로 재분류(1966.12.31)

0271

정/리/보/존/문/서/목/록

기록물종류	문서-일반공문서철	등록번호	944 9617	등록일자	2006-07-27
분류번호	741.12	국가코드	US	주제	
문서철명	한.미국 간의 상호방위조약 제4조에 의한 시설과 구역 및 한국에서의 미국군대의 지위에 관한 협정 (SOFA) 전59권. 1966.7.9 서울에서 서명 : 1967.2.9 발효 (조약 232호) *원본				
생산과	미주과/조약과	생산년도	1952 - 1967	보존기간	영구
담당과(그룹)	조약	조약	서가번호	--	
참조분류					
권차명	V.46 한.미국 양측 교섭안 비교				
내용목차	* 일지 : 1953.8.7 이승만 대통령-Dulles 미국 국무장관 공동성명 - 상호방위조약 발효 후 군대지위협정 교섭 약속 1954.12.2 정부, 주한 UN군의 관세업무협정 체결 제의 1955.1월, 5월 미국, 제의 거절 1955.4.28 정부, 군대지위협정 제의 (한국측 초안 제시) 1957.9.10 Hurter 미국 국무차관 방한 시 각서 수교 (한국측 제의 수락 요구) 1957.11.13, 26 정부, 개별 협정의 단계적 체결 제의 1958.9.18 Dawling 주한미국대사, 형사재판관할권 협정 제외 조건으로 행정협정 체결 의사 전달 1960.3.10 정부, 토지, 시설협정의 우선적 체결 강력 요구 1961.4.10 장면 국무총리-McConaughy 주한미국대사 공동성명으로 교섭 개시 합의 1961.4.15, 4.25 제1, 2차 한.미국 교섭회의 (서울) 1962.3.12 정부, 교섭 재개 촉구 공한 송부 1962.5.14 Burger 주한미국대사, 최규하 장관 면담 시 형사재판관할권 문제 제기 않는 조건으로 교섭 재개 통고 1962.9.6 한.미국 간 공동성명 발표 (9월 중 교섭 재개 합의) 1962.9.20~ 1965.6.7 제1-81차 실무 교섭회의 (서울) 1966.7.8 제82차 실무 교섭회의 (서울) 1966.7.9 서명 1967.2.9 발효 (조약 232호)					

마/이/크/로/필/름/사/항

촬영연도	*롤 번호	화일 번호	후레임 번호	보관함 번호
2006-11-24	I-06-0071	06	1-136	

0001

14/20

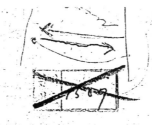

KOREAN AND U.S. DRAFTS

FOR

STATUS OF FORCES NEGOTIATION

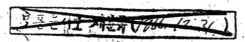

AMERICA SECTION

MINISTRY OF FOREIGN AFFAIRS

(.K.LEE)

0002

7/20

관리번호 15-7

C O N T E N T S

보통문서로 재분류(1966. 12. 31.)

K.J.K.

0003

PREAMBLE

Whereas the United States of America has disposed its armed forces in and about the territory of the Republic of Korea pursuant to the resolutions of the United Nations Security Council of June 25, 1950, June 27, 1950, and July 7, 1950, and pursuant to Article IV of the Mutual Defense Treaty between the United States of America and the Republic of Korea signed on October 1, 1953.

Therefore, the United States of America and the Republic of Korea, in order to strengthen the close bonds of mutual interest between their two countries, have entered into this Agreement regarding facilities and areas and the status of United States armed forces in the Republic of Korea in terms as set forth below:

Definitions Article

In this Agreement the expression

(a) "members of the United States armed forces" means the personnel on active duty belonging to the land, sea or air armed services of the United States of America when in the territory of the Republic of Korea except for personnel of the U.S. armed forces attached to the U.S. Embassy and personnel for whom status has been provided in the Military Advisory Group Agreement of January 26, 1950, as amended.

(b) "civilian component" means the civilian persons of the U.S. nationality who are in the employ, serving with, or accompanying the United States armed forces in the Republic of Korea, but excludes persons who are ordinarily resident in the Republic of Korea or who are mentioned in paragraph of Article.

For the purposes of the Agreement only, dual nationals, i.e. persons having both United States and Korean nationality, who are brought into the Republic of Korea by the United States shall be considered as United States nationals.

(c) "dependents" means

(1) Spouse and children under 21;

(2) Parents, and children over 21, or other relatives dependent for over half their support upon a member of the United States armed forces or civilian component.

Agreed Minute

With regard to subparagraph (b), it is recognized that persons possessing certain skills, not available from United States or Korean sources, who are nationals of third states may be brought into Korea by the United States armed forces solely for employment by the United States armed forces. Such persons, and third state nationals who are employed by, serving with, or accompanying the United States armed forces in Korea when this agreement becomes effective, shall be considered as members of the civilian component.

0006

Entry and Exit Article

1. The United States may bring into the Republic of Korea persons who are members of the United States armed forces, the civilian component, and their dependents, subject to the provisions of this Article. The Government of the Republic of Korea will be notified at regular intervals, in accordance with procedures to be agreed between the two Governments, of numbers and categories of persons entering and departing.

2. Members of the United States armed forces shall be exempt from Korean passport and visa laws and regulations. Members of the United States armed forces, the civilian component, and their dependents shall be exempt from Korean laws and regulations on the registration and control of aliens, but shall not be considered as acquiring any right to permanent residence or domicile in the territory of the Republic of Korea.

3. Upon entry into or departure from the Republic of Korea members of the United States armed forces shall be in possession of the following documents:

(a) personal identity card showing name, date of birth, rank and service number, service, and photograph; and

(b) individual or collective travel order certifying to the status of the individual or group as a member or members of the United States armed forces and to the travel ordered.

For purposes of their identification while in the Republic of Korea, members of the United States armed forces shall be in possession of the foregoing personal identity card which must be presented on request to the appropriate Korean authorities.

4. Members of the civilian component, their dependents, and

0007

the dependents of members of the United States armed forces shall be in possession of appropriate documentation issued by the United States authorities so that their status may be verified by Korean authorities upon their entry into or departure from the Republic of Korea, or while in the Republic of Korea.

5. If the status of any person brought into the Republic of Korea under paragraph 1 of this Article is altered so that he would no longer be entitled to such admission, the United States authorities shall notify the Korean authorities and shall, if such person be required by the Korean authorities to leave the Republic of Korea, assure that transportation from the Republic of Korea will be provided within a reasonable time at no cost to the Government of the Republic of Korea.

6. If the Government of the Republic of Korea has requested the removal from its Territory of a member of the United States armed forces or civilian component or has made an expulsion order against an ex-member of the United States armed forces or the civilian component or against a dependent of a member or an ex-member, the authorities of the United States shall be responsible for receiving the person concerned into its own territory or otherwise disposing of him outside the Republic of Korea. This paragraph shall apply only to persons who are not nationals of the Republic of Korea and have entered the Republic of Korea as members of the United States armed forces or civilian component or for the purpose of becoming such members, and to the dependents of such persons.

Agreed Minutes

1. With regard to Paragraph 3(a), United States Armed Forces law enforcement personnel (such as MP, SP, AP, CID and CIC), who engage in military police activities in the Republic of Korea, will carry a

0008

bilingual identity card containing the bearer's name, position, and the fact that he is a member of a law enforcement agency. This card will be shown upon request to persons concerned when the bearer is in the performance of duty.

2. The United States Armed Forces will furnish, upon request, to Korean authorities the form of the identification cards of the members of the United States Armed Forces, the civilian component, and their dependents and descriptions of the various uniforms of the United States Armed Forces in the Republic of Korea.

3. The final sentence of Paragraph 3 means that members of the United States Armed Forces will display their identity cards upon request but will not be required to surrender them to Korean authorities.

4. Following a change of status pursuant to Paragraph 5, the responsibilities of the United States authorities under Paragraph 6 shall arise only if the expulsion order is issued within a reasonable time after the notice under Paragraph 5 has been communicated to the Korean authorities.

0009

Health and Sanitation Article

Consistent with the right of the United States to furnish medical support for its armed forces, civilian component and their dependents, matters of mutual concern pertaining to the control and prevention of diseases and the coordination of other public health medical, sanitation, and veterinary services shall be resolved by the authorities of the two Governments in the Joint Committee established under Article ______.

142

<u>Taxation Article</u>

1. The United States armed forces shall not be subject to taxes or similar charges on property held, used or transferred by such forces in Korea.

2. Members of the United States armed forces, the civilian component, and their dependents shall not be liable to any any Korean taxes to the Government of Korea or to any other taxing agency in Korea on income received as a result of their service with or employment by the United States armed forces, including their activities provided for in Article ___. Persons in Korea solely by reason of being members of the United States armed forces, the civilian components, or their dependents shall not be liable to pay any Korean taxes to the Government of Korea or to any taxing agency in Korea on income derived from sources outside of Korea, nor shall periods during which such persons are in Korea be considered as periods of residence or domicile in Korea for the purpose of Korean taxation. The provisions of this Article do not exempt such persons from payment of Korean taxes on income derived <u>from Korean sources</u>, other than those sources referred to in the first sentence of this paragraph, nor do they exempt United States citizens who claim Korean residence for United States income tax purposes from payment of Korean taxes on income.

3. Members of the United States armed forces, the civilian component, and their dependents shall be exempt from taxation in Korea on the holding, use, transfer <u>inter se</u>, or transfer by death of movable property, tangible or intangible, the presence of which in Korea is due solely to the temporary presence of these persons in Korea, provided that such exemption shall not apply to property held for the purpose of investment or the conduct of business in Korea or to any intangible property registered in Korea.

Joint Committee Article

1. A Joint Committee shall be established as the means for consultation between the Government of the United States and the Government of the Republic of Korea on all matters requiring mutual consultation regarding the implementation of this Agreement except where otherwise provided. In particular, the Joint Committee shall serve as the means for consultation in determining the facilities and areas in the Republic of Korea which are required for the use of the United States in carrying out the purpose of this Agreement.

2. The Joint Committee shall be composed of a representative of the Government of the United States and a representative of the Government of the Republic of Korea, each of whom shall have one or more deputies and a staff. The Joint Committee shall determine its own procedures, and arrange for such auxiliary organs and administrative services as may be required. The Joint Committee shall be so organized that it may meet immediately at any time at the request of the representative of either the Government of the United States or the Government of the Republic of Korea.

3. If the Joint Committee is unable to resolve any matter, it shall refer that matter to the respective Government for further consideration through appropriate channels.

Agreed Minute

"The exception provided for in the first sentence of paragraph 1 is relevent only to paragraph 2, subparagraphs (b) and (c) of Article___

1144

Enrollment and Training of Reservists Article

The United States may enroll in its reserve forces and train, in Korea, eligible United States citizens who are in the Republic of Korea.

Meteorological Services Article

The Government of the Republic of Korea undertakes to furnish the United States armed forces with the following meteorological services in accordance with arrangements between the appropriate authorities of the two Governments:

(a) Meteorological observations from land and ocean areas including observations from ships;

(b) Climatological information including periodic summaries and historical data wherever available;

(c) Telecommunications service to disseminate meteorological information;

(d) Seismographic data.

Respect for Local Law Article

It is the duty of members of the United States Armed Forces, the civilian component, the persons who are present in the Republic of Korea pursuant to Article ____, and their dependents, to respect the law of Korea and to abstain from any activity inconsistent with the spirit of this Agreement, and, in particular, from any political activity in Korea.

Vehicle and Drivers License Article

1. Korea shall accept as valid, without a driving test or fee, the driving permit or license or military driving permit issued by the United States, or political subdivision thereof, to a member of the United States armed forces, the civilian component, and their dependents.

2. Official vehicles of the United States armed forces and the civilian component shall carry distinctive numbered plates or individual markings which will readily identify them.

3. The Government of the Republic of Korea will license and register those vehicles privately owned by members of the United States armed forces, the civilian component, or dependents. The names of the owners of such vehicles and such other pertinent information as is required by Korean law to effect the licensing and registration of such vehicles, shall be furnished to the Government of the Republic of Korea by officials of the United States Government through the Joint Committee. Except for the actual cost of the issuance of license plates, members of the United States armed forces, the civilian component, and their dependents shall be exempt from the payment of all fees and charges relating to the licensing, registration, or operation of vehicles in the Republic of Korea and, in accordance with the provisions of Article _____, from the payment of all taxes relating thereto.

Access by Vessels and Aircraft Article

1. United States and foreign vessels and aircraft operated by, for, or under the control of the United States for official purposes shall be accorded access to any port or airport of Korea free from toll or landing charges. When cargo or passengers not accorded the exemptions of this Agreement are carried on such vessels and aircraft, notification shall be given to the appropriate Korean authorities, and their entry into and departure from Korea shall be according to the laws and regulations of Korea.

2. The vessels and aircraft mentioned in paragraph 1, United States Government-owned vehicles including armor, and members of the United States armed forces, the civilian component, and their dependents shall be accorded to and movement between facilities and areas in use by the United States armed forces and between such facilities and areas and the ports or airports of Korea. Such access to and movement between facilities and areas by United States military vehicles shall be free from toll and other charges.

3. When the vessels mentioned in paragraph 1 enter Korean ports, appropriate notification shall, under normal conditions, be made to the proper Korean authorities. Such vessels shall have freedom from compulsory pilotage, but if a pilot is taken pilotage shall be paid for at appropriate rates.

Agreed Minutes

1. "United States and foreign vessels ... operated by, for, or under the control of the United States for official purposes" mean United States public vessels and chartered vessels (bare boat charter, voyage charter and time charter). Space charter is not incl

Commercial cargo and private passengers are carried by them only in exceptional cases.

2. The Korean ports mentioned herein will ordinarily mean "open ports".

3. An exception from making the "appropriate notification" referred to in paragraph 3 will apply only in unusual cases where such is required for security of the United States armed forces or similar reasons.

4. The laws and regulations of Korea will be applicable except as specifically provided otherwise in this Article.

Air Traffic Control and Navigational Aids Article

1. All civil and military air traffic control shall be developed in close coordination and shall be integrated to the extent necessary for the operation of this Agreement. Procedures, and any subsequent changes thereto, necessary to effect this coordination and integration will be established by arrangement between the appropriate authorities of the two Governments.

2. The United States is authorized to establish, construct and maintain aids to navigation for vessels and aircraft, both visual and electronic as required, throughout the Republic of Korea and in the territorial waters thereof. Such navigation aids shall conform generally to the system in use in Korea. The United States and Korean authorities which have established navigation aids shall duly notify each other of their positions and characteristics and shall give advance notification where practicable before making any changes in them or establishing additional navigation aids.

Agreed Minute

Installation by the United States Armed Forces of permanent navigational aids for vessels and aircraft outside of areas and facilities in use by the United States Armed Forces will be effected in accordance with the procedures established under paragraph 1 of Article_____.

Revision of the Agreement Article

Either Government may at any time request the revision of any Article of this Agreement, in which case the two Governments shall enter into negotiations through appropriate channels.

Military Post Offices Article

The United States may establish and operate, within the facilities and areas in use by the U.S. armed forces, United States military post offices for the use of members of the United States armed forces, the civilian component, and their dependents, for the transmission of mails between United States military post offices in Korea and between such military post offices and other United States post offices.

Agreed Minute

United States military post offices may be used by other office and personnel of the United States Government, and their dependents, ordinarily accorded such privileges abroad.

KOREA

Facilities and Areas

ARTICLE

1. The Government of the Republic of Korea grants, under Article IV of the Mutual Defense Treaty between the Republic of Korea and the United States of America, to the United States the use of the facilities and areas in the Republic of Korea as provided for in this Agreement. Arrangements as to the specific faciliti-es and areas shall be made by the two Governments through the Joint Committee.

2. Facilities and areas referred to in this Agreement include existing furnishings, equipment and fixtures necessary to the operation of such facilities and areas.

3. The facilities and areas of which the United States has the use at the time of entry into force of this Agreement, shall be regarded, for the purpose of this Agreement, as facilities and areas granted to the United States under this Agreement. For the purpose of this paragraph, all facilities and areas of which the United States has the use at the time of entry into force of this Agreement shall be surveyed and determined by the two Governments through the Joint Committee.

U. S.

Grant of F & A.

OK

Okeyed 33th

ARTICLE

Art. A-1 (a) The United States is granted, under Article IV of the Mutual Defense Treaty, the use of facilities and areas in the Republic of Korea. Agreements as to specific facilities and areas shall be concluded by the two Governments through the Joint Committee provided for in Article   of this Agreement. "Facilities and Areas" include existing furnishings, equipment and fixtures, wherever located, used in the operation of such facilities and areas.

means "necessary to"

Revised

(b) The facilities and areas of which the United States has the use at the effective date of this Agreement shall be considered as facilities and areas agreed upon between the two Governments in accordance with sub-paragraph (a) above.

4. With regard to the private property used as facilities and areas by the United States armed forces under this Agreement, the United States shall make reasonable compensation through the Government of the Republic of Korea to the owners of such facilities and areas with a view to alleviating their losses. Detailed arrangements, including the amounts of compensation, shall be made between the two Government through the Joint Committee.

5. The Governments of the United States bears without cost to the Republic of Korea all expenditures incident to the maintenance of the facilities and areas granted under this Agreement.

Art. D-1. It is agreed that the United States will bear for the duration of the Agreement without cost to the Republic of Korea all expenditures incident to the maintenance of the United States armed forces in the Republic of Korea, except those to be borne by the Republic of Korea as provided in paragraph 2.

6. At the request of either Government, the Government of the Republic of Korea and the Government of the United States shall review such arrangements referred to in paragraph 1 and may agree that such facilities and areas shall be returned to the Republic of Korea or that additional facilities and areas may be provided.

2. At the request of either Government, the Governments of the United States and the Republic of Korea shall review such arrangements and may agree that such facilities and areas or portions thereof shall be returned to the Republic of Korea or that additional facilities and areas may be provided.

Okeyed (16차)

7. The facilities and areas used by the United States shall be promptly returned to the Government of the Republic of Korea whenever they are no longer needed for the purpose of this Agreement, and the Government of the United States agrees to keep the needs for facilities and areas under continual observation with a view toward such return.	A 3. The facilities and areas used by the United States shall be returned to the Republic of Korea under such conditions as may be agreed through the Joint Committee whenever they are no longer needed for the purposes of this Agreement and the United States agrees to keep the needs for facilities and areas under continual observation with a view toward such return.
8. When facilities and areas are temporarily not being used by the United States, interim use by the authorities of the Republic of Korea or nationals may be arranged through the Joint Committee.	Okeyed (16차) A 4. (a) When facilities and areas are temporarily not being used and the Government of the Republic of Korea is so advised, the Government of the Republic of Korea may make, or permit Korean nationals to make, interim use of such facilities and areas provided that it is agreed between the two Governments through the Joint Committee that such use would not be harmful to the purposes for which the facilities and areas are normally used by the United States armed forces.
9. With respect to facilities and areas which are to be used by the United States for limited period of time, the Joint Committee shall specify in the agreements covering such facilities and areas the extent to which the provisions of this Agreement shall apply.	(16차) Oked (b) With respect to facilities and areas which are to be used by United States armed forces for limited periods of time, the Joint Committee shall specify in the agreements covering such facilities and areas the extent to which the provisions of this Agreement shall apply.

OK 16

not agreed

3차

- 21 -

0024

Measures which may be taken i

Okeyed (32nd)

10. Within the facilities and areas, the Government of the United States may take all the measures necessary for their establishment, operation, safeguarding and control. In order to provide access for the United States forces to the facilities and areas for their support, safeguarding and control, the Government of the Republic of Korea shall, at the request of the Government of the United States and upon consultation between the two Governments within the scope of applicable laws and regulations over land, territorial waters and airspace adjacent to, or in the vicinities of the facilities and areas. The Government of the United States may also take necessary measures for such purposes upon consultation between the two Governments through the Joint Committee.

11. The Government of the United States agrees not to take the measures referred to in paragraph 1 in such a manner as to interfere unnecessarily with navigation, aviation, communication, or land travel to or from or within the territories of the Republic of Korea.

Art. B-1. Within the facilities and areas, the United States may take all the measures necessary for their establishment, operation, safeguarding and control. Agreed Minute In an emergency, measures necessary for their safeguarding and control may also be taken in the vicinity thereof. In order to provide access for the United States armed forces to the facilities and areas for their support, safeguarding and control, the Government of the Republic of Korea shall, at the request of the United States armed forces and upon consultation between the two Governments through the Joint Committee, take necessary measures within the scope of applicable laws and regulations over land, territory waters and airspace adjacent to, or in the vicinities of the facilities and areas. The United States may also take necessary measures for such purposes upon consultation between the two Governments through the Joint Committee.

OK

B Okeyed 2. (a) The Government of the United States agrees not to take the measures referred to in paragraph 1 in such a manner as to interfere unnecessarily with navigation, aviation, communication, or land travel to or from or within the territories of the Republic of Korea.

All questions relating to frequencies, power and like matters used by apparatus employed by the Government of the United States designed to emit electric radiation shall be settled by arrangement between the appropriate authorities of the two Governments.	(b) All questions relating to telecommunications including radio frequencies for electromagnetic radiating devices, or like matters, shall continue to be resolved expeditiously in the utmost spirit of coordination and cooperation by arrangement between the designated military communications authorities of the two Governments.
12. Operations in the facilities and areas in use by the Government of the United States shall be carried on with due regard to the public safety.	3. Operations in the facilities and areas in use by the United States armed forces shall be carried on with due regard for the public safety.
	Art. B-2 (c) The Government of the Republic of Korea shall, within the scope of applicable laws, regulations and agreements, take all reasonable measures to avoid or eliminate interference with electromagnetic radiation-sensitive devices, telecommunications devices, or other apparatus required by the United States armed forces.
13. The Government of the United States is not obliged, when it returns facilities and areas to the Government of the Republic of Korea on the expiration of this Agreement or at an earlier date, to restore the facilities and areas to the conditions in which they were at the time they became available to the United	Art. C-1. The United States is not obliged, when it returns facilities and areas to the Republic of Korea on the expiration of this Agreement or at an earlier date, to restore the facilities and areas to the condition in which they were at the time they became available to the United States armed

Obeyed OK 18 Obeyed (18차) Obeyed (18차) OK 18 Return of OK OK

States, or to compensate the Government the Republic of Korea in lieu of such restoration. However, in case of private property extremely demolished by the use of the United States, the Government of United States shall, upon the request of the Government of the Republic of Korea pay due consideration to its restoration or compensation in lieu thereof.

14. The Government of the Republic of Korea is not obliged to make any compensation to the Government of the United States for any improvements made in the facilities and areas or for the buildings, structures, supply or any other materials left thereon on the expiration of this Agreement or the earlier return of the facilities and areas.

forces, or to compensate the Republic of Korea in lieu of such restoration.

2. The Republic of Korea is not obligated to compensate the United States for improvements made in United States facilities and areas or for the buildings or structures remaining thereon upon the return of the facilities and areas.

3. All removable facilities erected or constructed by or on behalf of the United States at its expense and all equipment, materials and supplies brought into or procured in the Republic of Korea by or on behalf of the United States in connection with the construction, development, operation, maintenance, safeguarding and control of the facilities and areas will remain the property of the United States Government and may be

removed from the Republic of Korea.

C 4. The foregoing provisions shall not apply to any construction which the Government of the United States may undertake under special arrangements with the Government of the Republic of Korea.

Compensation for the Use of F. & A.

Art. D-3. It is agreed that the Republic of Korea will furnish for the duration of this Agreement without cost to the United States and make compensation where appropriate to the owners and suppliers thereof all facilities and areas and rights of way, including facilities and areas jointly used such as those at airfields and ports as provided in Articles II and III. The Government of the Republic of Korea assures the use of such facilities and areas to the United States Government and will hold the United States Government as well as its agencies and employees harmless from any third party claims which may be advanced in connection with such use.

Revised Draft okeyed (32nd)

1. ......

(b) The facilities and areas of which the United States armed forces have the use at the effective date of this agreement together with those areas and facilities which the United States armed forces have returned to the Republ of Korea with the reserved right of re-entry, when these facilities and areas have been re-entered by U.S. forces, shall be considered as the facilities and areas agreed upon between the two Governments in accordance with sub-paragraph (a) above. Records of facilities and areas of which the United States armed forces have the use or right of re-entry shall be maintained through the Joint Committee after this Agreement comes into force.

OK

Okeyed (32nd)

AGREED MINUTE

It is agreed that in the event of an emergency, the United States armed forces shall be authorized to take such measures in the vicinity of the areas and facilities as may be necessary to provide for their safeguarding and control.

OK
32

31차
회의

0029

Customs

Customs Duties

1. Except as provided expressly to the contrary in this Agreement, members of the United States forces, the civilian component, and their dependents shall be subject to the laws and regulations administered by the customs authorities of the Republic of Korea. In particular the customs authorities of the Republic of Korea shall have the right, under the general conditions laid down by the laws and regulations of the Republic of Korea, to search members of the United States forces, the civilian component and their dependents and to examine their luggage, and to seize articles pursuant to such laws and regulations.

2. All materials, supplies and equipment imported by the United States forces or by the organizations provided for in Article ____ exclusively for the official use of the United States forces or those organizations or for the use of members of the United States forces, the civilian component and their dependents shall be permitted entry into Korea free from customs duties and other such charges. When such materials, supplies and equipment are imported, a certificate issued by the authorities of the United States forces

ARTICLE (Customs)

1. Save as provided in this Agreement, members of the United Stat[es] armed forces, the civilian component, and their dependents shall be subjec[t to] the laws and regulations administere[d] by the customs authorities of the Republic of Korea.

2. All materials, supplies and equipment imported by the United State[s] armed forces, including their authoriz[ed] procurement agencies and their non-appropriated fund organizations provid[ed] for in Article , for the official use of the United States armed forces or for the use of the members of the United States armed forces, the civilia[n] component, and their dependents, and materials, supplies and equipment which are to be used exclusively by the United States armed forces or are ultimately

in the form to be determined by the Joint Committee shall be submitted to the customs authorities of the Republic of Korea.

3. Property consigned to and for the personal use of members of the United States forces, the civilian component and

to be incorporated into articles or facilities used by such forces, shall be permitted entry into the Republic of Korea; such entry shall be free from customs duties and other such charges. Appropriate certification shall be made that such materials, supplies and equipment are being imported by the United States armed forces, including their authorized procurement agencies and their non-appropriated fund organizations provided for in Article , or, in the case of materials, supplies and equipment to be used exclusively by the United States armed forces or ultimately to be incorporated into articles or facilities used by such forces, that delivery thereof is to be taken by the United States armed forces for the purposes specified above. The exemptions provided in this paragraph shall extend to materials, supplies and equipment imported by the United States armed forces for the use of other armed forces in Korea which receive logistical support from the United States armed forces.

3. Property consigned to and for the personal use of members of the United States armed forces, the civilian

their dependents, shall be subject to customs duties, except that no such duties or charges shall be paid with respect to:

(a) Furniture, household goods and other personal effects for their private use imported by the members of the United States forces, the civilian component and their dependents at time of their first arrival in Korea.

(b) Reasonable quantities of clothing and household goods which are mailed into the Republic of Korea through the United States military post offices.

(c) Vehicles and parts imported by members of the U.S. armed forces or civilian component within two months after their first arrival in Korea for the private use of themselves or their dependents.

4. The exemption granted in paragraph 2 and 3 shall apply only to cases of importation of goods and shall not be

component, and their dependents, shall be subject to customs duties and other such charges, except that no duties or charges shall be paid with respect to:

(a) Furniture, household goods, and personal effects for their private use imported by the members of the United States armed forces or civilian component when they first arrive to serve in the Republic of Korea or by their dependents when they first arrive for reunion with members of such forces or civilian component;

(b) Vehicles and parts imported by members of the United States armed forces or civilian component for the private use of themselves or their dependents;

(c) Reasonable quantities of personal effects and household goods of a type which would ordinarily be purchased in the United States for the private use of members of the United States armed forces, civilian component, and their dependents, which are mailed into the Republic of Korea through United States military post offices.

4. The exemptions granted in paragraph 2 and 3 shall apply only to cases of importation of goods and shall

interpreted as refunding customs duties and domestic excises collected by the customs authorities at the time of entry in cases of purchases of goods on which such duties and excises have already been collected.

5. Customs examination shall be exempted only in the following cases:

(a) Units of the United States forces under orders entering or leaving the Republic of Korea;

(b) Official documents under official seal;

(c) Official mail in United States military postal channels;

(d) Military cargo shipped on a United States Government bill of lading.

6. Goods imported free from customs duties and other such charges pursuant to paragraphs 2 and 3 above:

(a) May be re-exported free from customs duties and other such charges;

(b) shall not be disposed of in the Republic of Korea, by way of either sale or gift, to person not entitled to import such goods free from duty, except as such disposal may be authorized on conditions

not be interpreted as refunding customs duties and domestic excises collected by the customs authorities at the time of entry in cases of purchase of goods on which such duties and excises have already been collected.

5. Customs examination shall not be made in the following cases:

(a) Members of the United States armed forces under orders entering or leaving the Republic of Korea;

(b) Official documents under official seal and mail in United States military postal channels;

(c) Military cargo consigned to the United States armed forces, including their authorized procurement agencies and their non-appropriated fund organizations provided for in Article.

6. Except as such disposal may be authorized by the United States and Korean authorities in accordance with mutually agreed conditions, goods imported into the Republic of Korea free of duty shall not be disposed of in the Republic of Korea to persons not entitled to import such goods free of duty.

7. Goods imported into the Republic of Korea free from customs

agreed between the authorities of the Republic of Korea and the United States.

7. (a) The authorities of the United States forces, in cooperation with the authorities of the Republic of Korea, shall take such steps as are necessary to prevent abuse of the privileges granted to the United States forces, members of such forces, the civilian component, and their dependents in accordance with this Article.

(b) In order to prevent offenses against customs and fiscal laws and regulations, the authorities of the Republic of Korea and of the United States forces shall assist each other in the conduct of inquiries and the collection of evidence.

(c) The authorities of the United States forces shall render all assistance within their power to ensure that articles liable to seizure by, or on behalf of, the customs authorities of the Republic of Korea are handed to those authorities.

duties and other such charges pursuant to paragraphs 2 and 3, may be re-exported free from customs duties and other such charges.

8. The United States armed forces, in cooperation with Korean authorities, shall take such steps as are necessary to prevent abuse of privileges granted to the United States armed forces, members of such forces, the civilian component, and their dependents in accordance with this Article.

9. (a) In order to prevent offenses against laws and regulations administered by the customs authorities of the Government of the Republic of Korea, the Korean authorities and the United States armed forces shall assist each other in the conduct of inquiries and the collection of evidence.

(b) The United States armed forces shall render all assistance within their power to ensure that articles liable to seizure by, or on behalf of, the customs authorities of the Government of the Republic of Korea are handed to those authorities.

(d) The autherities of the United States forces shall render all assistance within their power to ensure the payment of duties, taxes and penalities payable by members of the United States forces or the civilian component, or their dependents.	(c) The United States armed forces shall render all assistance within their power to ensure the payment of duties, taxes, and penalities payable by members of such forces or of the civilian component, or their dependents.
(e) The authorities of the United States forces shall provide all practicable assistance to the customs officials dispatched to military controlled piers and airports for the purpose of customs inspection.	
8. Vehicles and articles belonging to the United States armed forces seized by the customs authorities of the Government of the Republic of Korea in connection with an offense against its customs or fiscal laws or regulations shall be handed over to appropriate authorities of the force concerned.	(d) Vehicles and articles belonging to the United States armed forces seized by the customs authorities of the Government of the Republic of Korea in connection with an offense against its customs or fiscal laws or regulations shall be handed over to the appropriate authorities of the forces concerned.
<u>Agreed Minute</u>	<u>Agreed Minutes</u>
The Korean authorities may request the United States military authorities whatever information they deem necessary pertaining to all cargo consigned to the non-appropriated fund organizations and the United States military authorities shall promptly provide such infomation in the manner as is specified by the	1. The quantity of goods imported under paragraph 2 by non-appropriated fund organizations of the United States armed forces for the use of the members of the United States armed forces, the civilian component, and their dependents shall be limited to the extent reasonably required for such use.

Korean authorities.

2. Paragraph 3(a) does not require concurrent shipment of goods with travel of owner nor does it require single loading or shipment. In this connection, members of the United States armed forces or civilian component and their dependents may import free of duty their personal and household effects during a period of six months from the date of their first arrival.

3. The term "military cargo" as used in paragraph 5(c) is not confined to arms and equipment but refers to all cargo consigned to the United States armed forces, including their authorized procurement agencies and their non-appropriated fund organizations provided for in Article .

4. The United States armed forces will take every practicable measure to ensure that goods will not be imported into the Republic of Korea by or for the members of the United States armed forces, the civilian component, or their dependents, the entry of which would be in violation of Korean customs laws and regulations. The United States armed forces will promptly notify the Korean

customs authorities whenever the entry of such goods in discovered.

5. The Korean customs authorities m may, if they consider that there has been an abuse or infringement in connection with the entry of goods under Article , take up the matter with the appropriate authorities of the United States armed forces.

6. The words "The United States armed forces shall render all assistance within their power," etc., in paragraph 9 (b) and (c) refer to reasonable and practicable measures by the United States armed forces authorized by United States law and service regulations.

7. It is understood that the duty free treatment provided in paragraph 2 shall apply to materials, supplies, and equipment imported for sale through commissaries and non-appropriated fund organizations, under such regulations as the United States armed forces may promulgate, to those individuals and organizations referred to in Article____ and its Agreed Minute.

Proposed additional sentence, Agreed Minute #3:

"Pertinent information on cargo consigned to non-appropriated fund organizations will be furnished authorities of the Republic of Korea upon request through the Joint Committee."

Non-appropriated Fund Organizations

ARTICLE

1. (a) Navy exchanges, post exchanges, messes, commissaries, social clubs, theaters and other non-appropriated fund organizations authorized and regulated by the authorities of the United States armed forces may be established within the facilities and areas in use by the United States armed forces for the exclusive use of the members of such forces, the civilian component, and their dependents. Except as otherwise provided in this Agreement, such organizations shall not be subject to Korean regulations, license, fees, taxes or similar controls.

(b) When a newspaper authorized and regulated by the authorities of the United States armed forces is sold to the general public, it shall be subject to Korean regulations, license, fees, taxes or similar controls so far as such circulation is concerned.

2. No Korean tax shall be imposed on sales of merchandise and services by such organizations, except as provided in paragraph 1(b) but purchase within the Republic of Korea of merchandise and supplies by such organizations shall be subject to Korean taxes unless otherwise agreed between the two Governments.

ARTICLE

1. (a) Military exchanges, messes, social clubs, theaters, newspapers and other non-appropriated fund activities authorized and regulated by the United States military authorities may be established by the United States armed forces for the use of members of such forces, the civilian component, and their dependents. Except as otherwise provided in this Agreement, such activities shall not be subject to Korean regulations, licenses, fees, taxes, or similar controls.

(b) When a newspaper authorized and regulated by the United States military authorities is sold to the general public, it shall be subject to Korean regulations, licenses, fees, taxes or similar controls so far as such circulation is concerned.

2. No Korean tax shall be imposed on sales of merchandise and services by such organizations, except as provided in paragraph 1(b) of this Article. Purchases within the Republic of Korea of merchandise and supplies by such organizations shall be subject to the Korean taxes to which other purchasers

0039

3. Goods which are sold by such organizations shall not be disposed of in the Republic of Korea to persons not authorized to make purchases from such organizations. Administrative measures shall be taken by the authorities of the United States to prevent such disposition.

4. The quantity of goods imported by such organizations for use of the members of the United States armed forces, the civilian component, and their dependents shall be limited to the extent reasonably required for such use.

5. The organizations referred to in this Article shall provide such information to the authorities of the Republic of Korea as is required by Korean legislations.

of such merchandise and supplies are subject unless otherwise agreed between the two Governments.

3. Except as such disposal may be permitted by the United States and Korean authorities in accordance with mutually agreed conditions, goods which are sold by such activities shall not be disposed of in Korea to persons not authorized to make purchases from such activities.

4. The activities referred to in this Article shall, after consultation between the representatives of the two governments in the Joint Committee, provide such information to the Republic of Korea tax authorities as is required by Korean tax legislation.

Agreed Minute

The activities referred to in paragraph 1 may be used by other officers or personnel of the United States Government ordinarily accorded such privileges, by non-Korean persons whose presence in Korea is solely for the purpose of providing contract services financed by the United States Government, by the dependents of the foregoing, by organizations which are present in the Republic of Korea primarily for the benefit and service of the United States armed forces personnel, such as the American Red Cross and the United Service Organizations, and by the non-Korean personnel of such organizations and their dependents.

Revised Draft of the Agreed Minute

The United States Armed Forces may grant the use of the organizations referred to in paragraph 1 of Article___ to: (a) other officers or personnel of the United States Government ordinarily accorded such privileges; (b) those other non-Korean Armed Forces in Korea under the Unified Command which receive logistical support from the United States Armed Forces, and their members; (c) those non-Korean persons whose presence in the Republic of Korea is solely for the purpose of providing contract services financed by the United States Government; (d) those organizations which are present in the Republic of Korea primarily for the benefit and service of the United States Armed Forces, such as the American Red Cross and the United Service Organizations, and their non-Korean personnel; (e) dependents of the foreoging; and (f) other persons and organizations with the express consent of the Government of the Republic of Korea.

Utilities and Services

ARTICLE ____

1. The United States armed forces shall have the use of all public utilities and services belonging to or controlled or regulated by the Government of the Republic of Korea. The term "utilities and services" shall include, but not be limited to, transportation and communications facilities and systems, electricity, gas, water, steam, heat, light, power, and sewage disposal. In the use of such utilities and services the United States armed forces shall enjoy priorities under conditions no less favorable that those that may be applicable from time to time to the ministries and agencies of the Government of the Republic of Korea.

ARTICLE ____

O 1. ~~(a)~~ The United States armed forces shall have the use of all utilities and services~~, whether publicly~~ ~~or privately owned,~~ owned, which are controlled or regulated by the Government of the Republic of Korea or local administrative ~~political~~ subdivisions thereof. The term "utilities and services" shall include, but not be limited to, transportation and communications facilities and systems, electricity, gas, water, steam, heat, light, power, and sewage disposal ~~however produced,~~ and sewage disposal. The use of utilities and services as provided herein shall not prejudice the right of the United States to operate military transportation, communication, power and such other utilities and services ~~and facilities~~ deemed necessary for the operations of the United States armed forces.

O 2 ~~(b)~~ The use of such utilities and services by the United States shall be in accordance with priorities, conditions, and rates or tariffs no less favorable than those accorded any other user, ~~governmental or private.~~ ~~The Republic of Korea shall insure that by reason of legislation or otherwise, there shall be no discrimination again~~

2. (a) Specific arrangements as to the use of such public utilities and services by the United States armed forces and the payment therefor shall be made between the appropriate authorities of the two Governments or their agencies.

(b) The existing arrangements concerning the use of such public utilities and services by the United States armed forces at the effective date of this Agreement shall be regarded as the arrangements referred to in the foregoing paragraph.

Revised Draft

3. (a) The United States armed forces shall have the use of all utilities and services which are owned, controlled ore regulated by the Government of the Republic of Korea or local administrative subdivisions thereof. The term "utilities and services" shall include, but not be limited to, transportation and communications facilities and systems, electricity, gas, water, steam, heat, light, power,

the United States armed forces in the procurement of such utilities and services. Should the emergency operating needs of the United States armed forces so require, the Republic of Korea shall, upon notification thereon, take all measures to assure provision of utilities and services necessary to meet these needs.

Accounting Procedures

(b) It is agreed that arrangements will be effected between the Governments of the United States and the Republic of Korea for accounting applicable to financial transactions arising out of this Agreement.

Revised Draft of third and fourth sentences, paragraph 3(a)

The use of utilities and services as provided herein shall not prejudice the right of the United States to operate military transportation, communication, power and such other utilities and services deemed necessary for the operations of the United States armed forces. This right shall not be exercised in a manner inconsistent with the operation by the Government of the Republic of

0044

and sewage disposal. The use of utilities and services as provided herein shall not prejudice the right of the United States to operate military transportation, communication, power and such other utilities and services deemed necessary for the operations of the United States armed forces. This right shall not be exercised in a manner inconsistent with the operation by the Government of the Republic of Korea of its utilities and services.

(b) The use of such utilities and services by the United States shall be in accordance with priorities, conditions, and rates or tariffs no less favorable than those accorded any other user.

(4. Removed from this article; to be placed elsewhere in SOFA.)

Agreed Minute

1. The Joint Committee shall be given the opportunity of discussing any changes determined by the Korean authorities of priority or rates applicable to the United States armed forces prior to their effective date.

2. Paragraph 3 of Article ____ will not be construed as in any way abrogating the Utilities and Claims

Korea of its utilities and services.

Agreed Minute

1. It is understood that any change determined by the Korean authorities in priority, conditions, and ~~or increase in utility or service~~ rates applicable or tariffs, to the United States armed forces shall be the subject of ~~prior~~ consultation in the Joint Committee. prior to their effective date.

2. Paragraph 3 of Article ____ will not be construed as in any way abrogating the Utilities and Claims

Settlement Agreement of December 18, 1958, which continues in full force and effect unless otherwise agreed by the two governments.

3. ~~Should the~~ In an emergency ~~operating needs of the United States armed forces so require,~~ the Republic of Korea ~~shall, after consultation thereon,~~ agrees to take appropriate measures to assure provision of utilities and services necessary to meet ~~these~~ the needs of the United States armed forces.

Settlement Agreement of December 18, 1958 which continues in full force and effect unless otherwise agreed by the two Governments.

- 43 -

0046

Local Procurement　　*Agreed*

ARTICLE

1. The United States may contract for any supplies or construction work to be furnished or undertaken in the Republic of Korea for purposes of, or authorized by, this Agreement, without restriction as to choice of supplier or persons who does the construction work. Such supplies or construction work may, ~~upon~~ agreement between the appropriate authorities of the two Governments, also be procured through the Government of the Republic of Korea.

2. Materials, supplies, equipment and services which are required from local sources for the maintenance of the United States armed forces and the procurement of which may have an adverse effect on the economy of the Republic of Korea shall be procured in coordination with, and, when desirable, through or with the assistance of, the competent authorities of the Republic of Korea.

3. Materials, supplies, equipment and services procured for official purposes in the Republic of Korea by the United States armed forces, or by authorized procurement agencies of the United

ARTICLE

1. The United States may contract for any [materials, equipment and services (including] supplies ~~or~~ construction work) to be furnished or undertaken in the Republic of Korea for purposes of, or authorized by, this Agreement, without restriction as to choice of [contractor,] supplier or persons who [provides such services.] ~~does the construction work.~~ Such [materials,] supplies, [equipment and services] ~~or construction work~~ may, upon agreement between the appropriate authorities of the two Governments, also be procured ~~through the Government~~ of the Republic of Korea.

2. Materials, supplies, equipment and services which are required from local sources for the maintenance of the United States armed forces and the procurement of which ~~may~~ [may] have an adverse effect on the economy of the Republic of Korea shall be procured in coordination with, and, when desirable, through or with the assistance of, the competent authorities of the Republic of Korea.

3. Materials, supplies, equipment and services procured for official purposes in the Republic of Korea by the United States armed forces, including their authorized procurement agencies,

States armed forces upon appropriate certification shall be exempt from the following Korean taxes:

(a) Commodity tax

(b) Gasoline tax

(c) Electricity and gas tax

Materials, supplies, equipment and services procured for ultimate use by the United States armed forces shall be exempt from commodity and gasoline taxes upon appropriate certification by the United States armed forces. With respect to any present or future Korean taxes not specifically referred to in this Article which might be found to constitute a significant and readily identifiable part of the gross purchase price of materials, supplies, equipment and services procured by the United States armed forces, the two Governments will agree upon a procedure for granting such exemption or relief therefrom as is consistent with the purpose of this Article.

4. Neither members of the United States armed forces, civilian component, nor their dependents, shall by reason of this Article enjoy any exemption from taxes or similar charges relating to personal purchases of goods and

or procured for ultimate use by the United States armed forces shall be exempted from the following Korean taxes upon appropriate certification by the United States armed forces:

(a) commodity tax

(b) Traffic tax

(c) Petroleum tax

(d) Electricity and gas tax

(e) Business tax

With respect to any present and future Korean taxes not specifically referred to in this Article which might be found to constitute a significant and readily identifiable part of the gross purchase price of materials, supplies, equipment and services procured by the United States armed forces, or for ultimate use by such forces, the two Governments will agree upon a procedure for granting such exemption or relief therefrom as is consistent with the prupose of this Article.

4. Neither members of the United States armed forces, civilian component, nor their dependents, shall by reason of this Article enjoy any exemption from taxes or similar charges relating to personal purchases of goods and

services in the Republic of Korea chargeable under Korean legislation.

5. Except as such disposal may be authorized by the Korean and United States authorities in accordance with mutually agreed conditions, goods purchased in the Republic of Korea exempt from the taxes referred to in paragraph 3, shall not be disposed of in the Republic of Korea to persons not entitled to purchase such goods exempt from such tax.

services in the Republic of Korea chargeable under Korean legislation.

5. Except as such disposal may be authorized by the United States and Korean authorities in accordance with mutually agreed conditions, goods purchased in the Republic of Korea exempt from taxes referred to in paragraph 3, shall not be disposed of in the Republic of Korea to persons not entitled to purchase such goods exempt from such tax.

Agreed Minute

1. The United States armed forces will furnish the Korean authorities with appropriate information as far in advance as practicable on anticipated major changes in their procurement program in the Republic of Korea.

2. The problem of a satisfactory settlement of difficulties with respect to procurement contracts arising out of differences between Korea and United States economic laws and business practices will be studied by the Joint Committee or other appropriate ~~persons~~ representatives.

3. The procedures for securing exemptions from taxation on purchases of goods for ultimate use by the United States armed forces will be as follows:

(a) Upon appropriate certification by the United States armed forces that materials, supplies and equipment consigned to or destined for such forces, are to be used, or wholly or partially used up, under the supervision of such forces, exclusively in the execution of contracts for the construction, maintenance or operation of the facilities and areas referred to in Article   or for the support of the forces therein, or are ultimately to be incorporated into articles or facilities used by such forces, an authorized representative of such forces shall take delivery of such materials, supplies and equipment directly from manufacturers thereof. In such circumstances the collection of taxes referred to in Article   , paragraph 3, shall be held in abeyances.

(b) The receipt of such materials, supplies and equipment in the facilities and areas shall be confirmed by an authorized representative of the United States armed forces to the Korean authorities.

(c) Collection of the taxes on such materials, supplies and equipment shall be held in abeyance until

(1) The United States armed forces confirm and certify the quantity or degree of consumption of the above referred to materials, supplies and equipment, or

(2) The United States armed forces confirm and certify the amount of the above referred to materials, supplies, and equipment which have been ~~incorporated into~~ articles or facilities used by the United States armed forces.

(d) Materials, supplies, and equipment certified under (e) (1) or (2) shall be exempt ~~from taxes~~ referred to in Article , paragraph 3, insofar as the price thereof is paid out of United States Government appropriations or out of funds contributed by the Government of the Republic of Korea for disbursement by the United States.

4. Regarding paragraph 3, it is understood that "materials, supplies, equipment and services procured for official purposes" refers to direct procurement by the United States armed forces or its authorized procurement agencies from Korean suppliers. "Materials, supplies, equipment and services procured for ultimate use" refers to procurement by contractors of the United States armed forces from Korean suppliers of items to be incorporated into or necessary for the production of the end product of their contracts with the United States Armed Forces."

Contractors

ARTICLE

1. Persons, including corporations organized under the laws of the United States, and their employees who are ordinarily resident in the United States and whose presence in the Republic of Korea is solely for the purpose of executing contracts with the United States for the benefit of the United States armed forces, and who are designated by the Government of the United States in accordance with the provisions of the paragraph 2 below, shall, except as provided in this Article, be subject to the laws and regulations of the Republic of Korea.

2. The designation referred to in paragraph 1 above shall be made upon consultation with the Government of the Republic of Korea and shall be restricted to cases where open competitive bidding is not practicable due to security considerations, to the technical qualifications of the contractors involved, to the unavailability of materials or services required by United States standards, or to the limitations of United States law. The designation shall be withdrawn by the Government of the United States:

ARTICLE

1. Persons, including corporations, their employees, and the dependents of such persons, present in Korea solely for the purpose of executing contracts with the United States for the benefit of the United States armed forces or other armed forces in Korea under the Unified Command receiving logistical support from the United States armed forces, who are designated by the Government of the United States in accordance with the provisions of paragraph 2 below, shall, except as provided in this Article, be subject to the laws and regulations of Korea.

2. The designation referred to in paragraph 1 above shall be made upon consultation with the Government of Korea and shall be restricted to cases where open competitive bidding is not practicable due to security considerations, to the technical qualifications of the contractors involved, to the unavailability of materials or services required by United States standards, or to limitations of United States law. The designation shall be withdrawn by the Government of the United States:

(a) upon completion of contracts with the United States for the United States armed forces;	(a) upon completion of contracts with the United States for the United States armed forces or other armed forces in Korea under the Unified command receiving logistical support from the United States armed forces;
(b) upon proof that such persons are engaged in business activities in the Republic of Korea other than those pertaining to the United States armed forces; or	(b) Upon proof that such persons are engaged in business activities in Korea other than those pertaining to the United States States armed forces or other armed forces in Korea under the Unified Command receiving logistical support from the United States armed forces;
(c) when such persons are engaged in practices illegal in the Republic of Korea.	(c) Upon proof that such persons are engaged in practices illegal in Korea.
3. Upon certification by the appropriate authorities of the United States as to their identity, such persons and their employees shall be accorded the following benefits of this Agreement:	3. Upon certification by appropriate United States authorities as to their identity, such persons shall be accorded the following benefits of this Agreement:
	(a) Rights of accession and movement, as provided for Article , paragraph 2;
(a) Entry into the Republic of Korea in accordance with the provisions of Article ____;	(b) Entry into Korea in accordance with the provisions of Article ____;
(b) The exemption from customs duties and other such charges provided	(c) The exemption from customs duties, and other such charges provided

for in Article _____, paragraph 3 for members of the United States forces, the civilian component, and their dependents;

(c) If authorized by the Government of the United States, the right to use the services of the organizations provided for in Article _____;

(d) Those provided for in Article _____, paragraph 2, for members of the United States armed forces, the civilian component, and their dependents;

(e) If authorized by the Government of the United States, the right to use military payment certificates, as provided for in Article ____;

(f) The use of postal facilities provided for in Article _____;

for in Article _____, paragraph 3, for members of the United States armed forces, the civilian component, and their dependents;

(d) If authorized by the Government of the United States, the right to use the services of the activities provided for in Article ____;

(e) Those rights provided in Article _____, paragraph 2, for members of the United States armed forces, the civilian component, and their dependents;

(f) If authorized by the Government of the United States, the right to use military payment certificates, as provided for in Article _____;

(g) The use of postal facilities provided for in Article _____;

(h) Those rights accorded the United States armed forces by Article___, paragraph 3, relating to utilities and services;

(i) Those rights provided to members of the United States armed forces, the civilian component, and their dependents by Article ,
relating to driving permits and registration of vehicles;

(g) Exemption from the laws and regulations of the Republic of Korea with respect to terms and conditions of employment.

4. Such persons and their employees shall be subject to the Korean passport and visa regulations and shall possess passports with their status described therein. Their arrival, departure and their residence while in the Republic of Korea shall be notified by the United States to the Government of the Republic of Korea.

5. Upon certification by an authorized officer of the United States armed forces, such contractors and their employees shall be exempt from taxation in the Republic of Korea on the holding, use, transfer by death, or transfer to persons or agencies entitled to tax

(j) Exemption from the laws and regulations of Korea with respect to terms and conditions of employment, and licensing and registration of business and corporations.

4. The arrival, departure, and place of residence in Korea of such persons shall from time to time be notified by the United States armed forces to the Korean authorities.

5. Upon certification by an authorized representative of the United States armed forces, depreciable assets, except hourse, held, used or transferred by such persons exclusively for the execution of contracts referred to in paragraph 1 shall not be subject to taxes or similar charges of Korea.

6. Upon certification by an authorized representative of the United States armed forces, such persons shall be exempt from taxation in Korea on the holding, use, transfer by death, or transfer to persons or agencies entitled to tax exemption under this

exemption under this Agreement, of any movable property, the presence of which in the Republic of Korea is due solely to the temporary presence of these persons in the Republic of Korea, provided that such exemption shall not apply to property held for the purpose of investment those executing contracts as described in paragraph 1 of this Article in the Republic of Korea.

6. The persons and their employees referred to in paragraph 1 shall not be liable to pay income tax to the Government of the Republic of Korea or to any other taxing agency in the Republic of Korea on any income derived under a contract made in the United States with the Government of the United States in connection with the construction, maintenance or operation of any of the facilities or areas covered by this Agreement. The provisions of this paragraph do not exempt such persons from payment of income or corporation taxed on income derived from other engagement than those mentioned in this paragraph.

Agreement, of movable property, tangible or intangible, the presence of which in Korea is due solely to the temporary presence of these persons in Korea, provided that such exemption shall not apply to property held for the purpose of investment or the conduct of other business in Korea or to any intangible property registered in Korea.

7. The persons referred to in paragraph 1 shall not be liable to pay income or corporation taxes to the Government of Korea or to any other taxing agency in Korea on any income derived under a contract with the Government of the United States in connection with the construction, maintenance or operation of any of the facilities or areas covered by this Agreement. Persons in Korea in connection with the execution of such a contract with the United States shall not be liable to pay any Korean taxes to the Government of Korea or to any taxing agency in Korea on income derived from sources outside of Korea nor shall periods during which such persons are in Korea be considered periods of

residence or domicile in Korea for the purposes of Korean taxation. The provisions of this paragraph do not exempt such persons from payment of income or corporation taxes on income derived from Korean sources, other than those sources referred to in the first sentence of this paragraph, nor do they exempt such persons who claim Korean residence for United States income tax purposes from payment of Korean taxes on income.

7. The Korean authorities shall have the primary right to exercise jurisdiction over the contractors and their employees referred to in paragraph 1 of this Article in relation to offenses committed in the Republic of Korea and punishable by the law of the Republic of Korea. In those cases, in which the Korean authorities decide not to exercise such jurisdiction they shall notify the military authorities of the United States as soon as possible. Upon such notification they military authorities of the United States shall have the right to exercise such jurisdiction over the persons referred to as is conferred on them by the law of the United States.

Revised Draft	Revised Draft
6. The persons referred to in paragraph 1 shall not be liable to pay income or corporation taxes to the Government of the Republic of Korea or to any other taxing agency in Korea on any income derived under a contract with the Government of the United States in connection with the construction, maintenance or operation of any of the facilities or areas covered by this Agreement. The provisions of this paragraph do not exempt such persons from payment of income or corporation taxes on income derived from Korean sources, other than those sources referred to in the first such persons who claim Korean residence for United States income tax purposes from payment of Korean taxes on income. Periods during which such persons are in Korea solely in connection with the execution of a contract with the Government of the United States shall not be considered periods of residence or domicile in Korea for the purpose of such taxation.	3. Upon certification by appropriate United States authorities as to their identity, such persons shall be accorded the following benefits of this Agreement: (a) Accession and movement, as provided for in Article __, paragraph 2; (b) Entry into Korea in accordance with the provisions of Article ____; (c) The exemption from customs duties and other such charges provided for in Article ____, paragraph 3, for members of the United States armed forces, the civilian component, and their dependents; (d) If authorized by the Government of the United States, the use of the services of the activities provided for in Article ____; (e) Those provided in Article ____, paragraph 2, for members of the United States armed forces, the civilian component, and their dependents; (f) If authorized by the Government of the United States, the use of military payment certificates, as provided in Article ____;

(g) The use of postal facilities provided for in Article ____;

(h) The use of utilities and services in accordance with those priorities, conditions, rates, or tariffs accorded the United States armed forces by Article ___, paragraph 3, relating to utilities and services;

(i) Those provided to members of the United States armed forces, the civilian component, and their dependents by Article ____, relating to driving permits and registration of vehicles;

(j) Exemption from the laws and regulations of Korea with respect to terms and conditions of employment, and registration of businesses and corporations.

Agreed Minute

The execution of contracts with the United States in addition to those specified in paragraph 1 of Article ____ shall not exclude the persons provided for in Article____ from the application of that Article.

0059

Security of U.S. Armed Forces and Their Properties

ARTICLE

The Republic of Korea and the United States will cooperate in taking such steps as may from time to time be necessary to ensure the security of the United States armed forces, the members thereof, the civilian component, their dependents, and their property. The Government of the Republic of Korea agrees to seek such legislation and to take such other action as may be necessary to ensure the adequate security and protection within its territory of installations, equipment, property, records and official information of the United States, and for the punishment of offenders under the applicable laws of the Republic of Korea.

ARTICLE

The United States and the Republic of Korea will cooperate in taking such steps as may from time to time be necessary to ensure the security of the United States armed forces, the members thereof, the civilian component, the persons who are present in the Republic of Korea pursuant to Article , their dependents and their property. The Government of the Republic of Korea agrees to seek such legislation and to take such other action as may be necessary to ensure the adequate security and protection within its territory of installations, equipment, property, records, and official information of the United States, of the persons referred to in this paragraph, and their property and, consistent with Article , to ensure the punishment of offenders under the applicable laws of the Republic of Korea.

Foreign Exchange Control

ARTICLE	ARTICLE
1. Members of the United States armed forces, the civilian component, and their dependents shall be subject to the foreign exchange controls of the Government of the Republic of Korea.	OK 1. Members of the United States armed forces, the civilian component, and their dependents, shall be subject to the foreign exchange controls of the Government of the Republic of Korea.
2. The preceding paragraph shall not be construed to preclude the transmission into or outside of the Republic of Korea of the United States dollars or dollar instruments representing the official funds of the United States or realized as a result of service or employment in connection with this Agreement by members of the United States armed forces and the civilian component, or realized by such persons and their dependents from sources outside of the Republic of Korea.	2. The preceding paragraph shall not be construed to preclude the transmission into or out of Korea of United States dollars or dollar instruments representing the official funds of the United States or realized as a result of service or employment in connection with this Agreement by members of the United States armed forces and the civilian component, or realized by such persons and their dependents from sources outside Korea.
3. The United States authorities shall take suitable measures to preclude the abuse of the privileges stipulated in the preceding paragraphs or circumvention of the Korean foreign exchange controls.	3. The United States authorities shall take suitable measures to preclude the abuse of the privileges stipulated in the preceding paragraphs or circumvention of the Korean foreign exchange controls.
Agreed Minute	Agreed Minute
Payment in Korea by the United States armed forces and by those organizations provided in Article ___ to persons	Payment in Korea by the United State armed forces including those activities provided in Article ___, to persons

non appropriated fund

other than members of the United States armed forces, civilian component, their dependents and those persons referred to in Article ___ shall be effected in accordance with the Korean Foreign Exchange Control Law and regulations. In these transactions the "~~basic rate~~ of exchange" shall be used.

"effective official rate of exchange"
"at the buying rate of the foreign exchange bank" (53차)

other than members of the United Sta[tes] armed forces, civilian component, the[ir] dependents and those persons referred in Article ___ shall be effected in accordance with the Korean Foreign Exchange Control Law and regulations. The funds to be used for these transactions shall be convertible into currency of the Republic of Korea at the highest rate in terms of the number of Korean Won per United State[s] dollar which, at the time the conversion is made, is not unlawful in the Republic of Korea.

"and is applicable in the transactions of foreign exchange banks" (한, 54차)

ok with this

55차 U.S. (170)

Military Payment Certificate

ARTICLE

1. (a) United States military payment certificates denominated in dollars may be used by persons authorized by the United States for internal transaction (within the facilities and areas in use by the United States forces.)

(b) The United States Government will take appropriate action to ensure that authorized personnel are prohibited from engaging in transactions involving military payment certificates except as authorized by United States regulations.

withdrew (17)

(c) The Government of the Republic of Korea will take necessary action to prohibit unauthorized person from engaging in transactions involving military payment certificates and with the aid of United States authorities will undertake to apprehend and punish any person or persons under its jurisdiction involved in the counterfeiting or uttering of counterfeit military payment certificates.

(d) It is agreed that the United States authorities will apprehend and punish members of the United States forces, the civilian component, or their dependents, subject to the Military Law of the United States, who tender military payment certificates to unauthorized persons and

ARTICLE

1. (a) United States military payment certificates denominated in dollar may be used by persons authorized by the United States for internal transactions. The Government of the United States will take appropriate action to ensure that authorized personnel are prohibited from engaging in transactions involving military payment certificates except as authorized by United States regulations.

After C.J.A.

(c) The Government of Korea will take necessary action to prohibit unauthorized persons from engaging in transactions involving military payment certificates and with the aid of United States authorities will undertake to apprehend and punish any person or persons under its jurisdiction involved in the counterfeiting or uttering of counterfeit military payment certificates.

(b) It is agreed that the United States authorities will "to the extent authorized by United States law," apprehend and punish members of the United States armed forces, the civilian component, or their dependents, subject to the Military Law of the United States, who

that no obligation will, after the date of coming into force of this Agreement, be due to such unauthorized persons or to the Government of the Republic of Korea or its agencies from the United States or any of its agencies as a result of any unauthorized use of military payment certificates within the Republic of Korea.

2. (a) In order to exercise control of military payment certificates the United States may designate certain American financial institutions to maintain and operate, under United States supervision, facilities for the use of persons authorized by the United States to use military payment certificates.

(b) Institutions authorized to maintain military banking facilities will establish and maintain such facilities physically separated from their Korean commercial banking business, with personnel whose sole duty is to maintain and operate such facilities. Such facilities shall be permitted to maintain United States currency bank accounts and to perform all financial transactions in connection therewith including receipt and remission of funds to the extent provided by Article ___,

tender military payment certificates to unauthorized persons and that no obligation will be due to such unauthorized persons or to the Government of Korea or its agencies from the United States or any of its agencies as a result of any unauthorized use of military payment certificates within Korea.

okeyed (1/7)

2. In order to exercise control of military payment certificates the United States may designate certain American financial institutions to maintain and operate, under United States supervision, facilities for the use of persons authorized by the United States to use military payment certificates. Institutions authorized to maintain military banking facilities will establish and maintain such facilities physically separated from their Korean commercial banking business, with personnel whose sole duty is to maintain and operate such facilities. Such facilities shall be permitted to maintain United States currency bank accounts and to perform all financial transactions in connection therewith including receipt and remission of funds to the extent

paragraph 2, of this Agreement.

X Agreed Minute

United States military payment certificates under custody of the Government of the Republic of Korea at the time of entry into force of this Agreement shall be disposed in accordance with the agreement between the two Government

provided by Article , paragraph 2, of this Agreement.

X Agreed Minute

Inasmuch as United States military Payment Certificates are property of the United States Government, any Military Payment Certificates which are in, or come into, the possession of the Government of the Republic of Korea shall be returned without compensation to the authorities of the United States armed forces as expeditiously as practicable.

Claims

ARTICLE	ARTICLE
1. Each Party waives all its claims against the other Party for damage to any property owned by it and used by its armed ~~services~~ *Forces*, if such damage --	1. Each Party waives all its *claims* against the other Party for damage *to any* property owned by it and used by its land, sea or air armed forces, if such damage:
(a) was caused by a member or an employee of the armed services of the other Party, in ~~execution~~ *performance* of his official duties; or	(a) was caused by a member or an employee of the armed forces of the other Party in the performance of his official duties; or
(b) arose from the use of any vehicle, vessel or aircraft owned by the other Party and used by its armed services, provided either that the vehicle, vessel or aircraft causing the damage was being used ~~in the execution~~ *for performance* of its official duty or that the damage was caused to property being so used.	(b) arose from the use of any vehicle, vessel or aircraft owned by the other Party and used by its armed forces, provided either that the vehicle, vessel or aircraft causing the damage was being used for official purposes, that the damage was caused to property being so used.
Claims for maritime salvage by one Party against the other Party shall be waived, provided that the vessel or cargo salved was owned by the other Party and being used by its armed services for official purposes.	Claims by one Party against the other Party for maritime salvage shall be waived provided that the vessel, or cargo salvaged was owned by a Party and being used by its armed forces for official purposes.
2. (a) In the case of damage caused or arising as stated in paragraph 1 to other property owned by either Party and located in the Republic of Korea, the issue of liability of the other Party shall be determined and the amount of	2. In the case of damage caused or arising as stated in paragraph 1 to other property owned by a Party: (a) each Party waives its claim up to the amount of $1400 or its equivalent in Korean currency at the rate

0066

damage shall be assessed, unless the two Governments agree otherwise, by a sale arbitrator selected in accordance with subparagraph (b) of this paragraph. The arbitrator shall also decide any counter-measures arising out of the same incidents.

(b) The arbitrator referred to in subparagraph (a) above shall be selected by agreement between the two Governments from amongst the nationals of the Républic of Korea who hold or have held high judicial office.

(c) Any decision taken by the arbitrator shall be binding and conclusive upon the Parties.

(d) The amount of any compensation awarded by the arbitrator shall be distributed in accordance with the provisions of paragraph 5(e) (i), (ii) and (iii) of this Article.

(e) The compensation of the arbitrator shall be fixed by agreement between the two Governments and shall, together with the necessary expenses incidental to the performance of his duties, be defrayed in equal proportions by them.

(f) Each Party waives its claim in any such case up to the amount equivalent of exchange provided for in the Agreed Minute to Article ____ at the time the claim is filed.

(b) Claims in excess of the amount stated in subparagraph (a) shall be settled by the Party against which the claim is made in accordance with its domestic law.

1,400

to 800 United States dollars or 104,000 won. In the case of considerable variation in the rate of exchange between these currencies the two Governments shall agree on the appropriate adjustments of these amounts.

3. For the purpose of paragraph 1 and 2 of this Article the expression "owned by a Party" in the case of a vessel includes a vessel on bare boat charter to that Party or requisitioned by it on bare boat terms or seized by it in prize (except to the extent that the risk of loss or liability is borne by some person other than such Party).

4. Each Party waives all its claims against the other Party for injury or death suffered by any member of its armed services while such member was engaged in the performance of his official duties.

5. Claims (other than contractual claims and those to which paragraph 6 or 7 of this Article apply) arising out of acts or omissions of members or employees of the United States armed forces, including those employees who are nationals of or ordinarily resident in the Republic of Korea, done in the performance of

3. For the purpose of paragraph 1 and 2 of this Article, the expression "owned by a Party" in the case of a vessel includes a vessel on bare boat charter to that Party or requisitioned by it on bare boat charter terms or seized by it in prize (except to the extent that the risk of loss or liability is borne by some other person than such Party).

4. Each Party waives all its claims against the other Party for injury or death suffered by any member of its armed forces while such member was engaged in the performance of his official duties.

5. Claims (other than contractual claims) arising out of acts or omissions of members or employees of the United States armed forces done in the performance of official duty, or out of any other act, omission or occurrence for which the United States armed forces are legally responsible, and causing damage

official duty, or out of any other act, omission or occurrence for which the United States armed forces are legally responsible, and causing damage in the Republic of Korea to third Parties, other than the Government of the Republic of Korea, shall be dealt with by the Republic of Korea in accordance with the following provisions:

(a) Claims shall be filed, considered and settled or adjudicated in accordance with the laws and regulations of the Republic of Korea with respect to the claims arising from the activities of its own armed forces.

(b) The Republic of Korea may settle any such claims, and payment of the amount agreed upon or determined by adjudication shall be made by the Republic of Korea in won.

(c) Such payment, whether made pursuant to a settlement or to adjudication of the case by a competent tribunal of the Republic of Korea, or the final adjudication by such a tribunal denying payment, shall be binding and conclusive upon the Parties.

(d) Every claim paid by the Republic of Korea shall be communicated to the appropriate United States authorities in the Republic of Korea to third parties, other than the two Governments shall be processed and settled in accordance with the applicable provisions of United States law. The United States Government shall entertain other non-contractual claims against members of the United States armed forces or of the civilian component and may offer an ex gratia payment in such cases and in such amount as is determined by the appropriate United States authorities.

together with full particulars and a proposed distribution in conformity with subparagraph (e) (i) and (ii) below.

In default of a reply within two months, the proposed distribution shall be regarded as accepted.

(e) The cost incurred in satisfying claims pursuant to the proceding subparagraph and paragraph 2 of this Article shall be distributed between the Parties as follows:

(i) Where the United States alone is responsible, the amount awarded or adjudged shall be distributed in the proportion of 15 per cent chargeable to the Republic of Korea and 85 per cent chargeable to the United States.

25

75

(ii) Where the Republic of Korea and the United States are responsible for the damage, the amount awarded or adjudged shall be distributed equally between them. Where the damage was caused by the armed forces of the Republic of Korea and the United States and it is not possible to attribute it specifically to one or both of those armed services, the amount awarded or adjudged shall be distributed equally between the Republic of Korea and the United States.

0070

(iii) Every half-year, a statement of the sums paid by the Republic of Korea in the course of the half-yearly period in respect of every case regarding which the proposed distribution on a percentage basis has been accepted, shall be sent to the appropriate authorities of the United States, together with a request for reimbursement. Such reimbursement shall be made, in won, within the shortest possible time.

(f) Members or employees of the United States armed forces, excluding those employees who are nationals of or ordinarily resident in the Republic of Korea, shall not be subject to any proceedings for the enforement of any judgement given against them in the Republic of Korea in a matter arising from the performance of their official duties.

(g) Except in so far as subparagraph (e) of this paragraph applies to claims covered by paragraph 2 of this Article, the provisions of this paragraph shall not apply to any claims arising out of or in connection with the navigation or operation of a ship or the loading, carriage, or discharge of a cargo, other than claims for death or personal injury to which paragraph 4 of this Article does

6. Claims against members or employees of the United States armed forces (except employees who are nationals of or ordinarily resident in the Republic of Korea) arising out of tortious acts or omissions in the Republic of Korea not done in the performance of official duty shall be dealt with in the following manner:

(a) The authorities of the Republic of Korea shall consider the claim and access compensation to the claimant in a fair and just manner, taking into account all the circumstances of the case, including the conduct of the injured persons, and shall prepare a report on the matter.

(b) The report shall be delivered to the appropriate United States authorities, who shall then decide without delay whether they will offer an ex gratia payment, and if so, of what amount.

(c) If an offer of ex gratia payment is made, and accepted by the claimant in full satisfaction of his claim, the United States authorities shall make the payment themselves and inform the authorities of the Republic of Korea of their decision and of the sums paid.

(d) Nothing in this paragraph shall affect the jurisdiction of the courts of the Republic of Korea to entertain an action against a member or an employee of the United States armed forces unless and until there has been payment in full satisfaction of the claim.

7. Claims arising out of the unauthorized use of any vehicle of the United States forces shall be dealt with in accordance with paragraph 6 of this Article, except in so far as the United States forces are legally responsible.

8. If a dispute arises as to whether a tortious act or omission of a member or an employee of the United States armed forces was done in the performance of official duty or as to whether the use of any vehicle of the United States armed forces was unauthorized, the question shall be submitted to an arbitrator appointed in accordance with paragraph 2(b) of this Article, whose decision on this point shall be final and conclusive.

9. For the purposes of this Article, each Party shall have the right to determine whether a member or employee of its armed forces was engaged in the performance of official duties and whether property owned by it was being used by its armed forces for official purposes.

9. (a) The United States shall not claim immunity from the jurisdiction of the courts of the Republic of Korea for

6. (a) A member or employee of the United States armed forces shall not be afforded immunity from the

members or employees of the United States armed forces in respect of the civil jurisdiction of the courts of the Republic of Korea except to the extent provided in paragraph 5(f) of this Article.

(b) In case any private movable property, excluding that in use by the United States armed forces, which is subject to compulsory execution under the Korean law, is within the facilities and areas in use by the United States armed forces, the United States authorities shall, upon the request of the courts of the Republic of Korea, possess and turn over such property to the authorities of the Republic of Korea.

(c) The authorities of the Republic of Korea and the United States shall cooperate in the procurement of evidence for a fair hearing and disposal of claims under this Article.

10. Disputes arising out of contracts concerning the procurement of materials, supplies, equipment, services by or for the United States armed forces, which are not resolved by the Parties to

jurisdiction of the civil courts of Korea except: (1) in a matter arising out of acts or omissions done in the performance of official duty; or (2) in respect to any claim where there has been payment in full satisfaction of the claimant.

(3) (b) In the case of any private movable property, excluding that in use by the United States armed forces, which is subject to compulsory execution under Korean law, and is within the facilities and areas in use by the United States armed forces, the United States authorities shall, upon the request of the Korean courts, render all assistance within their power to see that such property is turned over to the Korean authorities.

(4) 7. The authorities of the United States and Korea shall cooperate in the procurement of evidence for a fair disposition of claims under this Article.

-71-

0074

the contract concerned, may be submitted to the Joint Committee for conciliation, provided that the provisions of this paragraph shall not prejudice any right, which Parties to the contract may have, to file a civil suit.

11. Paragraphs 2 and 5 of this Article shall apply only to claims arising incident to non-combat activities.

8. Paragraphs 2 and 5 of this Article shall apply only to claims arising incident to noncombat activities.

12.

10. For the purposes of this Article, members of the Korean augmentation to the United States Army (KATUSA) shall be considered as member of the United States armed forces, and members of the Korean Service Corps (KSC) shall be considered as employees of the armed forces of the Republic of Korea.

Employees of USAF

13.

11. The provisions of this Article shall not apply to any claims which arose before the entry into force of this Agreement.

ROK

Agreed Minutes (Claims Article)

1. The amount to be paid to each claimant, under the provisions of paragraph 5(b) of this Article, except the cases being determined by adjudication, shall be communicated to the authorities of the United States before the payment is made.

In case any reply in favour of the decision is received from the U.S. side, or in default of a reply within one month of receipt of the communication envisaged above, the amount decided by the Korean Claims Authorities shall be regarded as agreed upon between the both Governments.

If, however, the authorities of the United States disagree to the amount decided by the Korean Claims Authorities and reply to this effect within the one-month period, the Korean Claims Authorities shall re-examine the case concerned. The amount decided as a result of the re-examination shall be final and conclusive. The Korean Claims Authorities shall notify the authorities of the United States of the result of re-examination as early as practicable.

The amount agreed upon between the both Governments or decided through the re-examination shall be paid to the claimant concerned without delay.

0076

협정 발효후 6개월 이후부터 발효한다.

2. The provisions of paragraph 5 of this Article will become effective after six months from the date of entry into force of this Agreement. Until such time the United States agrees to pay just and reasonable compensation in settlement of civil claims (other than contractual claims) arising out of acts or omissions of members of the United States armed forces done in the performance of official duty or out of any other act, omission or occurrence for which the United States armed forces are legally responsible. In making such payments United States authorities would exercise the authority provided under United States laws relating to Foreign Claims and regulations issued thereunder. In settling claims which are described as arising "..... out of any act, omission or occurrence for which the United States armed forces are legally responsible", United States authorities will take into consideration local law and practice.

0077

KATUSA.-U.S. members

KSC.-U.S. Employee

3. For the purpose of paragraph 5 of this Article, members of the Korean Augmentation to the United States Army (KATUSA) and members of the Korean Service Corps (KSC) shall be considered respectively as members and employees of the United States armed forces.

0078

1963

Claims Adjudicated
Nr. 839

Claims Disallowed
Nr. 159

Claims Allowed
Nr. 680

Claims Paid
Nr. 649

Amount Paid

$148,185.86 Won 19,264,162

1964 (as of 1 Sept)

Claims Adjudicated
Nr. 911

Claims Disallowed
Nr. 322

Claims Allowed
Nr. 589

Claims Paid
Nr. 576

Amount Paid

$101,433.52 Won 25,865,548

0079

80- 84

LABOR ARTICLE

Presented at 75th Session, Apr. 28, 65.

(Underlining indicates modifications from Korean draft of the Labor Article tabled at 69th session)

1. In this Article the expression:

(a) "employer" refers to the United States Armed Forces (including non-appropriated fund activities).

(b) "employee" refers to any civilian (other than a member of the civilian component of the United States Armed Forces) employed by an employer. Such civilian personnel shall be nationals of the Republic of Korea.

2. Employers may recruit, employ and administer their personnel. Recruitment services of the Government of the Republic of Korea shall be utilized to the maximum extent practicable. In case employers accomplish direct recruitment of employees. The United States Armed Forces shall provide such relevant information as may be required for labor administration to the Office of Labor Affairs of the Republic of Korea.

Presented at 73rd Session, Apr. 20, 65

(underlining indicates changes from U.S. draft of the Labor Article tabled on December 23, 1964)

1. In this Article the expression:

(a) "employer" refers to the United States Armed Forces (including nonappropriated fund activities) and the persons referred to in the first paragraph of Article (_______).

(b) "employee" refers to any civilian (other than a member of the civilian component) employed by an employer, except (1) a member of the paramilitary Korean Service Corps and (2) a domestic employed by an individual member of the United States Armed Forces, civilian component or dependent thereof.

2. Employers may recruit, employ and administer their personnel. Recruitment services of the Government of the Republic of Korea will be utilized insofar as is practicable. In case employers accomplish direct recruitment of employees, employers will provide such relevant information as may be required for labor administration to the Office of Labor Affairs of the Republic of Korea.

0080

Labor Procurement

81

ARTICLE

Revised Korean Draft of Labor Article

(The underlined parts are modification) (69th)

1. The United States Armed Forces and the organizations provided for in Article ____ (hereinafter referred to as "employer") may employ civilian personnel (hereinafter referred to as "employee") under this Agreement. Such civilian personnel shall be nationals of the Republic of Korea.

2. The employers may recruit, employ and administer their personnel Recruitment services of the Government of the Republic of Korea shall be utilized to the maximum extent practicable. In case employers accomplish direct recruitment of employees, the United States Armed Forces shall provide such relevant information as may be required for labor administration to the Office of Labor Affairs of the Republic of Korea.

3. Except as may otherwise be mutually agreed, the conditions of employment and work, such as those relating to wages and supplementary payments, the conditions for the protection and welfare of employees, compensations, and the rights of employees, concerning labor relations shall conform with those laid down by the legislation of the Republic of Korea. (revised at 65th, Oct. 28, 64)

protection of workers, and ... of workers concerning labor relations shall be those laid down by the legislation of the Republic of Korea.

(The Underlined portions above were proposed at the 46th Session)

ARTICLE

1. In this Article the expression

(a) "employer" refers to the United States armed forces (including non-appropriated fund activities) and the persons referred to in the first paragraph of Article ____.

(b) "employee" refers to any civilian (other than a member of the civilian component) employed by an employer, except (1) a member of the Korean Service Corps, who is an employee of the Government of Korea, and (2) a domestic employed by an individual member of the United States armed forces, civilian component or dependent thereof.

OK 2. Employers may recruit, employ and administer their personnel. Recruitment services of the Government of the Republic of Korea will be utilized insofar as is practicable. In case employers accomplish direct recruitment of employees, employers will provide available relevant information as may be required for labor administration to the Office of Labor Affairs of the Republic of Korea.

3. To the extent not inconsistent with the provisions of this article or the military requirements of the United States Armed Forces, the conditions of employment, compensation, and labor-management practices established by the United States Armed Forces for their employees will conform with the labor laws, customs and practices of the Republic of Korea. (Revised at 68th, Oct. 16, 64)

(Revised US draft tabled at 68th Session, 23 Dec. 1964)

-73-

0081

and the organizations provided for in Article ____ may employ civilian personnel under this Agreement. Such civilian personnel shall be nationals of the Republic of Korea.

0081

2. The employers provided for in paragraph 1 shall recruit and employ to the maximum extent practicable with the assistance of the Korean authorities.

In case the United States military authorities exercise direct recruitment and employment of laborers, employers shall provide such relevant information as may be necessary for labor administration to the Office of Labor Affairs of the Republic of Korea.

(Proposed at 65th, Oct. 25, 64)

2. Employers may accomplish the recruitment, employment and management of employees directly and upon request by the employer, with the assistance of the authorities of the Republic of Korea. In case employers accomplish direct recruitment of employees, employers will provide available relevant information as may be required for labor administration to the Office of Labor Affairs of the Republic of Korea.

(Revised at 64th, Oct. 16, 64)

0082

protection of workers, and ... of workers concerning labor relations shall be those laid down by the legislation of the Republic of Korea.

(The Underlined portions above were proposed at the 46th Session)

with the labor law ...

ices of the Republ...

(Revised at 64th, Oct. 16. 64)

withdrew it at 45th)

0084

-73-

O "3. The conditions of employment and work, such as those relating to wages and supplementary payments, the conditions for the protection and welfare of employees, compensations, and the rights of employees, concerning labor relations shall, unless otherwise agreed upon in this Article, conform with those laid down by the legislation of the Republic of Korea."

(Proposed at 65th, Oct. 28. 64)

relating to wages and supplementary payments, the conditions for the protection of workers, and the rights of workers concerning labor relations shall be those laid down by the legislation of the Republic of Korea.

(The Underlined portions above were proposed at the 46th Session)

recruitment, employment and management of employees directly "and upon request by the employer, with the assistance of the authorities

X 3. To the extent not inconsistent with the provisions of this article or the basic management needs of the United States Armed Forces, the condition of employment, the compensation, and labor-management practices ~~shall be~~ established by the United States armed forces for their employees will conform with the labor laws, customs and practices of the Republic of Korea.

(Revised at 66th, Oct. 16.64)

withdrew it at

0083

2. Local labor requirements of the United States armed forces and of the said organizations shall be satisfied <u>to the maximum extent practicable</u> with the assistance of the Korean authorities. <u>In case the United States military authorities exercise direct recruitment and employment of laborers, they shall provide the Government of the Republic of Korea with the relevant information required for labor administration</u>. The obligations for the withholding and payment of income tax and social security contributions, and, unless otherwise agreed upon in this article, the conditions of employment and work, such as those relating to wages and supplementary payments, the conditions for the protection of workers, and the rights of workers concerning labor relations shall be those laid down by the legislation of the Republic of Korea.

(The Underlined portions above were proposed at the 46th Session)

with the provisions of this article and management practices shall be establi- basic management needs of the United ~~shed by the United States~~ armed forces States Armed Forces, for their employees ~~in general~~ conform will with the labor laws, customs and practices of the Republic of Korea.

~~Moreover, the United States Government may terminate employment whenever the continuation of such employment would materially impair the accomplishment of the mission of the United States armed forces.~~

(proposed to carry over Agreed Minutes and withdrew it at 45th)

0084

-73-

5. To the extent not inconsistent with the provisions of this article and to the minimum extent practicable, the conditions of employment, compensation, and labor-management practices established by the United States Armed Forces for their employees will conform with the labor laws, customs and practices of the Republic of Korea.

(Revised US draft tabled at 68th session, 22 Dec. 1964)

0081

ARTICLE

shall recruit and employ

~~said organizations ... satisfied with~~

to the maximum extent practicable

the assistance of the Korean authorities.

The obligations for the withholding and payment of income tax and social security contributions, and, unless otherwise agreed upon in this article, the conditions of employment and work, such as those relating to wages and supplementary payments, the conditions for the protection of workers, and the rights of workers concerning labour relations shall be those laid down by the legislation of the Republic of Korea.

with the provisions of this article and the basic management needs of the United States Armed Forces, management practices shall be established by the United States armed forces for their employees ~~in general~~ will conform with the labor laws, customs and practices of the Republic of Korea.

Moreover, the United States Government may terminate employment whenever the continuation of such employment would materially impair the accomplishment of the mission of the United States armed forces.

(proposed to carry over Agreed Minutes and withdrew it at 45th)

0084

0084-1

85-86

3. To the extent not inconsistent with the provisions of this Article or except as may otherwise be mutually agreed, the conditions of employment and work, such as those relating to wages and supplementary payments, the conditions for the protection and welfare of employees, compensations, and the rights of employees, concerning labor relations shall conform with those laid down by the labor legislation of the Republic of Korea.

4. (a) With regard to any dispute between employers and any employees or labor unions which cannot be settled through the use of existing procedures of the United States Armed Forces, settlement shall be accomplished in the following manner:

(1) The dispute shall be referred to the Office of Labor Affairs of the Republic of Korea for conciliation.

79th (2) In the event that the dispute is not settled by the procedures described in (1) above within twenty (20) days, the dispute shall be referred to the Joint Committee, which may refer the matter to the Labor sub-Committee or to a specially-designated

committee

3. To the extent not inconsistent with the provisions of this article or the military requirements of the United States Armed Forces, the conditions of employment, compensation, and labor-management practices established by the United States Armed Forces for their employees will conform with the labor laws, customs and practices of the Republic of Korea.

membership or nonmembership in such groups shall not be a cause for discharge or non-employment.

4. (a) Employers will maintain procedures designed to assure the just and timely resolution of employee grievances.

(b) An employee may voluntarily organize and join a union or other employee group whose objectives are not inimical to the interests of the United States. Membership or non-membership in such groups shall not be a factor in employment or other actions affecting employees.

(c) Unions or other employee groups recognized by the armed forces of the United States, pursuant to sub-paragraph (b) above, will be accorded the right of consultation with appropriate authorities of the United States armed forces.

0085

0086

the mission of the United States armed forces.

4. (a) An employee shall have the same right to strike as an employee in a comparable position in the employment of the armed forces of the Republic of Korea. Such an employee may voluntarily organize and join a union or other employ group whose objectives are not inimical to the interests of the United States. Membership or nonmembership in such groups shall not be a cause for discharge or non-employment.

in conformity with the provisions laid down in Korean legislation (Labor)

4. Employers shall insure the just and timely resolution of employee grievances. (69th)

4. (a) Employers will maintain procedures designed to assure the just and timely resolution of employee grievances.

(b) An employee may voluntarily organize and join a union or other employee group whose objectives are not inimical to the interests of the United States.

Membership or non-membership in such groups shall not be a factor in employment or other actions affecting employees.

(c) Unions or other employee groups recognized by the armed forces of the United States, pursuant to sub-paragraph (b) above, will be accorded the right of consultation with appropriate authorities of the United States armed forces.

3. Should the United States armed forces dismiss a worker and a decision of a court or a Labour Commission of the Republic of Korea to the effect that the contract of employment has not terminated become final, the following procedures shall apply:

(a) The United States armed forces shall be informed by the Government of the Republic of Korea of the decision of the court or Commission;

(b) Should the United States armed forces not desire to return the

(3) In the event that the dispute is not settled by the procedures outlined above, the Joint Committee will resolve the dispute. The decisions of the Joint Committee shall be binding.

(4) Neither employee organizations nor employees shall engage in any practice disruptive of normal work requirements unless a period of seventy (70) days has elapsed without settlement after the dispute is referred to the Office of Labor Affairs mentioned in (1) above. is referred to the specially-designated committee mentioned in (2) above.

0087

(5) Failure of any employee organization or employee to abide by the decision of the Joint Committee on any dispute, or engaging in practices disruptive of normal work requirements in violation of the provisions laid down in (4) above, shall be considered cause for the depriviation of the rights and protection accorded by the relevant labor legislation of the Republic of Korea.

(b) The right concerning strike shall be accorded to employees except those whose exercise of the right is prohibited by the Joint Committee.

(d) Any dispute between employers and employees or any recognized employee organization, which cannot be settled through the use of procedures of the United States armed forces, shall be settled as follows:

(1) The dispute shall be referred to the Office of Labor Affairs, Ministry of Health and Social Affairs, Republic of Korea for conciliation.

(2) In the event that the dispute is not settled by the procedure described in (1) above, the matter will be referred to the Joint Committee, which may refer the matter to the Labor Sub-Committee or to a specially-designated committee, for further fact-finding, review, and conciliation efforts.

(3) In the event that the dispute is not settled by the procedures outlined above, the Joint Committee will resolve the dispute. The decisions of the Joint Committee shall be binding.

(4) Failure of any recognized employee organization or employee to bide by the decision of the Joint Committee on any dispute, or engaging in practices disruptive of normal work requirements during settlement procedures, shall be considered just cause for the withdrawal of recognition of that organization and the discharge of that employee.

0088

0087

nor employees shall engage in any practice disruptive of normal work requirements unless a period of seventy (70) days has elapsed without settlement after the dispute is referred to the Office of Labor Affairs mentioned in (1) above.

zations nor employees shall engage in any practices disruptive of normal work requirements unless the cooling-off period set forth in Article 14 of the Korean Labor Dispute Law has elapsed after the dispute is referred to the specially-designated committee mentioned in (2) above.

(5) Failure of any employee organization or employee to abide by the decision of the Joint Committee on any dispute, or engaging in practices disruptive of normal work requirements in violation of the provisions laid down in (4) above, shall be considered cause for the depriviation of the rights and protection accorded by the relevant labor legislation of the Republic of Korea.

(b) The right concerning strike shall be accorded to employees except those whose exercise of the right is prohibited by the Joint Committee.

(d) Any dispute between employers and employees or any recognized employee organization, which cannot be settled through the use of procedures of the United States armed forces, shall be settled as follows:

(1) The dispute shall be referred to the Office of Labor Affairs, Ministry of Health and Social Affairs, Republic of Korea for conciliation.

(2) In the event that the dispute is not settled by the procedure described in (1) above, the matter will be referred to the Joint Committee, which may refer the matter to the Labor Sub-Committee or to a specially-designated committee, for further fact-finding, review, and conciliation efforts.

(3) In the event that the dispute is not settled by the procedures outlined above, the Joint Committee will resolve the dispute. The decisions of the Joint Committee shall be binding.

(4) Failure of any recognized employee organization or employee to bide by the decision of the Joint Committee on any dispute, or engaging in practices disruptive of normal work requirements during settlement procedures, shall be considered just cause for the withdrawal of recognition of that organization and the discharge of that employee.

0088

within ten days after being informed by the latter of the decision of the court or Commission, and may temporarily withhold the worker from duty;

(c) Upon such notification, the Government of the Republic of Korea and the United States armed forces shall consult together without delay with a view to finding a practical solution of the case;

(d) Should such a solution not be reached within a period of thirty days from the date of commencement of the consultations under (c) above, the worker will not be entitled to return to duty. In such case, the Government of the United States shall pay to the Government of the Republic of Korea an amount equal to the cost of employment of the worker for a period of time to be agreed between the two Governments through the Joint Committee.

5. (a) Should the Republic of Korea adopt measures allocating labor, the United States Armed Forces shall be accorded allocation privileges no less favorable than those enjoyed by the Armed Forces of the Republic of Korea. 69th	ok 5. (a) Should the Republic of Korea adopt measures allocating labor, the United States armed forces shall be accorded employment privileges no less favorable than those enjoyed by the armed forces of the Republic of Korea.

0089

- 75 -

5. In the event of a national emergency, such as war, hostilities or situations where war or hostilities is imminent, the application of this Article shall be limited in accordance with the emergency measures taken by the Government of the Republic of Korea, and, in addition, the following arrangements will be made:

(a) Should the Government of the Republic of Korea adopt measures allocating labor, the United States Armed Forces shall be accorded allocation privileges no less favorable than those enjoyed by the Armed Forces of the Republic of Korea.

(b) Employees who have acquired skills essential to the mission of the United States Armed Forces will, upon request of the United States Armed Forces and through mutual agreement, be deferred from Republic of Korea military service or other compulsory services. The United States Armed Forces shall in advance furnish to the Government of the Republic of Korea lists of those employees deemed necessary.

6. Members of the civilian component of the United States Armed Forces shall not be subject to Korean laws or resulations with respect to their terms and conditions of employment.

(e) An employee shall be subject to the same legal provisions concerning strikes and other work stoppages as an employee in a comparable position in the employment of the armed forces of the Republic of Korea.

exempt from Republic of Korea military service or other compulsory service. The United States armed forces shall furnish to the Republic of Korea lists of those employees deemed essential.

5.

(a) Should the Republic of Korea adopt measures allocating labor, the United States Armed Forces shall be accorded allocation privileges no less favorable than those enjoyed by the Armed Forces of the Republic of Korea.

(b) In the event of a national emergency, such as war, hostilities, or situations where war or hostilities may be imminent, employees who have acquired skills essential to the mission of the United States Armed Forces shall, upon request of the United States Armed Forces, be deferred from Republic of Korea military service or other compulsory service. The United States Armed Forces shall furnish in advance to the Republic of Korea lists of those employees deemed essential.

6. Member of the civilian component shall not be subject to Korean laws or regulations with respect to their terms and condition of employment.

0090

(b) In the event of a national emergency such as war, hostilities, or other imminent situations, the employees who have acquired skills essential to the mission of the United States Armed Forces may, upon request of the United States Armed Forces, be deferred from Republic of Korea military service or other compulsory services. The United States Armed Forces shall in advance furnish to the Republic of Korea lists of those employees deemed essential.

6. Members of the civilian component shall not be subject to Korean laws or regulations with respect to their terms and conditions of employment.

AGREED MINUTES

1. The undertaking of the United States to conform with the labor legislation of the Republic of Korea does not imply any waiver by the United States Government of its immunities under international law.

the United States armed forces or the

(b) In the event of a national emergency, employees who have acquired skills essential to the mission of the United States armed forces shall be exempt from Republic of Korea military service or other compulsory service. The United States armed forces shall furnish to the Republic of Korea lists of those employees deemed essential.

6. Members of the civilian component shall not be subject to Korean laws or regulations with respect to their terms and conditions of employment.

Agreed Minutes

1. The Republic of Korea will make available, at designated induction points qualified personnel for Korean Service Corps units in numbers sufficient to meet the requirements of United States Armed Forces. The employment of a

69th

(b) In the event of a national emergency such as war, hostilities, or other imminent situations, the employees who have acquired skills essential to the mission of the United States Armed Forces may, upon request of the United States Armed [illegible] from Republic [illegible] service or o[illegible]ces. The United States Armed Forces shall in advance furnish to the Republic of Korea lists of those employees deemed essential.

6. Members of the civilian component shall not be subject to Korean laws or regulations with respect to their terms and conditions of employment.

1. The undertaking of the United States to conform with the labor legislation of the Republic of Korea does not imply any waiver by the United States Government of its immunities under international law.

1. It is understood that the Government of the Republic of Korea shall be reimbursed for costs incurred under relevant contracts between appropriate authorities of the Korean Government and the United States armed forces or the

0091-1

6. Members of the civilian component shall not be subject to Korean laws or regulations with respect to their terms and conditions of employment.

Agreed Minutes

1. The Republic of Korea will make available, at designated induction points, qualified personnel for Korean Service Corps units in numbers sufficient to meet the requirements of United States Armed Forces. The employment of a

92-98

AGREED MINUTES

1. The undertaking of the United States to conform to the labor legislation of the Republic of Korea does not imply any waiver by the United States Government of its immunities under international law.

2. It is understood that the Government of the Republic of Korea shall be reimbursed for direct costs incurred in providing assistance pursuant to Paragraph 2.

3. Employers will withhold from the pay of their employees, and pay over to the Government of the Republic of Korea withholdings required by the income tax legislation of the Republic of Korea.

4. In case where it is impossible for employers to conform to the labor legislations of the Republic of Korea applicable under paragraph 3 on account of the military requirements of the United States Armed Forces, the matter shall be referred, in advance, to the Joint Committee for mutual agreement. The Government of the Republic of Korea will give due consideration to the military requirements of the United States Armed Forces.

1. The Republic of Korea will make available, at designated induction points, qualified personnel for Korean Service Corps units in numbers sufficient to meet the requirements of United States Armed Forces.

2. It is understood that the Government of the Republic of Korea shall be reimbursed for direct costs incurred in providing assistance requested pursuant to paragraph 2.

3. The undertaking of the United States Government to conform to Korean labor laws, customs, and practices, does not imply any waiver by the United States Government of its immunities under international law. The United States Government may terminate employment at any time the continuation of such employment is inconsistent with the military requirements of the United States Armed Forces.

4. Employers will withhold from the pay of their employees, and pay over to the Government of the Republic of Korea withholdings required by the income tax legislation of the Republic of Korea.

5. When employers cannot conform with provisions of labor legislation of the Government of the Republic of Korea applicable under this Article on account of the military requirements of the United States Armed Forces, the matter shall be reported, in advance whenever possible, to the Joint Committee for its consideration and review.

0092

on the pay of their employees, and pay over to the Government of the Republic of Korea, withholdings required by the income tax legislation of the Republic of Korea.

3. It is understood that the Government of the Republic of Korea shall be reimbursed for direct costs incurred in providing assistance pursuant to Paragraph 2.

4. In case where it is impossible for the employers to conform, on account of the military requirements of the United States Armed Forces, with the Korean labor legislation under the provisions of Paragraph 3, the matter shall in advance be referred to the Joint Committee for mutual agreement. The Republic of Korea will give due consideration to the military requirements of the United States Armed Forces.

5. With regard to any dispute between the employers and any employees or labor unions which cannot be settled through the use of existing procedures of the United States Armed Forces, settlement shall be accomplished in the following manner:

(a) The dispute shall be referred to the Office of Labor Affairs of the Republic of Korea for conciliation.

(b) In the event that the dispute is not settled by the procedures described in (a) above, the dispute shall be referred to a special committee designated by the Joint Committee for further conciliation efforts.

(c) In the event that the dispute is not settled by the procedures outlined above, the Joint Committee will resolve the dispute. The decisions of the Joint Committee shall be binding.

(d) Neither employee organizations nor employees shall engage in any practices disruptive of normal work requirements unless the cooling-off period set forth in Article 14 of the Korean Labor Dispute Law has elapsed after the dispute is referred to the Office of Labor Affairs mentioned in (a) above.

(e) Failure of any employee organization or employee to abide by the decision of the Joint Committee on any dispute, or engaging in practices disruptive of normal work requirements in violation of the provisions of Paragraph (d) above, shall be considered cause for the

domestic by an individual member of the United States Armed Forces, civilian component or dependent thereof shall be governed by applicable Korean law and in addition by wage scales and control measures promulgated by the United States Armed Forces.

2. The undertaking of the United States Government to conform to Korean labor laws, customs, and practices, does not imply any waiver by the United States Government of its immunities under international law. The United States Government may terminate employment at any time the continuation of such employment is inconsistent with the military requirements of the United States Armed Forces.

(Revised US draft tabled at 68th Session, 23 Dec. 1964)

0093

3. It is understood that the Government of the Republic of Korea shall be reimbursed for direct cost incurred in providing assistance requested made pursuant to paragraph 2. (at 45th)

OK (65, Oct. 23, 64)

4. Employers will withhold from the pay of their employees, and pay over to the Government of the Republic of Korea, withholdings required by the income tax legislation of the Republic of Korea. (64th, Oct. 16, 64)

5. With regard to any dispute between employers and any recognized employee organization or employees which cannot be settled through the use of existing procedures of the United States Armed Forces, settlement shall be accomplished as provided below. During such disputes neither employee organizations nor employees shall engage in any practices disruptive of normal work requirements:

(a) The dispute shall be referred to the Office of Labor Affairs, Ministry of Health and Social Affairs, Republic of Korea, for conciliation.

(b) In the event that the dispute is not settled by the procedure described in (a) above, the matter may be referred to the Joint Committee, which may refer the matter to the Labor Sub-Committee or specially designated Committee, for further fact-finding, review and shall in advance be referred to the Joint Committee for mutual agreement.

The Republic of Korea will give due consideration to the military requirements of the United States Armed Forces.

5. With regard to any dispute between the employers and any employees or labor unions which cannot be settled through the use of existing procedures of the United States Armed Forces, settlement shall be accomplished in the following manner:

(a) The dispute shall be referred to the Office of Labor Affairs of the Republic of Korea for conciliation.

(b) In the event that the dispute is not settled by the procedures described in (a) above, the dispute shall be referred to a special committee designated by the Joint Committee for further conciliation efforts.

(c) In the event that the dispute is not settled by the procedures outlined above, the Joint Committee will resolve the dispute. The decisions of the Joint Committee shall be binding.

(d) Neither employee organizations nor employees shall engage in any practices disruptive of normal work requirements unless the cooling-off period set forth in Article 14 of the Korean Labor Dispute Law has elapsed after the dispute is referred to the Office of Labor Affairs mentioned in (a) above.

(e) Failure of any employee organization or employee to abide by the decision of the Joint Committee on any dispute, or engaging in practices disruptive of normal work requirements in violation of the provisions of Paragraph (d) above, shall be considered cause for the depriviation of the rights and protection accorded by the relevant laws of the Republic of Korea.

may terminate employment at any time the continuation of such employment is inconsistent with the military requirements of the United States Armed Forces.

(Revised US draft tabled at 68th Session, 23 Dec. 1964)

0093

3. It is understood that the Government of the Republic of Korea shall be reimbursed for direct cost incurred in providing assistance requested made pursuant to paragraph 2. (at 45th)

OK (65, Oct. 23, 64)

4. Employers will withhold from the pay of their employees, and pay over to the Government of the Republic of Korea, withholdings required by the income tax legislation of the Republic of Korea.

(64th, Oct. 16, 64)

5. With regard to any dispute between employers and any recognized employee organization or employees which cannot be settled through the use of existing procedures of the United States Armed Forces, settlement shall be accomplished as provided below. During such disputes neither employee organizations nor employees shall engage in any practices disruptive of normal work requirements:

(a) The dispute shall be referred to the Office of Labor Affairs, Ministry of Health and Social Affairs, Republic of Korea, for conciliation.

(b) In the event that the dispute is not settled by the procedure described in (a) above, the matter may be referred to the Joint Committee, which may refer the matter to the Labor Sub-Committee or specially designated Committee, for further fact-finding, review and conciliation efforts.

(c) In the event that the dispute is not settled by the procedure outlined above, the Joint Committee will resolve the dispute. The decisions of the Joint Committee shall be binding.

(d) Failure of any recognized employee organization or employee to bide by the decision of the Joint Committee on any dispute, or engaging in practices disruptive of normal work requirements during settlement procedures, shall be considered just cause for the withdrawal of recognition of that organization and the discharge of that employee.

0094

(Revised US draft tabled at 68th Session, 23 Dec. 1964)

organizations provided for in article ____ in connection with the employment of workers to be provided for the United States armed forces or such organizations.

2. It is understood that the term "the legislation of the Republic of Korea" mentioned in Paragraph 2, Article ____ includes decisions of the courts and the Labor Commissions of the Republic of Korea, subject to the provisions of Paragraph 3, Article ____.

3. It is understood that the provisions of Article ____, paragraph 3 shall only apply to discharges for security reasons including disturbing the maintenance of military discipline within the facilities and areas used by the United States armed forces.

(Proposed at 65th, Oct. 23. 64)

X4. "With regard to any dispute between the employers except the persons referred to in Paragraph 1, Article __, and employees or labor unions which cannot be settled through the use of existing procedures of the U.S. armed forces, settlement shall be accomplished in the following manner.

"(a). The dispute shall be referred to the Office of Labor Affairs, Ministry of Health and Social Affairs, Republic of Korea, for consiliation.

0095

Affairs, and the United States armed forces.

0096

Republic of Korea.

0098

d. During the period in which a dispute is being handled by the procedures mentioned in paras (a), (b) and (c) above, recognized employee organizations and employees shall not indulge in any practices disruptive of normal work requirements.

be considered just cause for the withdrawal of recognition of that organization and the discharge of that employee.

limitations provided for in article ____

in connection with the employment of workers to be provided for the United States armed forces or such organizations.

2. It is understood that the term "the legislation of the Republic of Korea" mentioned in Paragraph 2, Article ____ includes decisions of the courts and the

"(b). In the event that the dispute is not settled by the procedure described in (a) above, the matter may be referred to a Special Labor Committee appointed by the Office of Labor Affairs, Ministry of Health and Social Affairs, Republic of Korea, for mediation. This committee shall be tri-partite in composition and shall be consisted of equal representation from Labor Unions, the Office of Labor Affairs, and the United States armed forces.

0096

... of Korea.

0098

d. During the period in which a dispute is being handled by the procedures mentioned in paras (a), (b) and (c) above, recognized employee organizations and employees shall not indulge in any practices disruptive of normal work requirements.

be considered just cause for the withdrawal of recognition of that organization and the discharge of that employee.

obligations provided for in article ___ in connection with the employment of workers to be provided for the United States armed forces or such organizations.

2. It is understood that the term "the legislation of the Republic of Korea" mentioned in Paragraph 2, Article ___ includes decisions of the courts and the

"(c). In the event that the dispute is not settled by the procedures described in (a) and (b) above, the dispute shall be referred to the Joint Committee, or such sub-committee as may be established thereunder for arbitration to resolve the dispute. The decisions of the Joint Committee or sub-committee thereunder shall be binding."

0097

de... the rights and protection accorded by the relevant laws of the Republic of Korea.

0098

d. During the period in which a dispute is being handled by the procedures mentioned in paras (a), (b) and (c) above, recognized employee organizations and employees shall not indulge in any practices disruptive of normal work requirements.

be considered just cause for the withdrawal of recognition of that organization and the discharge of that employee.

organizations provided for in article ____ in connection with the employment of workers to be provided for the United States armed forces or such organizations.

2. It is understood that the term "the legislation of the Republic of Korea" mentioned in Paragraph 2, Article ____ includes decisions of the courts and the

(d) During the period in which a dispute is being handled by the procedures mentioned in paras (a), (b) and (c) above, authorities of the Republic of Korea shall urge labor unions and employees not to indulge in any practices disruptive of normal work requirements.

(e) Failure of any recognized employee organization or employee to abide by the decision of the Joint Committee or any sub-committee established thereunder on any dispute will be considered cause for the deprivation of the rights and protection accorded by the relevant laws of the Republic of Korea.

d. During the period in which a dispute is being handled by the procedures mentioned in paras (a), (b) and (c) above, recognized employee organizations and employees shall not indulge in any practices disruptive of normal work requirements.

be considered just cause for the withdrawal of recognition of that organization and the discharge of that employee.

0098

organizations provided for in Article ___ in connection with the employment of workers to be provided for the United States armed forces or such organizations.

2. It is understood that the term "the legislation of the Republic of Korea" mentioned in Paragraph 2, Article ___ includes decisions of the courts and the

e. Failure of any recognized employee organization or employee to abide by the decision of the Joint Committee or any sub-committee established thereunder on any dispute, or action in violation of para (d) above shall be considered just cause for the withdrawal of recognition of that organization and the discharge of that employee.

0098-1

Criminal Jurisdiction

ARTICLE

1. Subject to the provisions of this Article:

(a) The Military authorities of the United States shall have the right to exercise within the Republic of Korea criminal and disciplinary jurisdiction conferred on them by the law of the United States over all persons subject to the military law of the United States.

United States armed forces and the civilian components.

(b) the authorities of the Republic of Korea shall have jurisdiction over the members of the United States armed forces, the civilian component, and their dependents with respect to offenses committed within the territory of the Republic of Korea and punishable by the law of the Republic of Korea.

2. (a) The military authorities of the United States shall have the right to exercise exclusive jurisdiction over members of the United States armed forces and the civilian components with respect to offenses, including offenses relating to its security, punishable by the law of the United States, but not by the law of the Republic of Korea.

ARTICLE

1. Subject to the provisions of this Article,

(a) the authorities of the United States shall have the right to exercise within the Republic of Korea all criminal and disciplinary jurisdiction conferred on them by the law of the United States over members of the United States armed forces or civilian component, and their dependents.

(b) the civil authorities of the Republic of Korea shall have (~~the right to exercise~~) 삭제(58차 64.7.16.) jurisdiction over the members of the United States armed forces or civilian component, and their dependents, with respect to offenses committed within the territory of the Republic of Korea and punishable by the law of the Republic of Korea.

2. (a) The authorities of the United States shall have the right to exercise exclusive jurisdiction over members of the United States armed forces or civilian component, and their dependents, with respect to offenses, including offenses relating to its security, punishable by the law of the United States, but not by the law of the Republic of Korea.

- 78 -

0099

(b) The authorities of the Republic of Korea have the right to exercise exclusive jurisdiction over members of the United States armed forces, the civilian component, and their dependents with respect to offenses, including offenses relating to the security of the Republic of Korea, punishable by its law but not by the law of the United States.

(c) For the purpose of this paragraph and of paragraph 3 of this Article a security offense against a State shall include:

(i) treason against the State;

(ii) sabotage, espionage or violation of any law relating to official secrets of that State, or secrets relating to the national defense of that State.

3. In cases where the right to exercise jurisdiction is concurrent the following rules shall apply;

(a) The military authorities of the United States shall have the primary right to exercise jurisdiction over members of the United States armed forces or the civilian component in relation to:

(b) The authorities of the Republic of Korea shall have the right to exercise exclusive jurisdiction over members of the United States armed forces or civilian component, and their dependents, with respect to offenses, (including offenses relating to the security of the Republic of Korea,) punishable by its law but not by the law of the United States.

(c) For the purpose of this paragraph and of paragraph 3 of this Article, a security offense against a State shall include:

(i) treason against the State;

(ii) sabotage, espionage or violation of any law relating to official secrets of that State, or secrets relating to the national defense of that State.

3. In case where the right to exercise jurisdiction is concurrent the following rules shall apply:

(a) The authorities of the United States shall have the primary right to exercise jurisdiction over members of the United States armed forces or civilian component, and their dependents, in relating to:

official duty에서 관련성 양측 합의.

(i) offenses solely against the property or security of the United States, or offenses solely against the person or property of another member of the United States armed forces or the civilian component or of a dependent;

(ii) offenses arising out of any act or omission done in the performance of official duty(~~provided that such act or omission is directly related to the duty. The question as to whether offenses were committed in the performance of official duty shall be decided by a competent district public prosecutor of the Republic of Korea.~~

~~In case the offender's commanding officer finds otherwise, he may appeal from the prosecutor's decision to the Minister of Justice within ten days from the receipt of the decision of the prosecutor, and the decision of the Minister of Justice shall be final.~~)

(b) In the case of any other offenses the authorities of the Republic of Korea shall have the primary right to exercise jurisdiction.

(c) If the State having the primary right decides not to exercise jurisdiction, it shall notify the authorities of the other State as soon

(i) offenses solely against the property or security of the United States, or offenses solely against the person or property of another member of the United States armed forces or civilian component or of a dependent;

(ii) offenses arising out of any act of omission done in the performance of official duty;

52차에서 삭제키로 (64.5.20) 美측 제안을 제시.

(b) In the case of any other offense, the authorities of the Republic of Korea shall have the primary right to exercise jurisdiction.

(c) If the State having the primary right decides not to exercise jurisdiction, it shall notify the authorities of the other State as soon as practicable. The authorities of the State having the primary right shall give sympathetic consideration to a request from the authorities of the other State for a waiver of its right in cases where that other State considers such waiver to be of particular importance.

4. The foregoing provisions of this Article shall not imply any right for the military authorities of the United States to exercise jurisdiction over persons who are nationals of or ordinarily resident in the Republic of Korea, unless they are members of the United States armed forces.

5. (a) The military authorities of the United States and the authorities of the Republic of Korea shall assist each other in the arrest of members of the United States armed forces, the civilian component, or their dependents in the territory of the Republic of Korea and in handing them over to the authorities which is to exercise jurisdiction in accordance with the above provisions.

(b) The authorities of the Republic of Korea shall notify the military authorities of the United States of the arrest of any member of the United States armed forces, the civilian

accepts at 67th

as practicable. The authorities of the State having the primary right shall give sympathetic consideration to a request from the authorities of the other State for a waiver of its right in cases where that other State considers such waiver to be of particular importance.

(4) The foregoing provisions of this Article shall not imply any right for the authorities of the United States to exercise jurisdiction over persons who are nationals of or ordinary resident in the Republic of Korea, unless they are members of the United States armed forces.

5. (a) The authorities of the United States and the authorities of the Republic of Korea shall assist each other in the arrest of members of the United States armed forces, the civilian component, or their dependents in the territory of the Republic of Korea and in handing them over to the authority which is to have custody in accordance with the following provisions.

(b) The authorities of the Republic of Korea shall notify promptly the authorities of the United States of the arrest of any member of the United States armed forces, or civilian component, or ~~their~~ a ~~dependent~~.

(c) The military authority of the United States shall immediately notify the authority of the Republic of Korea of the arrest of a member of the United States armed forces, the civilian component, or a dependent, unless the United States authority has the right to exercise exclusive jurisdiction over such a person.

(d) An accused member of the

(d) "An accused member of the United States armed forces or civilian component over whom the Republic of Korea is to exercise jurisdi jurisdiction will, if he is in the hands of the United States, be under the custody of the United States during all judicial proceedings and until custody is requested by the authorities of the Republic of Korea. The Military authorities of the United States may transfer custody to the Korean authorities at any time and shall give sympathetic consideration to any request for the transfer of custody which may be made by the Korean authorities in specific cases."

NATO §22

(e) "In respect of offenses solely against the security of the Republic of Korea provided in paragraph 2(c), custody shall remain with the authorities of the Republic of Korea."

component, or a dependent.

(c) The custody of an accused member of the United States armed forces or civilian component, or of a dependent, over whom the Republic of Korea is to exercise jurisdiction shall, if he is in the hands of the United States, remain with the United States pending the conclusion of all judicial proceedings and until custody is requested by the authorities of the Republic of Korea. If he is in the hands of the Republic of Korea, he shall be promptly handed over to the authorities of the United States and remain in their custody pending completion of all judicial proceedings and until custody is requested by the authorities of the Republic of Korea. The United States authorities ~~will~~ shall promptly make any such accused available to the authorities of the Republic of Korea

- 82 -

0103

6. (a) The authorities of the Republic of Korea and the military authorities of the United States shall assist each other in the carrying out of all necessary investigations into offenses, and in the collection and production of evidence including the seizure and, in proper case, the handing over of objects connected with an offense. The handing over of such objects may, however, be made subject to their return within the time specified by the authority delivering them

(b) The authorities of the Republic of Korea and the military authorities of the United States shall notify each other of the disposition of all cases in which there are concurrent rights to exercise jurisdiction.

7. (a) A death sentence shall not be carried out in the Republic of Korea

upon their request for purposes of investigation and trial. {The authorities of the Republic of Korea shall give sympathetic consideration to a request from the authorities of the United States for assistance in maintaining custody of an accused member of the United States armed forces, the civilian component, or a dependent.}

6. (a) The authorities of the United States and the authorities of the Republic of Korea shall assist each other in the carrying out of all necessary investigations into offenses, and in the collection and production of evidence including the seizure and, in proper cases, the handing over of objects connected with an offense. The handing over of such objects may, however, be made subject to their return within the time specified by the authority delivering them.

(b) The authorities of the United States and the authorities of the Republic of Korea shall notify each other of the disposition of all cases in which there are concurrent rights to exercise jurisdiction.

7. (a) A death sentence shall not be carried out in the Republic of Korea

by the military authorities of the United States if the legislation of the Republic of Korea does not provide for such punishment in a similar case.

(b) The authorities of the Republic of Korea shall give sympathetic consideration to a request from the military authorities of the United States for assistance in carrying out a sentence of imprisonment pronounced by the military authorities of the United States under the provisions of this Article within the territory of the Republic of Korea.

by the authorities of the United States if the legislation of the Republic of Korea does not provide for such punishment in a similar case.

(b) The authorities of the Republic of Korea shall give sympathetic consideration to a request from the ① 제 92차 회의 P.102, 103 authorities of the United States for assistance in carrying out a sentence of imprisonment pronounced by the authorities of the United States under the provisions of this Article within the territory of the Republic of Korea. ② 미국 시설 이용

The authorities of the Republic of Korea shall also give sympathetic consideration to a request from the authorities of the United States for the custody of any member of the United States armed forces or civilian component or a dependent, who is serving a sentence of confinement imposed by a court of the Republic of Korea. If such custody is released to the authorities of the United States, the United States shall be obligated to continue the confinement of the individual in an appropriate confinement facility of the United States until the sentence to confinement shall have been served in full or until release from such

8. Where an accused has been tried in accordance with the provisions of this Article either by the authorities of the Republic of Korea or the military authorities of the United States and has been acquitted, or has been convicted and is serving, or has served, his sentence or has been pardoned, he may not be tried again for the same offense within the territory of the Republic of Korea by the authorities of the other State. However, nothing in this paragraph shall prevent the military authorities of the United States from trying a member of its forces for any violation of rules of discipline arising from an act or omission which constituted an offense for which he was tried by the authorities of the Republic of Korea.

9. Whenever a member of the United States armed forces, the civilian component or a dependent is prosecuted under the jurisdiction of the Republic of Korea he shall be entitled:

(a) to a prompt and speedy trial;

confinement shall be approved by competent Korean authority.

8. Where an accused has been tried in accordance with the provisions of this Article either by the authorities of the United States or the authorities of the Republic of Korea and has been acquitted, or has been convicted and is serving, or has served, his sentence, or his sentence has been remitted or suspended or he has been pardoned, he may not be tried again for the same offense within the territory of the Republic of Korea by the authorities of the other State. However, nothing in this paragraph shall prevent the authorities of the United States from trying a member of its armed forces for any violation of rules of discipline arising from an act or omission which constituted an offense for which he was tried by the authorities of the Republic of Korea.

9. Whenever a member of the United States armed forces or civilian component or a dependent is prosecuted under the jurisdiction of the Republic of Korea he shall be entitled:

(a) to a prompt and speedy trial

(b) to be informed, in advance of trial, of the specific charge or charges made against him;

(c) to be confronted with the witnesses against him;

(d) to have compulsory process for obtaining witnesses in his favor, if they are within the jurisdiction of the Republic of Korea;

(e) to have legal representation of his own choice for his defense or to have free or assisted legal representation under the conditions prevailing in the Republic of Korea;

(f) If he considers it necessary, to be provided with the services of a competent interpreter; and

(g) to communicate with a representative of the Government of the United States and to have such a representative present at his trial.

10. (a) Regularly constituted military units or formation of the United States armed forces shall have the right to police any facilities or areas which they use under Article IV of this Agreement. The military police of such forces may take all appropriate measures to ensure the maintenance of order and security within such facilities and areas.

(b) to be informed, in advance of trial, of the specific charge or charges made against him;

(c) to be confronted with the witnesses against him;

(d) to have compulsory process for obtaining witnesses in his favor, if they are within the jurisdiction of the Republic of Korea;

(e) to have legal representation of his own choice for his defense or to have free or assisted legal representation under the conditions prevailing for the time being in the Republic of Korea;

(f) if he considers it necessary, to have the services of a competent interpreter; and

(g) to communicate with a representative of the Government of the United States and to have such a representative present at his trial.

10. (a) Regularly constituted military units or formations of the United States armed forces shall have the right to police any facilities or areas which they use under Article ___ of this Agreement. The military police of such forces may take all appropriate measures to ensure the maintenance of order and security within such facilities and areas.

(b) Outside these facilities and areas such military police shall be employed only subject to arrangements with the authorities of the Republic of Korea and in liaison with those authorities and in so far as such employment is necessary to maintain discipline and order among the members of the United States armed forces.

(b) Outside these facilities and areas, such military police shall be employed only subject to arrangements with the authorities of the Republic of Korea and in liaison with those authorities and in so far as such employment is necessary to maintain discipline and order among the members of the United States armed forces, or ensure their security.

11. In the event of hostilities to which the provisions of Article II of the Treaty of Mutual Defense apply, the provisions of this Agreement pertaining to criminal jurisdiction shall be immediately suspended and the authorities of the United States shall have the right to exercise exclusive jurisdiction over members of the United States armed forces, the civilian component, and their dependents.

12. The provisions of this Article shall not apply to any offenses committed before the entry into force of this Agreement. Such cases shall be governed by the provisions of the Agreement between the United States of America and the Republic of Korea effected by an exchange of notes at Taejon, Korea on July 12, 1950.

Agreed Minutes

The provisions of this Article shall not affect existing agreements, arrangements, or practices, relating to the exercise of jurisdiction over personnel of the United Nations forces present in Korea other than forces of the United States.

RE Paragraph 1(b)

Combat zone

1. The authorities of the United States shall have the right to exercise exclusive jurisdiction over members of the United States armed forces or civilian component, and their dependents, if any, in the combat zone. The extent of the combat zone shall be defined by the Joint Committee and shall include the area from the demilitarization zone to the rear boundaries of the United States corps (group) and the Republic of Korea army-size unit deployed in that zone.

2. In the event that martial law is declared by the Republic of Korea, the provisions of this Article shall be immediately suspended in the part of the Republic of Korea under martial law, and the authorities of the United States shall have the right to exercise exclusive

jurisdiction over members of the United States armed forces or civilian component and their dependents, in such part until martial law is ended.

3. The jurisdiction of the authorities of the Republic of Korea over members of the United States armed forces or civilian component, and their dependents shall not extend to any offenses committed outside the Republic of Korea.

RE Paragraph 2

Waiver of Exclusive Jurisdiction

The Republic of Korea, recognizing the effectiveness in appropriate cases of the administrative and disciplinary sanctions which may be imposed by the United States authorities over members of the United States armed forces or civilian component, and their dependents, will give sympathetic consideration in such cases to requests in the Joint Committee for waivers of its right to exercise jurisdiction under paragraph 2.

RE Paragraph 2(c)

Both Governments shall inform each other of the details of all the security offenses mentioned in this subparagraph and the provisions governing such offenses in the existing laws of their respective countries.

RE Paragraph 2(c)

Each Government shall inform the other of the details of all security offenses mentioned in this subparagraph, and of the provisions regarding such offenses in its legislation.

111 - 117

Re. Para. 3(a) (ii) (52nd, May 20, 64)

1. "Where a member of the United States armed forces or civilian component is charged with an offense, a certificate issued by a staff judge advocate on behalf of his commanding officer stating that the alleged offense, if committed by him, arose out of an act or omission done in the performance of official duty, shall be sufficient evidence of the fact for the purpose of determining primary jurisdiction, unless the contrary is proved.

Para 3(a) (ii)
(42nd Session, Feb. 14, 1964)

(ii) offenses arising out of any act or omission done in the performance of official duty provided that such act or omission is directly related to the duty. The question as to whether offenses were committed in the performance of official duty shall be decided by a competent district public prosecutor of the Republic of Korea.

In case the offender's commanding officer finds otherwise, he may appeal from the prosecutor's decision to the Minister of Justice within ten days from the receipt of the decision of the prosecutor, and the decision of the Minister of Justice shall be final.

2. If the Chief Prosecutor of the Republic of Korea considers that there is proof contrary to the certificate of official duty, he will refer the matter to the Joint Committee for decision.

The above statements shall not be interpreted to prejudice in any way Article 308 of the Korean Code of Criminal Procedure."

...he nationals of the Republic of Korea ... instituting criminal proceedings.

To facilitate the expeditious ...osal of offenses of minor importance, ...ngements may be made between United States authorities and the competent authorities of the Republic of Korea to dispense with notification.

우리측이 수락용의 표시(52차)

Re Paragraph 3(a)

1. The authorities of the United States shall have the primary right to exercise jurisdiction over members of the United States armed forces in relation to offenses which, if committed by a member of the armed forces of the Republic of Korea, would be tried by court-martial rather than by a civilian court.

조정

Agreed Minute Re Para 3(a) (67th Session, Dec. 16, 1964)

2. Where a member of the United States armed forces or civilian components is charged with an offense, a certificate issued by competent authorities of the United States forces stating that the alleged offense, if committed by him, arose out of an act committed by him, arose out of an act or omission done in the performance

OK 대안 제시 (52차)

0111

111-117

2. If the Chief Prosecutor of the Republic of Korea considers that there is proof contrary to the certificate of official duty, he will refer the matter to the Joint Committee for decision.

The above statements shall not be interpreted to prejudice in any way Article 308 of the Korean Code of Criminal Procedure."

0112

Para 3(a) (ii)
(42nd Session, Feb. 14, 1964)

(ii) offenses arising out of any act or omission done in the performance of official duty provided that such act or omission is directly related to the duty. The question as to whether offenses were committed in the performance of official duty shall be decided by a competent district public prosecutor of the Republic of Korea.

In case the offender's commanding officer finds otherwise, he ...

and the nationals of the Republic of Korea from instituting criminal proceedings.

To facilitate the expeditious disposal of offenses of minor importance, arrangements may be made between United States authorities and the competent authorities of the Republic of Korea to dispense with notification.

우리측이 수락용의 표시(5차)

RE Paragraph 3(a)

1. The authorities of the United States shall have the primary right to exercise jurisdiction over members of the United States armed forces in relation to offenses which, if committed by a member of the armed forces of the Republic of Korea, would be tried by court-martial rather than by a civilian court.

조채

Agreed Minute Re Para 3(a) (67th Session, Dec. 16, 1964)

2. Where a member of the United States armed forces or civilian components is charged with an offense, a certificate issued by competent authorities of the United States forces stating that the alleged offense, if committed by him, arose out of an act or omission done in the performance

111 - 119

Para 3(a) (ii)
(42nd Session, Feb. 14, 1964)

(ii) offenses arising out of any act or omission done in the performance of official duty provided that such act or omission is directly related to the duty. The question as to whether offenses were committed in the performance of official duty shall be decided by a competent district public prosecutor of the Republic of Korea.

In case the offender's commanding officer finds otherwise, he may appeal from the prosecutor's decision to the Minister of Justice within ten days from the receipt of the decision of the prosecutor, and the decision of the Minister of Justice shall be final.

0113

and the nationals of the Republic of Korea from instituting criminal proceedings.

To facilitate the expeditious disposal of offenses of minor importance, arrangements may be made between United States authorities and the competent authorities of the Republic of Korea to dispense with notification.

우리측이 수락용의 표시(52차)

RE Paragraph 3(a)

1. The authorities of the United States shall have the primary right to exercise jurisdiction over members of the United States armed forces in relation to offenses which, if committed by a member of the armed forces of the Republic of Korea, would be tried by court-martial rather than by a civilian court.

Agreed Minute Re Para 3(a)(67th Session, Dec. 16, 1964)

2. Where a member of the United States armed forces or civilian components is charged with an offense, a certificate issued by competent authorities of the United States forces stating that the alleged offense, if committed by him, arose out of an act or omission done in the performance

and the nationals of the Republic of Korea from instituting criminal proceedings.

[To facilitate the expeditious disposal of offenses of minor importance, arrangements may be made between United States authorities and the competent authorities of the Republic of Korea to dispense with notification.]

우리측이 수락움의 도시(5자나)

0114

RE Paragraph 3(a) (ii)

The term "official duty" is not meant to include all acts by members of the United States armed forces or the civilian component during periods while they are on duty. Any departure from acts which are duly required to be done as a normal function of a particular duty shall be deemed as an act outside of his "official duty."

RE Paragraph 3(a)

1. The authorities of the United States shall have the primary right to exercise jurisdiction over members of the United States armed forces in relation to offenses which, if committed by a member of the armed forces of the Republic of Korea, would be tried by court-martial rather than by a civilian court.

Agreed Minute Re Para 3(a)(67th Session, Dec. 16, 1964)

2. Where a member of the United States armed forces or civilian components is charged with an offense, a certificate issued by competent authorities of the United States forces stating that the alleged offense, if committed by him, arose out of an act or omission done in the performance

0114

Para
(42n

act
manc
such
relat
as to
in th
shall
distr
Repub
In
offic
appea
to the
days
of the
of the
final.

2.
the Re
there
certif
will r
Commit
Th
be int
way Ar
of Cri

RE Paragraph 3(a) (ii)

The term "official duty" is not meant or include all acts by members of the United States armed forces or the civilian component during periods while they are on duty. Any departure from acts which are duly required to be done as a normal function of a particular duty shall be deemed as an act outside of his "official duty."

Re Paragraph 3(c)
(52nd Session, May 20, 1964)

"The authorities of the Republic of Korea will, upon the notification of individual cases falling under the waiver provided in Article ______ Paragraph 3(c) from the military authorities of the United States, waive its primary right to exercise jurisdiction under Article ______ except where they determine that it is of particular importance that jurisdiction be exercised by the authorities of the Republic of Korea."

In addition to the foregoing provisions,

Mutual procedures relating to waivers of the primary right to exercise jurisdiction shall be determined by the Joint Committee.

Trials of cases in which the authorities of the Republic of Korea waived the primary right to exercise jurisdiction, and trials of cases involving offenses described in paragraph 3(a) (ii) committed against the State or nationals of the Republic of Korea shall be held promptly in the Republic of Korea within a reasonable distance from the places where the offenses are alleged to have taken place unless other arrangements are mutually agreed upon. Representatives of the authorities of the Republic of Korea may be present at such trials.

arrangements may be made between United States authorities and the competent authorities of the Republic of Korea to dispense with notification.

우리측이 수락동의 돈시(5zlt)

RE Paragraph 3(a)

1. The authorities of the United States shall have the primary right to exercise jurisdiction over members of the United States armed forces in relation to offenses which, if committed by a member of the armed forces of the Republic of Korea, would be tried by court-martial rather than by a civilian court.

조치

Agreed Minute Re Para 3(a) (67th Session, Dec. 16, 1964)

2. Where a member of the United States armed forces or civilian components is charged with an offense, a certificate issued by competent authorities of the United States forces stating that the alleged offense, if committed by him, arose out of an act or omission done in the performance

0115

115

and the nationals of the Republic of Korea from instituting criminal proceedings.

To facilitate the expeditious disposal of offenses of minor importance, arrangements may be made between United States authorities and the competent authorities of the Republic of Korea to dispense with notification.

RE Paragraph 3(a)

1. The authorities of the United States shall have the primary right to exercise jurisdiction over members of the United States armed forces in relation to offenses which, if committed by a member of the armed forces of the Republic of Korea, would be tried by court-martial rather than by a civilian court.

Agreed Minute Re Para 3(a) (67th Session, Dec. 16, 1964)

2. Where a member of the United States armed forces or civilian components is charged with an offense, a certificate issued by competent authorities of the United States forces stating that the alleged offense, if committed by him, arose out of an act or omission done in the performance

(42nd) Feb. 14, 1964)

Mutual procedures relating to waivers of the primary right to exercise jurisdiction shall be determined by the Joint Committee.

Trials of cases in which the authorities of the Republic of Korea waived the primary right to exercise jurisdiction, and trials of cases involving offenses described in paragraph 3(a) (ii) committed against the State or nationals of the Republic of Korea shall be held promptly in the Republic of Korea within a reasonable distance from the places where the offenses are alleged to have taken place unless other arrangements are mutually agreed upon. Representatives of the authorities of the Republic of Korea may be present at such trials

0116

0114

RE Paragraph 3(a) (ii)

The term "official duty" is not meant

or include all acts by members of the

United States armed forces or the civilian

우리측이 수락용의 표시(52차)

조회

(42nd, Feb. 14, 1964)

2. Where a member of the United States armed forces or civilian component is charged with an offense, a certificate issued by or on behalf of his commanding officer stating that the alleged offense, if committed by him, arose out of an act or omission done in the performance of official duty, shall be conclusive for the purpose of determining primary jurisdiction.

0117

합의

OK 대안 제시 (52차)

and the nationals of the Republic of Korea from instituting criminal proceedings.

[To facilitate the expeditious disposal of offenses of minor importance, arrangements may be made between United States authorities and the competent authorities of the Republic of Korea to dispense with notification.]

우리측이 수락용의 표시(53차)

Re Paragraph 3(a)

1. The authorities of the United States shall have the primary right to exercise jurisdiction over members of the United States armed forces in relation to offenses which, if committed by a member of the armed forces of the Republic of Korea, would be tried by court-martial rather than by a civilian court.

조회

Agreed Minute Re Para 3(a)(67th Session, Dec. 16, 1964)

2. Where a member of the United States armed forces or civilian components is charged with an offense, a certificate issued by competent authorities of the United States forces stating that the alleged offense, if committed by him, arose out of an act or omission done in the performance of official duty shall be sufficient evidence of the fact for the purpose of determining primary jurisdiction.

In those exceptional cases where the chief prosecutor for the Republic of Korea considers that there is proof contrary to a certificate of official duty, it may be made the subject of review through discussions between appropriate officials of the Government of the Republic of Korea and the diplomatic mission of the United States in Korea.

(42nd) Feb. 14, 1964)

Mutual procedures relating to waivers of the primary right to exercise jurisdiction shall be determined by the Joint Committee.

Trials of cases in which the authorities of the Republic of Korea ... primary right to exercise

0118

Mutual procedures relating to waivers of the primary right to exercise jurisdiction shall be determined by the Joint Committee.

Trials of cases in which the authorities of the Republic of Korea waived the primary right to exercise jurisdiction, and trials of cases involving offenses described in paragraph 3(a) (ii) committed against the State or nationals

States armed forces or civilian component is charged with an offense, a certificate issued by or on behalf of his commanding officer stating that the alleged offense, if committed by him, arose out of an act or omission done in the performance of official duty, shall be conclusive for the purpose of determining primary jurisdiction.

우리측이 수락용의 표시(52차)

조제

ROK대안 제시 (52차)

0118-1

118-121

Re Paragraph 3
(67th Session, Dec. 16, 1964)

The Republic of Korea, recognizing that it is the primary responsibility of the United States authorities to maintain good order and discipline where persons subject to United States law are concerned, waives its primary right to exercise jurisdiction under paragraph 3 b. In accordance therewit the United States authorities shall notify the authorities of the Republic of Korea of their intention to exercise jurisdiction in such cases through the Joint Committee. When the authorities of the Republic of Korea, after consultation with United States authorities, are of the opinion that, by reason of special circumstances in a specific case involving an offense against the security of the Republic of Korea or of forcible rape, or of a malicious killing, the exercise of Korean jurisdiction is of vital importance to the Republic of Korea in that case, they will notify the United States authorities of that opinion within fifteen days after receipt of notification that the United States intends to exercise jurisdiction. The United States shall not have the right to exercise jurisdiction within those fifteen days. If any question arises concerning who is to exercise jurisdiction the United States

0119

118-121

diplomatic mission will be afforded an opportunity to confer with the proper authorities of the Republic of Korea before a final determination of this matter is made.

Trials of cases in which the authorities of the Republic of Korea waive the primary right to exercise jurisdiction, and trials of cases involving offenses described in para 3(a) (ii) committed against the state or nationals of the Republic of Korea will be held within a reasonable distance from the place where the offenses are alleged to have taken place unless other arrangements are mutually agreed upon. Representatives of the Republic of Korea may be present at such trials.

In the implementation of the provisions of Article ___ and this Minute, and to facilitate the expeditious disposal of offenses, arrangements may be made between the authorities of the United States and the Republic of Korea to dispense with notification.

0120

118-121

0121

RE Paragraph 3, (42nd Session, Feb. 14, 1964)

The Republic of Korea, recognizing that it is the primary responsibility of the United States authorities to maintain good order and discipline among the members of the United States Armed Forces and civilian component, and their dependents, waives the right of the authorities of the Republic of Korea to exercise jurisdiction under paragraph 3. The United States authorities shall notify the competent authorities of the Republic of Korea of individual cases falling under the waiver thus provided. If, by reason of special circumstances in a specific case, the authorities of the Republic of Korea consider that it is of particular importance that jurisdiction be exercised by the Republic of Korea in that case, they shall, within 15 days of receipt of the notification envisaged above, seek agreement of the Joint Committee to recall the waiver for that particular case.

Subject to the foregoing, the waiver granted by the Republic of Korea shall be unconditional and final for all purposes and shall bar both the authorities and the nationals of the Republic of Korea from instituting criminal proceedings.

To facilitate the expeditious disposal of offenses of minor importance, arrangements may be made between United States authorities and the competent authorities of the Republic of Korea to dispense with notification.

118-121

RE Paragraph 3

The Republic of Korea, [recognizing that it is the primary responsibility of the United States authorities to maintain good order and discipline among the members of the United States Armed Forces and civilian component, and their dependents,] waives the right of the authorities of the Republic of Korea to exercise jurisdiction under paragraph 3. The United States authorities shall notify the competent authorities of the Republic of Korea of individual cases falling under the waiver thus provided. If, by reason of special circumstances in a specific case, the authorities of the Republic of Korea consider that it is of particular importance that jurisdiction be exercised by the Republic of Korea in that case, they shall, within 15 days of receipt of the notification envisaged above, [seek agreement of the Joint Committee to recall the waiver for that particular case.]

Subject to the foregoing, the waiver granted by the Republic of Korea shall be unconditional and final for all purposes and shall bar both the authorities

0122

- 90 -

122-123

(Suggestion: Mutual Waiver)
"When the Korean authorities hold the view that by reason of special circumstances in a specific cases, major interests of the Korean administration of justice make imperative the exercise of the Korean jurisdiction, they will notify the military authorities of the United States of that opinion within a reasonable period. In case an understanding cannot be reached in discussion between the both sides, the U.S. military authorities will seek agreement of the Joint Committee within fifteen days from the date of receipt of such notification If the U.S. authorities do not reply within fifteen days, the request for waiver will be deemed to have recalled."

0123

122

RE Paragraph 4

Dual nationals, the Republic of ~~Korea~~ and United States, who are the members of the United States armed forces or the civilian component and are brought to the Republic of Korea shall not be considered as nationals of the Republic of Korea, but shall be considered as United States nationals for the purposes of this paragraph.

RE Paragraph 5(b)

In case the authorities of the Republic of Korea have arrested an offender who is a member of the United States armed forces, the civilian component or a dependent with respect to a case over which the Republic of Korea has the primary right to exercise jurisdiction, the authorities of the Republic of Korea will, unless they deem that there is adequate cause and necessity to retain such offender, release him to the custody of

1, Japan SOFA Re Para 5(1)에 a defendant 포함.

122-123

of the Republic of Korea shall be held promptly in the Republic of Korea within a reasonable distance from the places where the offenses are alleged to have taken place unless other arrangements are mutually agreed upon. Representatives of the authorities of the Republic of Korea may be present at such trials.

RE Paragraph 4

Dual nationals, the Republic of Korea and United States, who are the members of the United States armed forces or the civilian component and are brought to the Republic of Korea shall not be considered as nationals of the Republic of Korea, but shall be considered as United States nationals for the purposes of this paragraph.

RE Paragraph 5(b)

In case the authorities of the Republic of Korea have arrested an offender who is a member of the United States armed forces, the civilian component or a dependent with respect to a case over which the Republic of Korea has the primary right to exercise jurisdiction, the authorities of the Republic of Korea will, unless they deem that there is adequate cause and necessity to retain such offender, release him to the custody of

1. Japan SOFA Re Para 5(1)에도 a defendant 포함.

the United States military authorities provided that he shall, on request, be made available to the authorities of the Republic of Korea, if such be the condition of his release. The United States authorities shall, on request, transfer his custody to the authorities of the Republic of Korea at the time he is indicted by the latter.

RE Paragraph 6

1. A member of the United States armed forces or the civilian component shall, if sommoned by the authorities of the Republic of Korea as a witness in the course of investigations and trials, make himself available to the authorities of the Republic of Korea.

2. If any person sommoned as witness did not make himself available to the authorities of the Republic of Korea, they may take necessary measures in accordance with the provisions of the law of the Republic of Korea. Subject to the foregoing, the military authorities of the United States shall, upon presentation of a warrant issued by a judge of the Republic of Korea, immediately take all appropriate measures to ensure the execution of the warrant by the authorities of the Republic of Korea.

RE Paragraph 6

1. The authorities of the United States and the authorities of the Republic of Korea shall assist each other in obtaining the appearance of witnesses necessary for the proceedings conducted by such authorities within the Republic of Korea.

When a member of the United States armed forces in Korea is summoned to appear before a Korean court, as a witness or as a defendant, United States authorities shall unless military exigency requires otherwise, secure his attendance provides such attendance is compulsory under Korean law. If military exigency prevents such attendance, the authorities on the United States shall furnish a certificate stating the estimated duration of such disability.

Service of process upon a member of the United States armed forces or civilian component, or a dependent required as a witness or a defendant must be personal service in the English language. Where the service of process is to be effected by a Korean process server upon any person who is inside a military installation or area, the authorities of the United States shall take all measures necessary to enable the Korean process server to effect such service.

In addition, the Korean authorities shall promptly give copies of all criminal writs (including warrants, summonses, indictments, and subpoenas) to an agent designated by the United States authorities to receive them in all cases of Korean criminal proceedings involving a member of the United States armed forces or civilian component, or a dependent.

When citizens or residents of the Republic of Korea are required as witnesses or experts by the authorities of the United States, the courts and authorities of the Republic of Korea shall, in accordance with Korean law, secure the attendance of such persons. In these cases the authorities of the United States shall act through the Attorney General of the Republic of Korea, or such other agency as is designated by the authorities of the Republic of Korea.

Fees and other payments for witnesses shall be determined by the Joint Committee established under Article ____.

2. The privileges and immunities of witnesses shall be those accorded by

0126

the law of the court, tribunal or authority before which they appear. In no event shall a witness be required to provide testimony which may tend to incriminate him.

3. If, in the course of criminal proceedings before authorities of the United States or the Republic of Korea, the disclosure of an official secret of either of these States or the disclosure of any information which may prejudice the security of either appears necessary for the just disposition of the proceedings, the authorities concerned shall seek written permission to make such disclosure from the appropriate authority of the State concerned.

RE Paragraph 9(a)

The right to a prompt and speedy trial by the courts of the Republic of Korea shall include public trial by an impartial tribunal composed exclusively of judges who have completed their probationary period. A member of the United States armed forces or civilian component, or a dependent, shall not be tried by a military tribunal of the Republic of Korea.

RE Paragraph 9(b)

A member of the United States armed forces or civilian component, or a dependent, shall not be arrested or detained by the authorities of the Republic of Korea without adequate cause, and he shall be entitled to an immediate hearing at which such cause must be shown in open court in his presence and the presence of his counsel. His immediate release shall be ordered if adequate cause is not shown. Immediately upon arrest or detention he shall be informed of the charges against him in a language which he understands.

He shall also be informed a reasonable time prior to trial of the nature of the evidence that is to be used against him. Counsel for the accused shall, upon request, be afforded the opportunity before trial to examine and copy the statements of witnesses obtained by authorities of the Republic of Korea which are included in the file forwarded to the court of the Republic of Korea scheduled to try the case.

RE Paragraph 9(c) and (d)

A member of the United States armed forces or civilian component, or a dependent, who is prosecuted by the authorities of the Republic of Korea shall have the right to be present throughout the testimony of all witnesses, for and against him, in all judicial examinations, pretrial hearings, the trial itself, and subsequent proceedings, and shall be permitted full opportunity to examine the witnesses.

RE Paragraph 9(e)

The right to legal representation shall exist from the moment of arrest or detention and shall include the right to have counsel present, and to consult confidentially with such counsel, at all preliminary investigations, examinations, pretrial hearings, the trial itself, and subsequent proceedings, at which the accused is present.

RE Paragraph 9(f)

The right to have the services of a competent interpreter shall exist from the moment of arrest or detention.

RE Paragraph 9(g)

The right to communicate with a representative of the Government of the United States shall exist from the moment of arrest or detention, and no statement of the accused taken in the absence of such a representative shall be admissible as evidence in support of the guilt of the accused. Such representative shall be entitled to be present at all preliminary investigations, examinations, pretrial hearings, the trial itself, and subsequent proceedings, at which the accused is present.

2. Nothing in the provisions of paragraph 9(g) concerning the presence of a representative of the United States Government at the trial of a member of the United States armed forces, the civilian component or a dependent prosecuted under the jurisdiction of the Republic of Korea, shall be so construed as to prejudice the provisions of the Constitution of the Republic of Korea with respect to public trials.

0129

RE Paragraph 9

para 1 (1) A member of the United States armed forces or civilian component, or a dependent, tried by the authorities of the Republic of Korea shall be accorded every procedural and substantive right granted by law to the citizens of the Republic of Korea. If it should appear that an accused has been, or is likely to be, denied any procedural or substantive right granted by law to the citizens of the Republic of Korea, representatives of the two Governments shall consult in the Joint Committee on the measures necessary to prevent or cure such denial of rights.

Paragraph 9

1. The rights enumerated in this paragraph are guaranteed to all persons on trial in the Korean courts by the provisions of the Constitution of the Republic of Korea. In addition to these rights, a member of the United States armed forces, the civilian component or a dependent who is prosecuted under the jurisdiction of the Republic of Korea shall have such other rights as are guranteed under the Constitution and laws of the Republic of Korea to all persons on trial in the Korean courts.

para (2) In addition to the rights enumerated in items (a) through (g) of paragraph 9 of this Article, a member of the United States armed forces or civilian component, or a dependent, who is prosecuted by the authorities of the Republic of Korea:

(a) shall be furnished a verbatim record of his trial in English;

(b) shall have the right to appeal a conviction or sentence; in addition, he shall be informed by the court at the time of conviction or sentencing of his right to appeal and of the time limit within which that right must be exercised;

(c) shall have credited to any sentence of confinement his period of pretrial confinement in a United States or Korean confinement facility;

(d) shall not be held guilty of a criminal offense on account of any act or omission which did not constitute a criminal offense under the law of the Republic of Korea at the time it was committed;

(e) shall not be subject to a heavier penalty than the one that was applicable at the time the alleged criminal offense was committed or was adjudged by the court of first instance as the original sentence;

> (e) "Shall not be subject to a heavier penalty than the one that was applicable at the time the alleged criminal offense was committed or was adjudged by the court of the first instance as the original sentence when an appeal o[illegible] case is made by or on behalf of the accused."

(f) shall not be held guilty of an offense on the basis of rules of evidence or requirements of proof which have been altered to his prejudice since the date of the commission of the offense.

(g) shall not be compelled to testify against or otherwise incriminate himself;

(h) shall not be subject to cruel or unusual punishment;

(i) shall not be subject to prosecution or punishment by legislative or executive act;

Criminal Jurisdiction Article

Paragraph 3 of the Agreed Minute Re Paragraph 9

No confession, admission, or other statement, obtained by torture, violence, threat, deceit, or after prolonged arrest or detention, or which has been made involuntarily, will be considered by the courts of the Republic of Korea as evidence in support of the guilt of the accused under this Article.

0132

(k) "Shall be entitled to request the post-ponement of his presence at a trial if he is physically or mentally unfit to stand trial and participate in his defense; "

(j) shall not be prosecuted or punished more than once for the same offense.

(k) shall not be required to stand trial if he is physically or mentally unfit to stand trial and participate in his defense;

(l) shall not be subjected to trial except under conditions consonant with the dignity of the United States armed forces, including appearing in appropriate military or civilian attire and unmanacled.

(5) No confession, admission, or other statement, or real evidence, obtained by illegal or improper means will be considered by courts of the Republic of Korea in prosecutions under this Article.

(6) In any case prosecuted by the authorities of the Republic of Korea under this Article no appeal will be taken by the prosecution from a judgment of not guilty or an acquittal nor will an appeal be taken by the prosecution from any judgment which the accused does not appeal, except upon grounds of errors of law.

The authorities of the United States shall have the right to inspect any

Korean confinement facility in which a member of the United States armed forces, civilian component, or dependent is confined, or in which it is proposed to confine such an individual.

In the event of hostilities, the Republic of Korea will take all possible measures to safeguard members of the United States armed forces, members of the civilian component, and their dependents who are confined in Korean confinement facilities, whether awaiting trial or serving a sentence imposed by the courts of the Republic of Korea. The Republic of Korea shall give sympathetic consideration to request for release of these persons to the custody of responsible United States authorities. Necessary implementing provisions shall be agreed upon between the two governments through the Joint Committee.

Facilities utilized for the execution of a sentence to death or a period of confinement, imprisonment, or penal servitude, or for the detention of members of the United States armed forces or civilian component or dependents, will meet minimum standards as agreed by the Joint Committee. The United States

Where seizure, search, or inspection with respect to persons or property within facilities and areas in use by the United States armed forces or with respect to property of the United States armed forces in the Republic of Korea is desired by the authorities of the Republic of Korea, the United States military authorities shall, upon request, make such seizure, search, or inspection. In the event of a judgement concerning such property, except property owned or utilized by the United States Government or its instrumentalities, the United States shall turn over such property to the authorities of the Republic of Korea for disposition in accordance with the judgement.

U.S

The United States military authorities may, under due process of law, arrest within or in the vicinity of a facility or area any person in the commission of an offense against the security of that facility or area. Any such person not subject to the jurisdiction of the United States armed forces shall immediately be turned over to the authorities of the Republic of Korea.

시설주변
US에도 있음

(1) within or all arrests (日本)에서 경우
(2) under due process of law 의 뜻은?

0137

외교문서 비밀해제: 주한미군지위협정(SOFA) 17

주한미군지위협정(SOFA) 서명 및 발효 17

초판인쇄 2024년 03월 15일
초판발행 2024년 03월 15일

지은이 한국학술정보(주)
펴낸이 채종준
펴낸곳 한국학술정보(주)
주 소 경기도 파주시 회동길 230(문발동)
전 화 031-908-3181(대표)
팩 스 031-908-3189
홈페이지 http://ebook.kstudy.com
E-mail 출판사업부 publish@kstudy.com
등 록 제일산-115호(2000. 6. 19)

ISBN 979-11-7217-028-8 94340
979-11-7217-011-0 94340 (set)